D0305465

A Woman of Spirit

A WOMAN OF SPIRIT

Nora Kay

Hodder & Stoughton
LONDON SYDNEY AUCKLAND

Kay, Nora

A woman of
spirit / Nora
Kay
                    FT

772586

F
772586

Copyright © 1994 Nora Kay

First published in Great Britain in 1994 by Hodder and Stoughton
A Division of Hodder Headline PLC

Reprinted in this edition 1994 by Hodder and Stoughton

The right of Nora Kay to be identified as the author
of this work has been asserted by her in accordance with the
Copyright, Designs and Patents Act 1988.

10 9 8 7 6 5 4 3 2 1

All rights reserved. No part of this publication may be
reproduced, stored in a retrieval system, or transmitted,
in any form or by any means, without the prior written
permission of the publisher, nor be otherwise circulated
in any form of binding or cover other than that in which
it is published and without a similar condition being
imposed on the subsequent purchaser.

All characters in this publication are fictitious
and any resemblance to real persons, living or dead,
is purely coincidental.

British Library Cataloguing in Publication Data

Kay, Nora
Woman of Spirit. – New ed
I. Title
823 [F]

ISBN 0-340-61337-8

Typeset by Hewer Text Composition Services, Edinburgh
Printed and bound in Great Britain by Mackays of Chatham plc

Hodder and Stoughton Ltd
A Division of Hodder Headline PLC
338 Euston Road
London NW1 3BH

To Bill and Raymond

CHAPTER ONE

On that last day of January 1885 a bitterly cold, contemptuous wind swept through the Lanarkshire village of Aranvale, flattening outhouses and sending slates crashing to the ground. Perched on the highest ground, Aran Heights braved the storm to suffer no more than a broken stable door left hanging drunkenly by its one remaining hinge.

Hamish MacFarlane, owner of the Aranvale Papermill, had had the house built to withstand the elements. Aran Heights was a grand mansion house without in any way being pretentious. Curved stone steps led up to the heavy oak door. The windows followed a precise pattern even to those in the attic and no unnecessary embellishments or fussiness of stone work detracted the eye from its classic simplicity and grace. Hamish MacFarlane was proud of his home and it would have surprised him greatly to know that his wife, Sarah, found it cold and forbidding. Only their daughter, Susan, shared her father's love of Aran Heights.

Hamish MacFarlane considered that he and his family were indeed fortunate to have the best of both worlds. Aranvale had all the attractions of a village with its low houses, small shops, its kirk and manse, two public houses and a railway station, yet was no more than fifteen miles from Glasgow. None would deny that this city of contrasts had some of the finest buildings in Scotland. The rich lived in splendid mansions in spacious streets while the poor were housed in disgusting hovels. Slowly these were disappearing and tenements taking their place, but with the owners demanding rents that most could not afford there was a great deal of bad feeling.

Years before, Samuel MacFarlane, Hamish's grandfather, had come to this part of Lanarkshire and seen the potential for a papermill at Aranvale. With a little money and a great deal of enthusiasm Samuel and a small band of helpers had worked from morning light until darkness to erect a jumble of rough buildings near to the artificial reservoir. Shrewdly he had recognised that the controlled flow of water would ensure a constant supply for manufacturing purposes.

When his son, Thomas, took over, the mill was already showing a healthy profit. New buildings had replaced the old and modern machinery had been added. With more and more orders coming in a larger workforce was needed. The papermill had become the life-blood of Aranvale and the surrounding villages. Now with Hamish in charge the Aranvale Papermill was one of the finest in the country. Even so society was not yet ready to open its doors to the MacFarlanes. The new rich were not yet accepted.

Overnight the wind had almost worn itself out and a weak sun slanted through the curtains of the room where Susan MacFarlane was at the window and her mother warming her hands in front of the log fire.

'Did the storm keep you awake, Mama?'

'Of course it did. As you very well know I have difficulty getting to sleep at the best of times. But we were not discussing the storm.' Then she added irritably, 'Come away from that window.'

Susan moved slowly away to join her mother at the fireside.

In her younger days Sarah MacFarlane had been considered a beauty but now only a faded prettiness remained and despite a daily battle with ever tighter laced corsets her figure had spread.

Half a head taller than her mother, Susan was slimly built with a lovely figure. She had high cheekbones, a velvety smooth skin and eyes of a deep blue but perhaps her real claim to beauty was the glorious silver fairness of her hair.

'I'm only nineteen, Mama,' Susan said quietly.

Seeing her daughter looking so composed brought the angry colour to Sarah's face.

2

'You'll soon be twenty,' the voice shrilled. 'At your age I was married to your papa.'

'Yes, Mama.' Having heard it all before Susan made the mistake of allowing weariness to creep into her voice and, hearing it, Sarah's fragile control snapped. From where she was standing her raised hand caught Susan's face a stinging slap and Susan, taken aback, stared at her mother in wide-eyed shock.

All the colour had left Sarah's face, leaving it grey and a shaking hand went up to cover her mouth.

'I'm sorry, so very sorry,' she mumbled, 'but it was your manner, your insolence.'

Expelling a shaky breath Susan touched her inflamed cheek. No one had ever raised a hand to her before and she was both outraged and humiliated.

Sarah's ample bosom rose and fell and when next she spoke her voice was softer and a hint of pleading had crept in.

'Edward Brodie would make an excellent husband.'

'For someone else I'm sure he would and don't misunderstand me: I don't dislike Edward, in fact I quite like him but I don't want to get married.'

'Did you tell him that?'

'Yes, I did,' Susan said spiritedly. 'Better to tell him the truth surely.'

'Really, Susan, you are quite impossible. At your age I wouldn't have dared disobey my parents.' Her lips curled. 'Would you rather end up a spinster like your Aunt Rachel?'

Susan didn't take the trouble to answer. Her mother and Papa's sister had never got on but Susan had a very real affection for her eccentric and often embarrassingly outspoken aunt. Rachel MacFarlane could have married but didn't. She was a practical, intelligent woman full of energy and she led a full and independent life.

Abruptly Sarah sat down on the couch and leaned her head against the plump upholstery, managing to lose a hairpin in the process.

'Believe me, Susan, you'll have to learn and learn quickly that your own inclinations are unimportant.' She bit her lip.

3

'John and Lilian Brodie are going to be very upset at your dismissal of Edward and small wonder.' She paused and looked bleak. 'My own position is going to be difficult. Mrs Brodie may decide to exclude me from further invitations to Croft House.' There was a pinched look about her mouth and Susan guessed that that was what concerned her mother most. The Brodies were accepted by society and through Lilian Sarah was edging her way into that exclusive circle.

'Surely Mrs Brodie wouldn't do that, Mama?'

Sarah's eyes darted to the marble clock on the mantelshelf of the splendid Italian fireplace and she gasped. 'Oh, dear, I almost forgot. Your papa wants to see you in the library at ten. Get up there now, it's almost that,' she said warningly.

The warning wasn't needed. Hamish MacFarlane demanded punctuality and Susan had no wish to incur more wrath than that which she had little doubt awaited her. The hand moved to three minutes before the hour.

Checking her face in the mirror and relieved to see no tell-tale signs of her earlier distress, she moved to the door then spoke hesitantly.

'Mama, how is Papa this morning?'

'Your papa has a touch of bronchitis and Dr Sullivan insists that he remains indoors for the next week or two.'

With the closing of the drawing-room door Sarah continued to sit where she was. Much of the room's magnificent splendour was due to her unrestricted expenditure. The exquisite gold-inlaid escritoire, Hepplewhite table and delicate Venetian glass were in perfect taste. Paintings and tapestries adorned the walls and in a locked cabinet, on glass shelves, were placed crinoline figures and other treasured pieces of porcelain. The drawing-room at Aran Heights was a showplace. Sarah loved it and spent as much time as possible there but the rest of the family much preferred the more comfortable and smaller rooms at the back of the house.

In those early days Hamish had been loath to curtail his wife's spending and indeed had admired her choice of furniture and furnishings. Much of the pleasure derived from such a fine display disappeared as the bills began to arrive. Sternly he had

4

reminded Sarah that money did not grow on trees and that one never knew what lay ahead. Sarah had agreed tearfully to exercise restraint in future but it angered her, knowing as she did that the paper-making industry was enjoying a boom in trade.

Amidst all this splendour, as always, her eyes went to the mantelshelf – drawn there to the face smiling out from the gold frame. She could never look at it without her lip trembling and wondered anew if the pain would ever lessen. Here in this same room the news had been broken to her, and closing her eyes she relived the horror of that cruel icy day in January, a year ago now, when tragedy had struck.

Only that previous week her handsome, darling, first-born son had celebrated his twenty-first birthday with a magnificent party. A superb horseman, no one knew how it could have happened but somehow Ralph had been thrown from his horse and in the fall his head had smashed against the stone dyke. The riderless horse had returned to the stables and that same night a distraught and grief-stricken father had ordered the beast to be destroyed.

CHAPTER TWO

Before entering, Susan gave a light knock on the library door.

'Good morning, Papa.' Knowing it would only irritate him she didn't ask after his health.

'Good morning, Susan,' he grunted, turning away from the window.

'Mama said you wished to see me.'

He nodded, his expression stern. For some time he kept her standing and with each passing moment her apprehension grew. Only now was she beginning to realise the enormity of what she had done and her mouth went dry. She had dared to disobey her parents, gone against an arrangement made by two powerful men to unite their families. Worse still, Edward had been agreeable, more than agreeable. She shivered.

Though heavily built there was a refinement about Hamish MacFarlane and a certain grace to his movements. He had a square-jawed face framed by a beard and sideburns and his dark brown hair, just beginning to grey, was still plentiful and curled to his collar.

Keeping his daughter standing had not been entirely to add to her discomfort. Hamish was enjoying looking at her, proud of her beauty and at other times he would have been secretly amused at her stubbornness, a trait she had inherited from him. However her refusal to become betrothed to Edward Brodie had come as an unpleasant shock. The marriage would take place, he would see to that, but meantime he would go easy on her. Susan, like most women, could be led but not driven. He would do well to exercise patience.

Carefully lowering himself into the spacious leather chair,

he motioned for Susan to be seated and she sat down gratefully in the nearest chair.

'Well, young woman,' he rasped, 'what have you got to say for yourself?'

'I'm sorry, Papa,' she whispered.

'And so you should be.' He frowned, drawing his brows together. 'This is going to cause embarrassment between our families. Your mother is most upset.'

'I know.'

'What's wrong with Edward?' he demanded.

'Nothing.'

'You'll soon be twenty as your mother has reminded me, time you were settled.'

Her stomach was churning with nerves but she had to ask now.

'The last thing I want to be, Papa, is a burden to you and that's why' – she faltered – 'may – may I ask something?'

'Go on.'

'I – I know how much you miss Ralph, we all do – ' She saw the pain her words had produced but hurried on. 'Papa, please let me take on some of the responsibility Ralph was shouldering. More than anything I want to learn about the mill.'

He was silent for so long that she thought he wasn't going to answer at all. Then she saw that he was struggling for control but whether it was anger at her temerity or grief for Ralph she couldn't decide.

'Don't be ridiculous,' he said at last, 'the very idea is outrageous.'

Before her courage failed she plunged on. 'It's thanks to you, Papa, that I'm well educated. Sharing lessons with Matthew has given me a knowledge of subjects most girls aren't allowed to study.'

My, but she was a plucky one bringing that up, Hamish thought as he hid a smile. If the truth were known he hadn't been particularly interested in his daughter's education but he wasn't one to waste money. Having the twins educated by one tutor made economical sense.

'Oh, you have an aptitude for figures, I won't deny that. It's just a pity your brother wasn't similarly blessed.' He gave a deep sigh. 'Instead I have a son of great charm, little brain and absolutely no ambition.'

'Papa, that's not fair!' Susan rushed to her twin's defence. 'Mr Clapperton is very impressed with Matthew and says he has the makings of a fine farmer.'

'I'm well aware where Matthew's interests lie,' he said irritably, 'and at one time I may have agreed to his taking up farming, but surely even he must see that it's out of the question now. Matthew's place is in the mill with me and the sooner he realises that the better.'

'Then my education has been a complete waste,' she said angrily and beyond caring now. 'And you who always say how much you hate waste.'

He glowered across the desk and pointed a stubby finger. 'If you filled your days with ladylike pursuits it would be better for all concerned. From what your mother tells me you have few accomplishments and your needlework is a disgrace.'

Susan felt a suffocating tightness in her throat.

'That's because I hate it and I couldn't bear to spend my life as Mama does.'

His expression softened but he gave a shake of his head.

'A woman's place is in the home, my dear, bringing up a family and organising the servants. Maybe one day society will look at it differently but it won't be in my time.'

'You employ women,' she said accusingly.

'Women of that class need to earn money.'

'But Papa –'

'Not another word, young woman, my patience is exhausted.' To show it and hasten her departure he lifted his pen and dipped it into the inkwell.

Sick at heart, Susan stumbled from the library, almost colliding with a startled maid in her rush for the privacy of her own bedroom. Once there she gave in to a storm of weeping, pounding the pillow with her clenched fist. It wasn't fair, nothing was fair. Just because she was a female so many doors were closed. Marriage seemed to be the only escape

9

and in time she was pretty sure that would become its own prison. As she grew calmer she felt ashamed at her outburst and got up from the bed. The covers were in disarray and she smoothed them then went over to the jug on the marble slab. A little water remained, cold now, and she poured it into the china basin and splashed her face. A brisk rub with the towel brought back her colour. Glancing in the mirror above she saw a mouth set in a stubborn line. Nobody, but nobody would force her into a marriage she didn't want. But even as she thought it she wondered how long she could hold out against her parents' wishes.

Hamish MacFarlane allowed himself a tired smile. The lass had a lot of character and a good head on her shoulders but that was no answer to his own problem. Hunched over his desk his eyes were troubled and to add to his difficulties he felt drained of his usual energy. Sarah's insistence on calling Dr Sullivan had resulted in him being confined to the house but truth to tell he didn't feel able to face a day's work at the mill.

'Ease up, man,' Dr Sullivan had said in his blunt manner, 'or you'll drive yourself into an early grave.' The two had been friends since their youth and believed in plain speaking.

'A touch of bronchitis is hardly likely to prove fatal,' Hamish said scornfully.

'With sensible precautions I quite agree but when have you ever been sensible where that mill is concerned?'

'Huh!'

'February is a treacherous month so you keep yourself indoors for the next week or ten days then we'll see.'

'Good God, man! You know that's impossible.'

'Nonsense. Takes a bit of rearranging that's all. Nothing to hinder you having the work needing your personal attention brought to you at Aran Heights and have enough confidence in your staff to delegate the rest.'

'Well, maybe –' Hamish said doubtfully.

'No maybe about it.' His finger pointed to a bottle of brown liquid. 'Don't be treating that as an ornament, the dosage is marked, see and take it regularly and I'll get on my way.'

10

Overweight and without the height to carry it, the doctor heaved himself up. 'Mistake to sit too long, Hamish. Could be that age is catching up with us,' he said cheerfully.

'Speak for yourself,' Hamish growled. He didn't like to be reminded that he was already well into middle age.

CHAPTER THREE

By late afternoon Susan was anxious to get out of the house and the disapproving atmosphere. Putting an old cloak over her plain dark gown that she wore in the mornings and should have changed, and a bonnet to cover her hair, she let herself out of the side door and into the cobbled courtyard. Aran Heights, set high on the hilliest part of Aranvale, seemed to grow out of the stark and harsh landscape of the hills and caught the full blast of the north wind which for much of the winter months howled and shrieked through the fields. As she moved across the courtyard a single frisky wind caught at her cloak and whipped it about her legs.

Keeping to the paths around the gardens Susan didn't at first hear the carriage and only when she heard her name shouted did she turn to see Matthew hurrying after her.

'Where are you off to?' Then he grinned. 'No, don't tell me,' he said, falling into step. 'You're in the dog-house.'

In spite of herself she giggled. 'You're an idiot, Matthew, and what are you doing home? Shouldn't you be hard at it in the mill?'

He scowled. Matthew was over six feet tall, loose-limbed, handsome and well aware of the effect his fair good looks had on young women.

'Chalmers was bringing some ledgers and stuff for Father and I decided to accompany him home.'

'You're absolutely hopeless, Matthew, no wonder Papa despairs of you.'

She saw his boyish face darken and then he burst into a sulky tirade.

'Would you believe this?' He sounded horrified. 'Father is insisting I familiarise myself with each stage of paper-making.

13

Heaven knows the office is bad enough but that God-awful clanking of machinery will slowly but surely drive me mad,' he said, clapping a hand to his brow.

'Try to stick it, Matt. After a while you'll hardly notice the noise and in any case you'll be spending most of the time in the office with Papa. He wants you ready to take over and you can't blame him for that, the mill is his whole life.'

'Exactly! As you so rightly say the mill is his whole life. He enjoys it, he got what he wanted and it would have been the same for Ralph.' He kicked viciously at a mound of frozen snow. 'Why did Ralph have to be so stupid as to go and get himself killed?'

'Matthew!' Susan was shocked.

'Sorry, I was thinking out loud. But can't you see, can't anyone see I'm different?' He spread out his hands in a gesture of hopelessness. 'I'm not interested in the mill or in making huge profits.'

'You're quite good at getting through your allowance,' she said tartly.

He glared angrily. 'Whose side are you on?'

'Matthew, I'm not taking sides.'

'Yes, you are.'

She forced a laugh. 'You don't know how ironic this is. What you are rebelling against is what I want. More than anything I want to work with Papa.'

'Wrong sex,' he said bluntly.

'No. Not the wrong sex just the wrong attitude from yours.'

He looked surprised and not a little put out.

'You're beginning to sound just like those females – you know, the ones fighting for God-knows-what.'

'They know what they're fighting for, the right to make use of their talents.'

While walking they had wandered away from the grounds of Aran Heights and Matthew stopped suddenly. 'This far enough for you?'

'I'm in no hurry to get back.'

'Come on then, we'll go round by Moorend.'

'Where else but Clapperton farm?' she said, amused.

'We needn't call in.'

'We won't be calling in,' Susan said firmly as she went ahead to take the road forking away from the farm road. She thought of Winnie Clapperton so obviously in love with Matthew and he only giving her the time of day because of his interest in the farm. Frowning at her thoughts, she turned to look at her brother and was surprised by a look of naked longing in his face as his eyes roved the peaceful country scene. Until that moment she hadn't fully realised just how deep went his passion for the land. Whatever the future held she couldn't see Matthew settling in the mill.

'You gone deaf or something?'

'Sorry, Matt.' She laughed, 'I was miles away. What were you saying?'

'One day Winnie will have all this.' His hand swept the surrounding acres and acres of fields and she heard his sigh. 'Pity she's so plain but I suppose it's a small price to pay for all this.' He gave his sister a sidelong glance.

'Stop it, Matthew,' Susan said sharply, 'Don't make use of people for your own ends and certainly not Winnie. I happen to be fond of her.'

'I wasn't serious.'

'I'm not so sure. I wouldn't put it past you but remember this, Matthew MacFarlane, I don't want Winnie hurt. In fact I might go as far as warn her.'

'Calm down for any favour and she wouldn't, you know – get hurt I mean. She'd be getting exactly what she wants,' he said smugly.

'Don't be so disgustingly sure of yourself. Winnie is no fool.'

'That I do know. When it comes to the farm she's almost as knowledgeable as old Clapperton and I happen to know that there isn't very much done without first discussing it with Winnie.'

Nothing more was said as they walked the rough pitted road. In the distance they could see smoke coming from the chimneys of the Old Mill House where Hamish had been

15

born and where his unmarried sister, Rachel, lived with her housekeeper and a small staff of servants.

'Susan!' Matthew gripped her arm. 'I've had an absolutely brilliant idea.' Then as she looked at him enquiringly he loosened his hold. 'No, I haven't, you've mucked it up by refusing Edward.'

'Mucked up what?'

'Edward hates playing second fiddle to that pompous ass Thomas.' He paused for Susan's reaction but there was none. 'What I'm trying to say is that Edward would be happier with some responsibility in the papermill rather than the way he's placed in the distillery.'

'Thomas is not a pompous ass, the description pompous applies more to Edward. Thomas is the elder son and naturally he'll succeed his father; Edward's trouble is that he doesn't like taking orders from anyone. That said, where is this supposed to be leading?'

'Nowhere,' he said morosely, 'unless you decide to marry Edward after all.' He brightened. 'Why not, Susan? Edward's all right, plenty after him and you could do worse.'

'You're the absolute limit, do you know that?'

'Just realistic. Married to you Edward becomes family and Father would welcome him with open arms, he'd be an asset to the mill. Later the pair of you will no doubt produce the longed-for grandson and all our troubles will be over.'

'Meaning you get what you want?'

'You won't come out of it so badly.'

'You're right I won't because, my dear brother, I have no intention of marrying Edward,' she said sweetly.

'Could be you'll have to, but speak of the devil, isn't that the Brodie carriage drawing up in the yard?'

She craned her neck and saw with a sinking heart that it was indeed the Brodie carriage. Even at that distance she could make out Edward's broad figure moving away from the carriage and walking towards the front entrance.

'What does he want here?' she muttered crossly.

'Come! Come! Susan, you must know that someone as persistent as our Edward won't be disheartened at the first

16

rebuff. Take it from me he won't be so easy to shake off.'
Seeing her expression he sobered. 'Why shouldn't he call?
Much more embarrassing if he didn't.' He grinned wickedly.
'Think of poor Mother if the Brodies were to shun Aran
Heights. She'd be inconsolable if her climb into society were
to be so cruelly halted.'

'That's going too far, Matthew,' Susan said coldly. 'Mama
has a wide circle of friends.'

'Agreed, but they're still way behind the high and mighty
Brodies.'

They were hardly inside and closing the vestibule door before
Sarah MacFarlane, in a pale lavender gown that rustled as she
moved, greeted her son warmly and turned to Susan.

'I do wish, Susan, that you had the good manners to tell
me before you go out,' she said petulantly. 'Edward is here,
he's with Papa at the moment.'

'My fault, Mother, don't blame Susan,' Matthew said
carelessly as he shrugged himself out of his coat. 'We were
both in need of a spot of fresh air.'

'Very well, but hadn't you better hurry and change?' she
said, looking with distaste at Susan's outdoor clothes.

'I was about to, Mama,' Susan said, anxious to make her
escape but it wasn't to be. The drawing-room door opened
and they heard Edward taking his leave of Hamish. Then,
catching sight of Susan, his eyebrows shot up and he was
smiling as he took the few strides along the passageway to
where they stood in the large square-shaped hall.

Moving away from the heat of the fire, Sarah excused
herself with a sweet smile to Edward and a warning look
in her daughter's direction. After a few pleasantries Matthew
followed his mother out.

Left together, Susan's first thought was that no matter
when one saw Edward he was always immaculately dressed.
Sarah liked such attention to appearance but Susan was
slightly put off by it. To her Edward just stopped short of
being a dandy.

Reaching for her hand he squeezed her fingers gently.

17

'Susan, let's not be awkward with one another; you were perfectly entitled to give me the answer you did.' He frowned as a maid arrived to add more logs to the hall fire. 'Couldn't we take a short stroll since you're dressed for outdoors?'

'Like this?'

He smiled. 'Not your best I gather but I have to be on my way shortly.'

At twenty-four Edward had the easy assurance of his class and was proud of his family history. His forebears had been Glasgow merchants engaged in the tobacco trade with the American colonies. Huge fortunes had been made and when trade declined the 'tobacco lords' as they were called bought other concerns. Seeing potential in the Granton Distillery, Joseph Brodie set about acquiring it and once it became his property began a programme of expansion. Pouring so much money into the hugely competitive whisky trade had not been without its risks, for though popular locally the Granton blend was virtually unknown outside Lanarkshire.

Aggressive marketing spread its fame and the Granton blend became known and approved. Profits soared and the Brodie family became one of the richest and most influential in Lanarkshire.

Once Susan and Edward were clear of the house Edward took her arm.

'Let me make one thing clear, Susan, the suddenness of my proposal was in no way influenced by your parents or mine.'

She felt laughter bubbling up in her throat. 'Come on, Edward, be completely honest, it had a good deal to do with it.'

'You're wrong about that.' His eyes met and held hers. 'Ralph knew how much I admired you. I even told him that you were the girl I was going to marry.'

'And what did Ralph have to say?' She couldn't stop herself asking.

'I'm happy to say he approved.'

And that was probably true, she thought. Ralph thought a lot of Edward, and Edward had been devastated by his friend's death. But it didn't alter anything as far as she was concerned.

'I wish it were different,' she said softly, 'but it's better to be honest. I like you but I don't love you.'

'That would come.' And when she didn't answer there was alarm in his voice. 'There isn't anyone – I mean you're not – '

She shook her head. 'No, Edward, there is no one,' she said truthfully.

His face relaxed. It was a nice face with well-defined features and light blue eyes but the mouth was too thin and could twist into a cruel line. Both Thomas and Edward owed their sandy colouring to their mother but that was all the brothers had in common. Whereas Thomas was small made with narrow shoulders Edward was built like his father and stood just short of six feet.

'That's a relief, you had me worried.' And as she made to speak he held up his hand. 'Don't worry, I'm not going to keep badgering you but at least I can go on hoping you'll change your mind.'

'You're a dear, Edward,' she said impulsively, 'and I know that for most girls marriage is the most important step in their life. One day maybe I'll feel that way too.'

'But not yet?'

'No, not yet. Before that I mean to do something with my life.'

'Such as?' His eyes were amused.

'Such as persuading Papa to give me some responsibility in the mill.'

Edward looked even more shocked than Papa had.

'Mr MacFarlane would never agree to that. Take my advice and don't suggest such a thing.'

'I already have,' she said haughtily.

'May I ask what he had to say?'

'Oh, he'll take a bit of persuading,' she said airily, 'but I don't give up easily.'

'Susan, I'm not suggesting that you are not intelligent – '

'How kind of you,' she said sarcastically, 'and how strange that one of my sex should be credited with brains.'

19

His face darkened with anger. 'All I meant was that business is a man's world and there is no place in it for a woman.'

'Why not? Are we fit only to do the master's bidding and bear his children?' she flashed back.

'Most women seem well satisfied with their lot,' he said grimly.

'What choice have they? I'm in a different position. Matthew wants to take up farming so Papa may have need of me.'

He nodded, some of his former annoyance evaporating. 'Yes, I know of Matthew's reluctance to be involved in the mill and how worrying it is for Mr MacFarlane. We were just discussing that.' About to say more he checked himself and in a blinding flash Susan saw it all. Matthew's brilliant idea hadn't been his alone. She could see that it would be to everyone's advantage if she were to marry Edward. Papa would welcome Edward into the mill but only as a son-in-law. Matthew wouldn't be under the same pressure and, last, but certainly not least, Mama's place in society would be assured if the families were united through marriage.

Well, she wouldn't let herself be used. She would stand up against the lot of them and if life became intolerable there was always Aunt Rachel. Aunt Rachel would understand as no one else would. The light of battle was in her eyes as she said frostily, 'I'm beginning to feel chilled, Edward. This is far enough and I'd like to return home now.'

CHAPTER FOUR

In the library, a very masculine wood-panelled room where Hamish MacFarlane had ruled out any interference from Sarah, Susan sat stiffly in a chair across from a desk littered with papers. On the floor on either side of her father's chair was a stack of ledgers and, seeing the questioning look in her eyes, he gave one of his rare smiles.

'You could say the office has been transferred to Aran Heights.'

Not knowing the reason for her summons some of the unease lifted and she smiled in relief.

Placing his elbows on his desk and with the tips of his fingers pressed together, Hamish looked at his daughter thoughtfully.

'I hadn't quite dismissed your suggestion of assisting me. No, don't get carried away,' he said as she leaned forward eagerly. 'Your presence in the mill is out of the question.'

'Then how can I – '

'Kindly stop interrupting.'

'I'm sorry,' she murmured, looking down at her clasped hands.

'Quite! Now if you will allow me to continue. It occurred to me that working from Aran Heights, though tedious and unsatisfactory for me, could be the answer in your case and since you are so keen to learn you can take on some of the work here at home.'

'Thank you, Papa.'

He frowned. 'Let me add that this is all very much against your mother's wishes and it might be prudent if you were to spend some of your time following the pursuits of a normal,' he stressed normal, 'young lady.' His eyebrows

21

beetled and he growled. 'That shouldn't be beyond your capabilities.'

'No, Papa,' she said demurely. 'I'll promise to try and please Mama.' Inwardly she was doubtful of success but at least she would try.

'Good!' he said as if that disposed of a tiresome problem. Rising from his chair she took as a signal for her departure and got up hastily.

'No, don't go just yet. This seems as good a time as any to initiate you into the business your great-grandfather founded.' He waved a hand. 'Bring your chair forward and we'll make a start and if you prove yourself useful I may consider having a desk brought in for your own use.'

Her father proved to be a good teacher. In a clear and unhurried manner he began to explain how a papermill functioned, emphasising the importance of each worker no matter how humble. She listened carefully, even venturing some questions and those he answered at length. She could sense that he was pleased. Time flew and too soon for Susan, her father closed the ledgers.

'Enough for one day, young woman.'

'I'm not a bit tired,' she protested.

'I dare say,' he said drily, 'but I am.'

Guiltily she remembered then that he was convalescent and, looking, she saw the tiredness etched on his face. She bit her lip. 'I ought to have remembered that Dr Sullivan – '

'Dr Sullivan is an old woman. A lot less fussing and I'd be a deal happier.' Then seeing her face and the concern there his voice softened. 'Teaching an able student is no hardship; my one regret is that you were blessed with the MacFarlane brains rather than Matthew. However that's the way it is,' he ended heavily.

'When may I come back?'

'Mmmmm. Mornings straight after breakfast, I think. I'll set you some work and – ' his eyes went to the bookshelves. 'You're not obliged to read them but if you're interested in the history of paper-making by all means take those you want.' His head went down and she knew that the time allotted to her had expired. Quietly she went out, closing the door behind her. Hardly had the door closed than her mother's voice reached her.

'Susan, come down here at once.'

'Coming, Mama.' Hurrying along the corridor and down to the dining-room Susan found her mother inspecting the polished furniture for traces of dust and, finding none, turned to her daughter.

'Where have you been all this time?' she snapped.

'With Papa, I told you.'

The dining-room was almost as big as the drawing-room and was used only when there were guests. The family dined in the breakfast-room or the small dining-room at the back of the house and nearer the kitchens.

'You think you've got your own way,' she smirked.

'Papa wants me – '

Sarah cut her off. 'What possible good it will do you is beyond me and what our friends would have to say if they found out – '

'Why should that matter?'

'Because, you stupid girl, well-brought-up young ladies do not interest themselves in such things. I'm surprised at your papa, more than surprised.'

'All I'll be doing is spending a few hours in the library and I would like to please you,' Susan said quietly, remembering her promise to her father.

'Then you may remain with me while I discuss the week's menus with Mrs Doig.'

Working closely with her father Susan got an insight into the real man. Not the harsh disciplinarian some saw but a man who had the good of his workers at heart. On self-inflicted troubles he poured out scorn but to those of his employees in genuine need he turned a sympathetic ear and there were many who had reason to bless the Master of Aranvale.

Loudly protesting yet recognising the necessity in this damp and foggy weather, Hamish MacFarlane extended his time at home. Each morning after breakfast Matthew left for

23

the mill and Susan joined her father in the library. Early on they had come to an agreement that outside the time allocated to her she would make no demands, ask no questions. For Susan this was no hardship; what she failed to grasp she took note of for their next session.

A lot of her day was spent closeted with her father in the library and if he noticed the lengthening of the day he made no remark. After all, having her own desk and working area meant no more than the scratching of two pens instead of one.

Before long Hamish was involving her in discussions or rather, she supposed, he was thinking out loud and happy to have an interested listener. On the last of these days Susan looked across to where her father sat and felt a wave of depression.

'You can't imagine how much I'm going to miss all this.'

'Some work will continue to be brought to you but it's high time I was back, Susan. Even the most conscientious workers need supervision.' He nodded his head knowingly. 'Human nature being what it is, when there is no one to oversee, slackness invariably happens. And another thing, no matter how much they grumble the workers recognise the need for strict and fair supervision, in fact they welcome it.'

'I'm sure you're right, Papa, but is there no chance – '

'Of working alongside me? Absolutely none so let's have no more of that. Instead consider yourself fortunate that I have allowed you this far.'

'I am grateful.'

He smiled. 'An intelligent interest I expected but you have surpassed my expectations and there is just the possibility that someone will be instructed to come to Aran Heights to teach you our method of book-keeping. That is if I can spare a clerk.'

It was around ten o'clock on a Wednesday morning that Susan crossed to the shelves for another book on the history of paper-making. On the way to her desk she glanced out of the window and at that angle could just make out the figure of a young man before he disappeared round to the side of the house. Idly she wondered whom he might be. Not a visitor or he would have arrived by carriage and there was no carriage in the courtyard. Mrs Dunbar, the housekeeper, would deal with him and if not she would have to go down. Mrs MacFarlane was indisposed with a headache and likely to keep to her bedroom for most of the day.

Turning the pages of the book before beginning serious reading, she was interrupted by the maid announcing that a Mr David Cameron had an appointment with Miss Susan MacFarlane.

'Indeed! Did he state his business?'

'No, Miss Susan. I put him in the mornin' room like the mistress told me. Did I do right?' she asked anxiously.

'Yes, Polly.' Susan nodded kindly to the new maid. 'I'll come down right away.'

When she entered the morning-room the stranger turned from his study of the view and as their eyes met Susan's heart fluttered and she had the strangest sensation that nothing would ever be quite the same again. It was alarming and ridiculous and to hide her confusion she drew herself up and spoke more haughtily than she intended.

'Kindly state your business, Mr Cameron.'

He gave a small bow and spoke with icy politeness.

'My business, Miss MacFarlane, is to spend two hours twice weekly teaching you the basics of book-keeping.' He managed to convey that the task ahead afforded him little pleasure.

Embarrassed at being caught out and angered at his tone she faltered.

'I – I beg your pardon. No one warned me of your coming.' She shouldn't have used the word 'warn' but really this common and forward young man was having such a disturbing effect on her. 'In any case,' she rushed on, making matters worse, 'I would have expected my father to engage an older and more senior clerk.'

The dark almost black eyes looked at her steadily.

'Miss MacFarlane, the task is not of my choosing and it so happens that the more elderly clerks are not accountants.'

25

Her lips tightened. He was, she thought, quite the most odious and at the same time the most handsome man she had ever met. Tall and very dark, he held himself with a soldierly erectness yet without stiffness. His features were regular, his chin determined and his eyes, darkly lashed, appeared almost black in a clean-shaven face.

'Am I right in assuming that your duties begin immediately, Mr Cameron?'

'Whenever you are ready,' he said mockingly.

'Then be good enough to follow me to the library,' she said crisply.

Very conscious of those dark eyes following her, Susan was glad when they reached the library. Once inside she saw his eyes move quickly round the room then linger on the book-laden shelves and widen in appreciation.

'Where do we work?' he asked politely.

Quickly she went to her desk and sat down. 'Bring a chair for yourself.' She pointed to one.

Without a word he picked up the heavy high-backed chair as though it were a lightweight, set it well apart from her and sat down. From the folder he had been carrying he extracted a bundle of papers and proceeded to spread them across the desk.

'Am I correct in assuming you have no knowledge of the subject, Miss MacFarlane?' he asked but the answer was there in his voice.

Susan set her lips and didn't answer. Let him find out, she thought.

'Very well, we'll begin at the beginning.'

'Where else?' she said sweetly, earning herself a dark look.

Clearly and precisely he gave his explanations and in a manner that would have been acceptable to someone of limited intelligence. Not having to dwell on the content, Susan studied his voice instead. Pleasant enough, she conceded and well modulated but his articulation was too careful and shrewdly she recognised that here was someone trying to rise above his station and to do so he was obviously emulating others. As he moved his head she frowned in concentration. For a fleeting tantalising moment he had reminded her of someone, then it was gone and she saw that he had stopped talking. Putting down his pen he leaned back in his chair and she saw a nerve twitch.

'For at least five minutes, Miss MacFarlane, you haven't heard a word I've said. Either I'm not making myself clear and you fail to understand or you already have some knowledge of the subject.'

She knew she'd angered him, deserved his reproach and she tried to redeem herself. 'Revision is seldom wasted, Mr Cameron, and I have to admit that some of it is familiar.'

'Then had you taken the trouble to inform me,' he said with icy coldness, 'your time and mine might have been saved.'

'I'm sorry, I do apologise,' she said, having the grace to blush. 'Allow me to show you the stage I have reached.' Taking out some of her own workings she put the neat columns of figures before him and saw his start of surprise.

'You did these?'

Feeling absurdly pleased she nodded. 'You seem to find it unusual in a female but figures have always held an interest for me. My brother and I shared lessons so I had a good grounding.'

'Forgive me saying so but your brother couldn't produce that kind of work, not with any amount of tuition.'

'Perhaps not,' she said coldly, feeling he was overstepping himself, 'my brother's talents take another direction.'

'I'm sure they do.' He selected another paper and began doing calculations while she looked on.

After he'd gone Susan felt her legs suddenly weak and sat down in the chair David Cameron had vacated. Her hands went to her hot cheeks and she wondered what was happening to her. Nothing or no one had ever made her feel this way and it was humiliating that a brash young man, a mere employee at the mill should have this effect on her. Then she tried to make excuses for herself, blaming it on the unexpectedness of his arrival.

Nevertheless it was the young accountant's mocking dark eyes she remembered as she lay awake well into the night.

David Cameron's first impression of Susan MacFarlane was of a spoilt and pampered young woman very much aware of her position and not likely to let him forget it either. As they would any full-blooded young man her beauty and poise had attracted him but it was her quick mind that had him captivated. In his short experience of the opposite sex beauty and brains seldom mixed yet here at Aran Heights he found that combination. Far from dreading his next visit to Aran Heights he found to his surprise that he was looking forward to teaching Miss Susan MacFarlane.

Taken aback by Mr MacFarlane's request – not a request, an order – to teach his daughter some book-keeping, David had resigned himself to the boredom of imparting information to someone incapable of understanding the first thing about such a complex subject. How wrong he had been to imagine that the master of the mill would indulge even his own daughter unless it were to prove profitable.

That had him wondering as he walked home to the humble cottage he shared with his mother. With the elder son dead and the other so obviously unsuited to follow his father, the master must be worried. Was it possible that Miss Susan MacFarlane was being coached and trained to become the controlling influence with her twin merely the figurehead? David had a shrewd suspicion that it could well be the case. What other explanation could there be?

A clever, ambitious young man, David had every intention of going far. The fact that he had been born out of wedlock did not greatly trouble him. Indeed after what he'd had to put up with it had prepared him to stand up for himself and given him the ruthlessness needed to succeed.

All that he had ever learned from his mother was that he had been fathered by a gentleman. Natural curiosity had urged him to ask more but his questions had been met with a tight-lipped refusal. For all her gentleness Eliza Cameron was a strong-willed and deeply religious woman. To her a

28

vow such as she had made was a sacred promise and nothing would make her break it. Only her sister knew and the secret was safe with her.

Employed as a table-maid in one of Lanarkshire's finest houses, Eliza's fresh young beauty had not gone unnoticed by the master of the house and as her figure blossomed into the shapeliness of womanhood so his interest in the young maid had increased.

More flattered than repulsed by the attention of a man old enough to be her father it had never occurred to Eliza Cameron to do other than obey. Wasn't he the master and hadn't her mother, fearful of her daughter losing such a sought-after position, drummed into her repeatedly the need to be obedient at all times?

Finding herself pregnant the sixteen-year-old Eliza had been terrified. With no one to turn to and only too well aware that her strict parents would show her the door, she had blurted out her condition to the master. Not that she expected any help from that quarter, indeed it could only hasten her departure from his house but he had noticed her distress and demanded to know the reason for it. As she stammered out the awful truth his face had grown grave and his long silence had unnerved her, bringing her to the verge of hysteria.

What was to become of her? Where could she go? From gossip in the kitchen she was vaguely aware of the method used by some girls who found themselves in this position and wanted rid of their unwanted babies. But that was a sin and Eliza Cameron had a healthy fear of the wrath of God and His punishment.

Not an unkind man, the master had drawn her gently to him and looked into her swimming eyes. Of course, he'd said gently, there was no question but that she must leave his employ and quickly but not without some support. How grateful she had been for those gold coins. A fortune in her eyes. Between sniffs and sobs she had poured out her gratitude, only too happy to agree to his terms. In return for such generosity she was to move away from the area and give him her vow of silence. No one must know that he was responsible for her condition. Everything he said had been agreed to willingly and, no doubt relieved to be rid of her so easily, he had pressed a further sum to help her educate the child if it were a boy.

Eliza Cameron had guarded that money for her son's education and even when she was at her wits' end as to where their next crust of bread was coming from she had never been tempted to dip into it. Now she was reaping her reward. David was a good son and he had worked hard at his studies, gaining praise from his teachers. Eliza was bursting with pride when he secured a position as junior accountant with the Aranvale Papermill and when he had insisted that she no longer took in washing or went out scrubbing she had been touched. Reluctant at first, she had eventually given in to his wishes. With careful budgeting, and she was used to that, his salary would cover their needs.

CHAPTER FIVE

Other than a Sunday morning, breakfast at Aran Heights was most often eaten in silence or at best in whispered conversation. Mr MacFarlane disliked talk at this time in the morning and indeed the family seldom sat down together. More and more in recent weeks the lady of the house was having a tray sent up to her bedroom and Matthew, always a late arrival for breakfast, allowed himself only sufficient time to swallow a few mouthfuls before joining his father in the carriage which would be ready and waiting for them in the drive.

This morning for some reason the entire family was to breakfast together. Susan was humming under her breath as she helped herself to breakfast from the hot plates on the dresser.

'Someone's happy,' Matthew whispered as he piled bacon on to his plate.

'Maybe I am but what's come over you? All of ten minutes to eat your bacon and eggs, that's unheard of.'

He grinned. 'Spring is in the air tra-la.'

'Susan,' her mother said plaintively, 'did you have a caller yesterday? I thought I heard voices but my head was pounding so painfully that I couldn't be sure.'

'A Mr Cameron from the mill called – ' Susan began.

'Sarah,' her husband said irritably, 'you knew Mr Cameron was expected. Damn it, I told you to tell Susan.'

'I'm sorry, Hamish, it completely slipped my mind.'

'Must have been a bit of a surprise for you, Susan?'

'Yes, it was.' Hastily she dropped her eyes as she felt her colour rising.

'Not overgifted with patience our Mr Cameron but a good

31

head on him so pay attention and you'll learn a lot.'

'Really, I must object to this nonsense,' Sarah said sharply, putting down the finger of toast she had been nibbling. She touched her lips delicately with a corner of her napkin. 'This is complete folly and it has gone far enough. What possible use can Susan be to you?'

'At one time I would have said none, my dear, but I have the future to think about. I won't always be here – '

'Don't talk like that,' Sarah interrupted sharply, 'it upsets me.'

'Then it shouldn't. We all have to leave this world one day and I want a MacFarlane ready to take over when that day comes.'

'Of course I understand that and by then Matthew will be ready to do so.'

'Unfortunately Matthew has shown himself to be completely useless.'

Matthew had half risen, his face had gone white and his eyes smouldered with anger.

'Useless in the mill, Father! Yes, I couldn't agree more. I hate the place and I'm beginning to suffocate in that vile atmosphere.' His eyes switched to Susan. 'By all means teach Susan; it's what she wants. You'll find her a willing and I don't doubt able student and think about it, Father, if you haven't already done so. If, or is it when, she marries Edward Brodie you'll have a good team: two business heads instead of one.'

Susan rounded on him furiously. 'You've no right to say such a thing.'

'Why not?' her mother said, opening her eyes wide. 'As regards Edward, Matthew is only stating what your papa and I have agreed is best for you.'

'Papa, it's not true.' Her eyes were pleading. 'You wouldn't make me marry Edward?'

'You're too young to know what is best for you,' he barked angrily and scraping back his chair strode out of the room, leaving his breakfast unfinished. Three pairs of eyes watched his departure then Mrs MacFarlane spoke warningly.

'Matthew, dear, you had better hurry.'

Drawing a hand through his unruly fair hair he sighed resignedly, gave Susan a ruefully apologetic grin which she ignored and, rising from his chair, followed his father out. At that moment, to Susan's intense relief, the maid arrived and stood hesitantly within the doorway awaiting instructions.

'Yes, you may clear up.' Sarah signalled to the table with a flurry of a white hand. Then without a glance at Susan she got up and swept from the room.

Susan watched the maid for a few minutes then collected an old coat from the stand in the hall and went out into the garden for a breath of fresh air and to get a grip on herself. The mist was lifting from the hills and a glint of sun peeked out to give the promise of a fine day but Susan scarcely noticed. She felt betrayed and hurt yet honesty forced her to see it from her father's position and in her heart she couldn't blame him. What other course was open to him? Both sons had failed him – Ralph by his untimely death and Matthew by his reluctance to work in the mill. With his own health giving cause for alarm was it any wonder that he now turned to his daughter to make a suitable marriage. And Edward would be eminently suitable. His background was excellent and he had a keen brain, just what the papermill required.

In a fit of depression she thought perhaps it would be wiser just to fall in with everyone's wishes and marry Edward. Respect and liking were quite enough for marriage as both her parents had been at pains to point out. And it could be worse, much worse; some girls were forced into marriage with someone old and repugnant and Edward was certainly neither of these. Why then, as she almost decided her fate, did a pair of mocking eyes rise up to taunt her?

In rather less than an hour David Cameron was due at Aran Heights and still Susan hadn't made up her mind as to what she would wear. Four gowns lay in an untidy heap on the bed, having been discarded for various reasons. Finally she decided on a skirt of black taffeta and a crisp white blouse with a high frilled neckline and fastened down the front with tiny pearl buttons.

Ten minutes before the appointed hour saw Susan behind her desk. Her silver blonde hair was swept up into a pompadour and secured with two tortoise-shell combs, leaving a slender column of neck above the frilled neckline. There was a soft tell-tale flush on her cheeks as she bent her head in a pretence of working. All the time her ears were alert for the sounds of Mr Cameron's arrival.

David Cameron was prompt; he would not have dared be otherwise. Remembering Miss Susan's instructions, careful instructions, the housekeeper had the maid show David to the library immediately on his arrival. The task was very much to the liking of the saucy young maid who eyed the strikingly handsome young man with bold, inviting eyes. But the boldness fast disappeared when she met his cold stare. With a tightening of her own lips she saw his curl in disgust and she gave an angry toss of her head. Walking ahead of him with an exaggerated swing to her hips she led the way along a passage with a stone floor and drab painted walls to stairs which divided the servants' quarters from the main house. Where the carpet began huge oil paintings dignified the impressive staircase and the length of wall to the library.

Susan answered the sharp rap on the door and, dismissing the maid with a curt nod, David entered. At that precise moment the grandfather clock in the hall boomed out the hour and Susan smiled with amusement.

'Good morning, Mr Cameron, you are prompt.'

'Good morning, Miss MacFarlane,' he said gravely. 'I take great pains to be punctual but seldom manage it to the minute.'

She gave him her warm smile then laughed. 'Believe me, I do know of my father's insistence on punctuality, it extends to his family as well.' She indicated the vacant chair next to her own. 'Please sit down then we can get started.'

Behind hastily lowered lashes she watched his tall figure cross the room and felt the quickening of her heartbeat as he took his seat beside her. At once his eyes went to the papers neatly placed on his end of the desk and a ledger open to display a completed balance sheet.

34

'Very good! You've done the work I set you?' He managed to sound both pleased and surprised.

Her delicate eyebrows shot up. 'Didn't you expect me to do it?'

'Thought maybe I'd overdone it – shades of the class-room!'

'Not at all,' she said stiffly, 'you're here to teach and I to learn and I may add that my father will expect results.'

'That I don't doubt.'

She looked at him quickly but he had turned his attention to her workings and she saw him frown. When he put a question mark in the margin she said, 'Why? What have I done wrong?'

'Nothing at all, you've arrived at the right answer.'

'Well then?'

'It was a long laborious way to get there. Let me show you.'

He took her each step of the way, occasionally looking up to see if she were following. At the end she said apologetically, 'How very much simpler and how stupid of me.'

He put down his pen and regarded her unsmilingly. 'There was nothing stupid about it. This is merely a way of saving time and effort and now we'll get on with the next part. I can see with the progress you're making that my services will very shortly become unnecessary.'

'I'm sure I still have a great deal to learn,' she said hastily, then, seeing his amusement, coloured and looked away.

An hour later she rubbed at her neck, feeling a stiffness.

'Too long holding your head in one position. I used to suffer from that,' he said sympathetically.

'A short break will do us both good, Mr Cameron.' She had a sudden, urgent need to learn more about Mr David Cameron.

'What made you decide to be an accountant?'

He thought before answering. 'There's security in this type of work and figures fascinate me just as they do you.'

'So your ambition has been realised?'

'Not at all though you may well be right.' He paused. 'A

friend I studied with has written recently to tell me of the good opportunities there are down south. He's doing well and suggests I should join him.'

'But you wouldn't?' she said swiftly. It was ridiculous the depth of disappointment she felt at the thought of him leaving Aranvale.

'I'm not free to go otherwise I most certainly would pack my bags and seek my fortune.' He stopped. 'If it's not an impertinence may I make a personal remark?'

She nodded. Of course she shouldn't encourage him, she knew that well enough, but she wanted to hear what he had to say.

'You have beauty and intelligence, something rarely found together.'

She blushed. 'Thank you but your view is limited. Many women are gifted but have no outlet for their talents.'

'Is it possible that one day the Aranvale Papermill may have a woman at its head?'

'Would that be so terrible?'

'Any departure from the normal is looked on with suspicion,' he said carefully.

'You for one wouldn't welcome it?' What was she thinking of, talking like this to an employee of her father?

'I didn't say that. In my opinion it would be far better to have a capable, intelligent woman in a position of authority than a man lacking in those qualities. Problem would be getting the respect from the workers.'

'Yes, you're probably right,' she said, opening one of the ledgers. For the remainder of the two hours the dark head and the fair head were bent over papers bearing the crest of the Aranvale Papermill.

'Time is up, Miss MacFarlane.' Did she detect a note of regret or was it wishful thinking?

'You're not finding the task too arduous?'

'On the contrary it has been a privilege and a pleasure.'

Getting to her feet she disturbed the papers on the desk and a few fluttered to the floor. Simultaneously they made a grab and in doing so their fingers touched. Susan drew back as though she had been scorched and for a long moment they both seemed to be holding their breath. In that short interval she could have sworn he was equally shaken but if so he quickly recovered and she was left wondering if she had imagined it. What wasn't imagination was the alarming effect this young man had had on her right from the first moment of meeting and suddenly she was afraid . . .

Those electrifying moments had shaken David Cameron more than he would have believed possible. Only by a supreme effort had he conquered an overwhelming desire to take her in his arms and crush her to him. That she was not totally indifferent to him he knew by the shock in those startlingly blue eyes. Yet what a ridiculous situation. He would do well to remember his place if he wished to remain in the employ of the Master of Aranvale.

Embarrassment had brought out her frostiness and as he prepared to leave she gave him a cool smile of dismissal.

'I'll get the maid to see you out.'

'No need for that, Miss MacFarlane,' he said, matching her tone for coolness. 'I have mastered the geography of the servants' quarters and can very well see myself out.'

Once outside, his folder beneath his arm, David gave in to an impulse and walked round to the front of Aran Heights where a broad sweep of gravel gave ample room for a carriage to turn. At the wide open ornamental gates he stood and looked in and for him the joy of this magnificent structure lay in its stark simplicity, its compelling beauty. Here was classic undertstatement. The precision in the spacing of the windows, in the tall stately chimneys and weather-beaten stone walls. Uncluttered with mouldings and innocent of decorative patterns, each window had a long, graceful line which continued to the windows of the attics. A forest of trees and olive green firs gave protection to the house from the worst of the weather. In the distance he could see the bobbing heads of the gardeners hoeing the ground and hear the trundling of barrows.

To dwell in such a house! To have servants to do one's

bidding and a carriage for convenience. Susan MacFarlane had all this, this was where she belonged. Thinking of the humble, damp cottage he shared with his mother David almost laughed out loud. Miss MacFarlane might occupy his thoughts but that was all it would ever be.

A lane behind the main street of Aranvale led to a row of badly maintained cottages and the end one was home to David and his mother. It was a but and ben and Eliza's bed was in a hole in the wall covered during the day by a curtain. Waxcloth worn in places covered the stone floor. The carefully black-leaded range gleamed in the light from the gas mantle. Because of the dampness the fire was never allowed to go out even in the summer. Each night it was banked up with dross and left to slow burn. In the middle of the room was a wooden table covered in a green plush cloth and under it two kitchen chairs. Here David and his mother ate their meals. As a schoolboy and later as a student it had served as a desk for his books and on washing days old blankets were spread on it to iron the clothes. This was done with a flat iron heated at the fire and spat on to test for the correct heat. Eliza was a dab hand at ironing, her expertise gained by years of ironing for the well-to-do who paid little but expected much. Two shabby cushioned chairs sat either side of the range and on the opposite wall stood a dresser with a wally dog on each side.

A door gave directly into the other room where David slept.

At the sink in front of the curtained window Eliza Cameron, wearing a coarse apron over her skirt, scraped at a potato with a kitchen knife. Then she added it to the others in the thick black pot and closed her eyes until the sharp pain reduced to a small, nagging annoyance. Her brow was beaded in sweat and she used a rag to wipe it away. Wearily she started on the carrots and turnip. David needed a good nourishing meal when he got home. Once it was under way and the table set she'd settle down in the chair for a rest. It would help her get through the rest of the evening without alarming David. She didn't want him to be worried about her health.

David lifted the sneck and let himself in. The sound was usually enough to bring his mother but not tonight. He hung up his coat on a hook attached to the wall and called out, 'I'm home, Mother.'

She was asleep in front of the range where two pots spluttered and steam rose from the heavy black kettle. For a few moments he looked down at her. Her head was bent forward and some of the grey hairs had escaped the coiled plait and hung loose and untidy on her neck. Blue-veined, papery hands that had done a lifetime of scrubbing and cleaning rested in her lap. Suddenly she gave a snort, her head jerked up and she looked at him with startled, uncomprehending eyes.

'It's only me, Mother,' David said gently.

She roused herself. 'Dearie me, I must have dropped off. You're early,' she said accusingly as she made to get up.

'No, Mother, it's my usual time but stay where you are. I'm perfectly capable of serving my own meal.'

'"deed and you'll do no such thing and you been workin' all day.' Pushing his arm away she staggered to her feet then held on to the back of the chair to regain her balance. 'Some would be sayin' your mother's had a drop too much,' she said with an attempt at humour.

'Folk know better than that, Mother.' He frowned. 'I'm worried about you and after we eat I'm going for Dr Anderson. This has gone on long enough.'

'You'll do no such thing, my lad. Can't a body be tired without all this fuss,' she said with a spurt of anger.

'All right,' he said soothingly, 'but promise me you'll see the doctor if this continues?'

'Take your meal while there's some good in it and stop worryin'. The Lord won't take me afore my time.'

CHAPTER SIX

Mr Cameron was seldom out of her thoughts and Susan felt strangely excited. She couldn't understand it or the sensation which twisted her stomach and sent her heart beating wildly. Getting up and wandering over to the window she watched the gardeners weeding and hoeing and replanting the flower-beds for the summer and longed to be out of doors.

'Susan, what is the matter with you?'

'Nothing, Mama.' She turned from the window as her mother put down the embroidery she had been working on. Then, after folding it carefully, put cloth, threads and scissors into a drawer of the small table and glanced at the clock.

'It's time I was getting ready. Susan, go and tell Mrs Dunbar to have the carriage brought round.'

Susan thought depressingly of the social calls ahead which played such an important part in her mother's day and, as if reading her thoughts, Sarah added, 'You won't be required to accompany me this afternoon.'

'In that case may I visit Moorend?' she asked, hiding her relief.

'By all means go over and spend some time with Winnie. Poor girl, her aunt can't be much company.'

It never ceased to surprise Susan that her mother encouraged the visits to Moorend when her own papa and Winnie's father barely spoke when they were in the same room.

Less than a mile from Aran Heights, it was a pleasant walk to Moorend. Sometimes she took the short cut across the fields but in the sunshine she decided on the longer route that took her past the kirk and the manse. Strains of organ music reached her ears from the open door which would be Mr McKay practising for the Sabbath worship.

Moorend, or Clapperton country as it was sometimes called, was by far the largest of the farms in the district and straddled the outward road. Like Hamish MacFarlane he was a fair employer and well respected by the farmhands.

From the window of the farmhouse Winnie Clapperton had spotted her visitor and she was at the door to meet Susan, her plain face wreathed in smiles. She was a tall, ungainly girl who looked older than her twenty years. Her face was sallow and framed by light mousy brown hair scraped back unbecomingly from her high forehead. Her eyes were of a soft velvety brown with amber flecks and hidden under the drab grey skirt was her only claim to beauty – her long, shapely legs hinted at only by the occasional glimpse of a neat ankle.

On the doorstep the two girls embraced then went indoors.

'Susan, how lovely of you to call and you couldn't have come at a better time,' Winnie said delightedly. 'Papa has just left for the market and Aunt Tina is in the village visiting one of her lame ducks so we can have a decent chat without interruptions.'

Susan was glad that Aunt Tina was not at Moorend. Not that she disliked Winnie's aunt, far from it; she was a kindly soul but with a tongue that would clip clouts as Papa once said on the one and only occasion she was at Aran Heights.

Shabby by Aran Heights' standard the parlour into which Winnie led her was a good-sized room with two large windows. From one could be seen the spire of the kirk where both the MacFarlanes and the Clappertons put in an appearance most Sabbath days. From the other windows the tall chimney of the papermill loomed high against the distant hills.

In protest against the violation of her comfortable quarters, Tabby, one of the farm cats, unfurled herself, mewed resentfully and slunk away to take refuge under one of the two leather armchairs drawn close on either side of the hearth. The rest of the furniture in the parlour was good and solid but here at Moorend polishing was an occasional rather than

42

a daily event. Nevertheless its faded elegance never ceased to please Susan. Here was homeliness, something her mother had never achieved at Aran Heights. In her book tidiness came next to Godliness and even the smallest ornament out of place offended her eye and had to be corrected immediately.

Neither of the women at Moorend was particularly house-proud and as a consequence few alterations had been made since the time that Winnie's mother had been its mistress. Betsy Clapperton had been a frail, sweet-faced woman and her death at the age of twenty-nine had been a devastating blow to Euan Clapperton and a bewildering loss to the nine-year-old Winnie.

A widower and a well-to-do one at that, it was expected that Euan Clapperton would be deluged with offers of help from the unattached ladies of Aranvale and beyond but their hopes of becoming the next mistress of Moorend were rudely shattered when his outspoken and embarrassingly tactless spinster sister, Tina, arrived to take charge of her brother and his little daughter. Some said sourly that but for Tina Clapperton her brother would have taken to himself a second wife if for no better reason than to give him a son to inherit Moorend.

That he would have welcomed a son there was no denying but his hopes were now firmly pinned on Winnie making a suitable marriage and in time presenting him with a grandson. When that day came Euan Clapperton would be a contented man.

Susan grinned with amusement as Tabby re-emerged to stretch herself and rub against Susan's skirt before taking up her rightful position in the middle of the hearthrug.

'Rules the house that one does,' Winnie said, giving the cat a playful dig with her foot. 'Give me your cloak, Susan, and I'll tell Lydia we're in the parlour. She can bring in tea later.'

Susan sat back contentedly in the comfortable softness of the armchair, only sitting forward when Winnie took the seat opposite.

'If it gets uncomfortably hot in here tell me and I'll have a window opened.'

43

'I'm very comfortable,' Susan said, shifting under the other's steady scrutiny.

'Something different about you.'

'What makes you say that?'

'I'm not sure,' Winnie said slowly, 'you seem keyed up and just not yourself.'

'You know me too well, that's the trouble,' Susan said ruefully.

'We're friends, talk if you want, I'm a good listener but if you prefer not to I won't probe.'

'I do need someone to talk to.' She swallowed. 'Edward proposed but maybe Matthew told you?'

'No, he didn't but isn't this a call for celebration?'

'I refused him.'

'Oh!'

'Does that surprise you?'

'I suppose so. You two seemed so well suited and he is nice.'

'That's not enough. I'm not in love with him.'

'How do you know?'

'I just do. He doesn't excite me in the least.'

'Well, that could be because you've always known him. Don't tell me you're waiting for someone to sweep you off your feet,' Winnie teased. 'If it comes to that aren't we all but that's the stuff of romantic novels not real life.'

'Maybe it does happen, Winnie, and not just in novels.'

'You've met someone, haven't you?'

'Of course not.'

'Then why are you blushing?'

'I'm not.' Then was furious with herself when she felt her cheeks hot.

'Susan, I'm only teasing.'

'There isn't anyone, not in the way you mean.' Her eyes flew to the door as if expecting someone to come in. Her voice dropped to a whisper. 'If I tell you something do I have your solemn promise that you'll never breathe a word to anyone?'

'You should know better than ask that,' Winnie said, sounding hurt.

44

'Of course I trust you it's just that – well – it's so stupid I know you're going to laugh.'

'I promise I won't.'

'You do know I'm doing some work for the mill?'

'Matthew mentioned it and I'm delighted.'

'Papa has arranged for an accountant to come to Aran Heights and teach me.'

'And this accountant is responsible – '

'It's awful, Winnie,' Susan said miserably. 'Mama would die if she knew and Papa would do something awful but I can't help myself. I think of him constantly yet he's rude and arrogant and quite common. Honestly, do you know he actually had the nerve to tell me he considered his time wasted though later he did concede that I wasn't the feather-brained female he'd expected.' She took a deep breath. 'What do you think of that?'

Winnie tried to stifle a giggle. 'Surely it was a compliment. Poor soul, he was probably petrified and putting a brave face on it because, if you'll forgive me saying so, you can act the haughty young miss when you have a mind to.'

'He has to be kept in his place.'

'You sound like your mama but tell me, what is this disturbing young man's name?'

'Mr Cameron – David Cameron,' she said dreamily. 'He's very dark and as tall as Matthew and unbelievably handsome. The proud way he carries himself – I mean if I hadn't known him to be an employee of Papa's I might well have mistaken him for a gentleman.'

'Depends on your interpretation of a gentleman,' Winnie said drily.

Susan studied the floor. 'Winnie, I can only tell you this but even just speaking about him I feel – I can't describe it – but they are wicked feelings and I'm ashamed.'

'Nothing wicked about them,' Winnie said matter-of-factly, 'you're just more honest than most in admitting to them.'

'You're not just saying that,' Susan said, looking uncertain and embarrassed.

'I'm a farmer's daughter, Susan,' Winnie said gently. 'Much

45

of what is unspeakable in your world is not in mine. But,' she added warningly, 'feelings like that can be dangerous so don't be foolish and meet this young man secretly.'

'How do you know – well – about that kind of feeling?'

'I'm a woman.' She smiled. 'We all have our dreams, even plain old me.'

'I wouldn't dream of meeting him secretly,' she bristled.

'Then there's nothing to worry about. Incidentally has Mrs MacFarlane met this David Cameron?'

'No, and it's highly improbable she ever will.' Susan grinned mischievously. 'Papa told her he was sending an accountant but she believes him to be one of the mill's elderly clerks and anyway he comes straight to the library by the servants' wing and Mama never goes near the library.'

'Susan, don't take this the wrong way but it could be because he doesn't belong to your circle that you find him so attractive. Blame it on that rebellious streak in you.'

'It isn't that, I know it isn't.' Susan thought it was time they got off the subject of Mr Cameron. 'Tell me, what's been happening at Moorend?'

'Precious little. Unlike you, handsome young men don't fall over themselves seeking my company.'

'A little encouragement might help.'

'I doubt it,' she said wistfully. 'If you but knew the times I've looked in the mirror and wept floods of tears. Why instead of resembling the Clappertons couldn't I have looked like my mother?'

Susan felt sympathy but exasperation too. 'You make no attempt to make the most of yourself. Mama says few women are born beautiful but the clever ones play up their good points. For a start you take no interest in clothes and scraping your hair back that way makes you look severe.'

Susan saw the slow colour spread into the sallow cheeks and when she spoke it was hesitantly unlike her usual brisk tones.

'Strange you should say that. Papa has been complaining that I don't spend enough on myself and I'd made up my mind

46

to splash out on a whole new wardrobe.' she paused. 'I'll get Aunt Tina to help me choose – '

'Over my dead body.'

Winnie giggled. 'Meaning her dress sense is as appalling as mine?'

'Your aunt dresses to suit her age,' Susan said dismissively, then broke off as Lydia knocked and entered with a tray. Once tea had been dispensed and Lydia taken her leave, Susan took up the subject of clothes again. 'Do let me help you choose, I'd love to.'

'Would you, Susan? Would you really? I mean this ugly duckling isn't going to turn into a swan and I'm not expecting miracles.'

'There are times when I could shake you,' Susan said with mock severity. She played with her lip the way she did when she was thinking. 'I could try and persuade Mama to come, she adores ordering new gowns and she does have good taste.'

'I know she always looks wonderful and I do know that Papa would be pleased. He has a great admiration for your mother. In fact,' her voice dropped to a conspiratorial whisper, 'Aunt Tina let it slip one day that my papa was once very sweet on your mama.'

'Really! That's news to me but she certainly has a soft spot for you. Maybe she sees you as the daughter she may have had.'

'And breathes a sigh of relief she had you instead,' Winnie said with a peal of laughter.

Susan giggled. 'Funny but it's difficult to think of one's parents doing – well, you know what I'm trying to say.'

'No, I don't.'

'Yes, you do. I mean falling in love and then all the rest of it.'

'I don't find it difficult. My papa and yours don't like each other, have you noticed?'

'Yes.'

Winnie looked thoughtful. 'Does Mr MacFarlane object to Matthew calling so often?'

'I don't imagine he knows.'

'You see, Susan,' Winnie said slowly, 'until recently Matthew came to Moorend to talk farming with Papa but it seems I'm the attraction now.'

The silence lengthened then Susan said unhappily, 'Matthew can be the limit, Winnie. Much as I love my brother I'm not blind to his faults.' She stopped. 'There isn't an easy way to say this.'

'Then let me say it for you. Matthew's interest can only be in the farm not in me?'

Susan was genuinely distressed. 'I wasn't going to say that at all. Matthew has a great admiration for you and that is true.'

'In my knowledge of farming, yes, I think he does, but listen to me, Susan. Offers of marriage won't come flooding my way unless from those with an eye on Moorend and I'm well aware that Matthew falls into that category.'

'Don't let him do that to you,' Susan said harshly.

'Why not if it happens to be what I want too?'

Matthew's words exactly, Susan remembered. She would be getting what she wants was what he'd said and here was Winnie confirming it.

'You'd be taking a big risk.'

'A calculated risk. You see,' she said softly, 'I've always loved Matthew and I want to get married while I'm young enough to have a family, the larger the better. Papa's dearest wish is to have a grandson and he's made it clear to me that he would welcome Matthew as a future son-in-law.'

Susan was unprepared for her own anger.

'That takes care of Moorend but what about the papermill?'

'Matthew's heart is in the land, Susan, he would never be happy in the mill.'

'That's beside the point. His place is in the mill and Papa is only having me trained to help behind the scenes.'

'Matthew wouldn't be any good in the mill and he'd be miserable.'

'And what is my father supposed to do?'

Winnie smiled. 'Much the same as mine. Just hope that his daughter makes a suitable match.'

'Now I see why you're so keen for me to marry Edward. It would suit you both. Well I'm not going to oblige,' Susan said, her blue eyes flashing dangerously.

'Whether or not you marry Edward has nothing to do with me but I will tell you this, if Matthew proposes marriage I shall accept.'

'Do you imagine he'll remain faithful?' she asked scornfully. 'Matthew has never been short of girls, beautiful girls,' she said cruelly.

'Don't be so naïve, Susan. Do you think I don't know that? Anyway I wouldn't be alone. How many husbands do we both know who look elsewhere for their comforts?'

'Then you wouldn't mind?'

'Of course I'd mind, I'd mind terribly but I'll have the good sense I hope not to make a scene.' She smiled. 'Maybe by that time I'd have a child or two to fill my life.'

'How little we really know each other,' Susan said wonderingly. 'You're really quite calculating.'

'Realistic, Susan, but I would never willingly hurt anyone, least of all you. We've been friends since we were small and I'd hate that to end. In any case Matthew may find marriage to me too big a price to pay for Moorend.'

There was the sound of a door opening and voices.

'Wheesht! Here's Aunt Tina,' Winnie said warningly as a stout, rather aggressive-looking woman stuck her grey head round the door and, seeing Susan, came in.

'How nice to see your bonny face, Susan.' She smiled then took the lid off the teapot. 'Tea still drinkable, Winnie?'

'No, I'll ring for Lydia.'

'Don't bother her just yet, she's busy instructing that young scullery maid and by the look of the lass she's none too bright.'

'How are you, Miss Clapperton?' Susan asked when she could get a word in.

'Thankful to be off my feet, Susan,' she said, sitting down heavily. 'Some folk can be so trying. No matter how helpful one tries to be one's efforts are invariably looked on as interference.'

'I'm sure they are grateful,' Susan said dutifully but with some sympathy for those people. Aunt Tina was like a small steam-roller and folk took a while to recover from her visits.

'Then all I can say is they have a queer way of showing it.' She wheezed and patted her bosom. 'Winnie's not neglected these days,' she said with a knowing smile. 'That brother of yours is just about making this his second home.'

Winnie frowned with annoyance and Susan, anxious to get away, stood up.

'You will excuse me, Miss Clapperton, but I've been here longer than I intended and Mama will be expecting me back.'

'I'll come part of the way with you,' Winnie said, disappearing and returning with Susan's cloak and her own coat.

Goodbyes said, the girls walked along the cart track where the ground bore the imprint of cattle and horses' hooves. Both of them were silent and for the first time uneasy with each other. Anxious to get back to their old friendly footing Winnie put her arm through Susan's.

'I've been too outspoken and upset you.'

'No, some of it is my fault.' She shrugged. 'I suppose it will all work out for the best.'

'Our friendship will survive?'

'Of course it will.'

'May I say one last thing?'

'I'm listening.'

'Whatever you feel for Edward he does love you, it's obvious the way he looks at you. Believe me I'd give anything to have someone love me for myself,' she said wistfully. Then in her usual brisk fashion added, 'Edward could get tired of waiting for you and look elsewhere; with his looks and position he can take his pick.'

'Then I wish he would.' But did she? She didn't want him herself but – everything was impossibly difficult and she didn't know what she wanted. A visit to Moorend should have helped but instead she was more confused than ever.

The roads diverged and Winnie stopped. 'About the spending spree, will you mention it to Mrs MacFarlane? But no pressure, mind, and only if she wants.'

'Mama is never pressurised into doing something she doesn't want but I'll let you know.'

'Thank you.'

With a final wave they took leave of each other just as a threatening dark cloud hovered overhead. Seeing it darken further, Susan quickened her pace to a half run. As Aran Heights came into view she felt the first large splashes of rain which almost at once developed into a downpour and, lifting her skirts, she raced to the entrance just as a carriage hurtled through the gates, sending a shower of muddy water over her. Fuming at the carelessness of the coachman and in her bedraggled state, she altered course and sped round to the side entrance.

Once in her room she stripped out of her wet clothes, leaving them on the floor, and changed completely. A bonnet had kept the worst of the rain off her hair but some of it was wet and she dabbed at it with a towel. Then she went in search of her mother and found her in the drawing-room, embroidery on her lap but her hands idle.

'Sorry I'm late, Mama, I stayed longer than I intended at Moorend and then I got caught in a downpour.'

'That's quite all right, dear,' Sarah said, without a trace of a reprimand. 'You missed Mrs Brodie. She called unexpectedly and fortunately I was at home.'

'So that's who the carriage belonged to! I got half drenched the way it hurtled past and didn't see who it was.'

'That doesn't surprise me. Why the Brodies keep that coachman I'll never understand. I wouldn't care to risk life and limb.'

Whatever had transpired between the ladies must have pleased Mama, Susan thought. She looked almost smug.

'Did you change out of your wet clothes?'

'Yes, I had to.'

'Have you told one of the maids to remove them for laundering?'

'Not yet.'

'Go and do it now.'

Susan went in search of a maid and returned in a few minutes. 'Lottie is on her way up.'

'Very well. Now sit down, I want to talk. You can't begin to know the relief it was to me to see Mrs Brodie. There was no awkwardness at all. In fact,' she preened herself, 'I have been invited to accompany her to select a few new gowns. Apparently she admires my taste.'

'Everyone does,' Susan said generously, 'and I know that Winnie would value your guidance too. Mr Clapperton has been urging her to spend more on herself.'

'And not before time, but where do I come in?'

'She was to ask her aunt to accompany her and I had to do something.'

'I should think so. Tina would be completely useless,' Sarah said aghast, 'she wouldn't have the least idea how to advise a young lady on dress.'

'I thought perhaps you would advise Winnie.'

'Let me consult my engagement book but I should be able to fit something in and knowing Mr Clapperton he'll be more than generous.'

'Winnie will be delighted.'

'Poor girl, she hasn't had your advantages.' She broke off as if at a sudden thought. 'I wonder what brought this on! Undoubtedly there will be a few young men and perhaps a few not-so-young who will be looking hopefully in Winnie's direction. Let's hope she chooses sensibly. Do you know if there is anyone special, has she mentioned any young man?'

Susan shook her head but wondered what her mother would say if she knew that Matthew was the young man Winnie had set her heart on.

'She'll tell you when she's ready to do so.' She smiled. 'This is going to be quite a challenge. Winnie with the right clothes and a little poise may surprise us all and herself most of all.'

'She goes on about being plain but does nothing about it.'

'You can help by encouraging her to change her hairstyle.'

'You're fond of Winnie, aren't you?'

'Yes, I am. I want a good marriage for her. Mr Clapperton made a mistake in his choice of wife. Betsy was quite unsuitable.'

'I understood that he was heartbroken when she died?'

'Of course he was. Betsy was a pleasant girl but unsuited to be mistress of Moorend. Even before marrying Euan she was in delicate health and giving birth to Winnie nearly cost her her life. After that there was no question of her bearing more children. Such a disappointment not to have a son to carry on the farm.'

Next morning it wasn't just a headache, Mrs MacFarlane complained of feeling very unwell and the coachman was hurriedly despatched to bring back Dr Sullivan. Susan's offer to sit with her was declined; her mother just wanted to be left alone. While the doctor was with her mother Susan went out into the garden and walked between the rose beds. The gardens were at their best during the summer months with climbing roses, pink and blue rhododendron bushes and the sweet smell of honeysuckle was all around. One corner had been given over to the native heathers with their purples just beginning to show. Susan was complimenting the head gardener on the lovely show when she saw the doctor looking over in her direction. Excusing herself she hurried to join him.

'How is Mama, Dr Sullivan?'

'Nothing serious, my dear, a touch of indigestion that's all. Painful and disagreeable though it is, it'll pass and I've given her something to help.' He stood back and gave her a lengthy look which from anyone else would have angered her. But as well as being the doctor who brought her into the world he was also a family friend.

'The picture of health and bonnier by the day.'

'Flatterer.' She laughed but then she saw his face turn grave and all the banter gone.

'Susan, I don't want to alarm you – '

She felt a sudden, cold chill. 'What is it?'

'It's about your papa – '

She paled. 'Papa's not ill again?'

'He will be if he doesn't ease up.'

'You mean – '

'He's worried, Susan.' He sounded exasperated. 'I try to reason with my patients, let them see that worry is a killer. Get that across and a doctor's load would be halved. It doesn't make one whit of difference to the problem, all it does is damage the health.'

'But how do we stop Papa worrying?' she said despairingly.

'You can't, only he can do that. What you can do, however, is make sure he isn't upset needlessly, otherwise, my dear . . .' He shrugged his shoulders and left the rest unsaid.

Susan clutched at his arm. 'He isn't going to – I couldn't bear it if anything happened to Papa,' she choked.

'There! There! Don't be upsetting yourself, it isn't as bad as that. Your father has a lot of good years ahead of him if he would just try and remember that a man of his years can't expect to do what he did twenty years ago.'

'I'll try, I'll do my very best, Dr Sullivan.'

'That I know, that's why it's you I'm telling. Your mother would just get herself into a state.' He smiled and patted her arm. 'Between us, lass, we'll look after him and now if you'll excuse me there's some others needing or thinking they need my attention.'

Biting back the tears Susan watched him get into the carriage and it move away, then slowly she turned back to the house. It must be serious. Dr Sullivan was not one to spread alarm, and thinking back she could recall the tell-tale signs, the irritableness over trifles, the way in unguarded moments his hands would clench, and a terrible fear gripped her. Life without Papa, the thought was too awful to contemplate.

Mrs MacFarlane and the two girls left the station and went out to where a few carriages were lined up. At a signal the nearest coachman got down from his perch, touched his cap and listened to Mrs MacFarlane's instructions.

'You know, Susan, it's ages since I was in Glasgow,' Winnie remarked.

'Then you sit at the window and I'll be piggy in the middle.'

'Susan, really!' But her mother was smiling and shaking her head.

They moved off and soon were trundling over the cobbles into West George Street and on to Buchanan Street with its fashionable shops. A cart had toppled and there was a hold-up until it was righted, then they were into St Vincent Street. Soon they were in Gordon Street and stopping outside the premises belonging to Charlotte Beattie. The coachman was paid and dismissed and the three ladies went inside. The young assistant, recognising Mrs MacFarlane and her daughter, asked them to be seated while she went in search of Miss Beattie.

The owner arrived slightly out of breath. She was a short, dumpy woman with a pronounced double chin, sharp intelligent eyes and the clear complexion enjoyed by so many auburn-haired women. Born into poverty but with a determination to better herself and a firm belief that she had the talent to do so the young Lottie had worked long hours, much of it in bad light, learning to be a seamstress. The pitiful wages were barely enough to survive but very early on she began to recognise her worth as the more exacting work came her way. The demand for more wages had been a bold step and a grave risk but in the end her stubbornness had paid off and her request grudgingly granted.

From then on Lottie had studied fashion, used her creative talent and against all the difficulties, and they were many, she had become a top designer, an astute business woman and a demanding though fair employer.

Civilities over, the ladies were seated on blue padded chairs in the perfumed room where floor-length velvet curtains in a darker shade of blue were partly drawn over the window. An otherwise dull corner was brought to life by a beautiful display of flowers in a tall oriental vase.

'We're here, Miss Beattie, to find something for Miss Clapperton but perhaps I, too, may be tempted.'

Miss Beattie acknowledged that with a smile then turned

her trained eye on Winnie, noting her sallow complexion, her gaucheness and the unbecoming clothes she wore.

'Miss Clapperton, would you mind standing, please?'

Winnie got up and as the moments grew so did her embarrassment but at last Miss Beattie nodded and she sat down. Later she was to confess to Susan that in those moments she had felt herself examined like a prize animal at an auction.

'Be proud of your height, Miss Clapperton, and don't be tempted to stoop, a common fault with tall young ladies. Anna,' she beckoned to her assistant, 'take this lady to the cubicle and help her out of her gown while I take a look through my stock.'

Showing a marked lack of eagerness, Winnie followed Anna and once they heard the sound of the curtain rail being drawn, Susan took a fit of the giggles.

'Hardly enthusiastic is she?'

'Behave yourself, Susan.' But her own lips twitched as she turned to examine some materials.

Winnie came slowly towards them and at Miss Beattie's request she pirouetted for them. The warm shade of pink removed much of the sallowness of her skin and the flowing line of the russet silk with just a hint of bustle took away the heaviness of her figure.

'Winnie, it's lovely and you do suit it. Doesn't she, Mama?'

'Yes, Winnie, that's very nice.'

Winnie's eyes shone. 'I'll have it, I do like it.'

'Tut-tut!' Miss Beattie looked shocked. 'The colour is good but the neckline is too fussy. Tell me, is this for a special occasion?'

'Oh, no, I'm just replenishing my wardrobe,' but there was a faint flush on her cheeks.

'Perhaps three day dresses and two more for formal occasions. What do you think, Winnie?' Mrs MacFarlane asked.

'That would do very well.'

'Now that I know what is required.' Miss Beattie spoke to her assistant: 'Anna, after you help Miss Clapperton out of that gown hurry along to the workroom and bring the green silk and the yellow brocade.' She saw Mrs MacFarlane examining the samples of materials. 'Our new designs are on the table should you care to look at them.'

'May I see them with you, Mama?'

'Of course, I had intended that you have a new gown.'

If only Mother were always like this, Susan thought. She could be so charming when she wanted.

After some swithering a delighted Winnie decided on a stylish gown in rose pink and another in a brilliant green silk. The pink needed a small alteration and the others were to be made up in a different material with slight adjustments to the style.

Then it was Susan's turn and when she came out in the golden yellow gown it was as if they all held their breath.

'Well, what do you think?' Susan said, not at all sure what the silence denoted.

'Lovely,' breathed Winnie, 'absolutely perfect on you.'

'Mama?'

A smile played around her mother's mouth. 'Many years ago I had a gown in just that shade. Yes, Susan, you must have it.' Miss Beattie departed to the workroom.

'I adore it and it is such a lovely surprise. Thank you, Mama.'

'Only to be worn on special occasions but I have a feeling we won't have too long to wait.' She looked coyly at Winnie. 'Perhaps two special occasions?'

The girls exchanged startled glances but Mrs MacFarlane had forgotten them. Miss Beattie had arrived and she was too absorbed in selecting a gown for herself.

She was much more difficult to please and Susan marvelled at the patience Miss Beattie displayed. If she was wearied she didn't show it though Anna was visibly drooping from the many visits paid to the workroom where busy hands were putting the finishing touches to the season's collection.

Out in the street Mrs MacFarlane touched her throat. 'I don't know about you two but I'm parched and I seem to remember a delightful teashop nearby.'

'Just round the next corner, Mama. I remember too.'

'You know I'm really enjoying this day out,' Winnie said as she looked about her. 'I must do it more often.'

'I remember Papa taking us to George Square when we were little to see the statue of Sir Walter Scott. It was supposed to be a statue of King George III and that is why it's called George Square.'

'Fancy you remembering all that, Susan, I don't.'

'You weren't there, we left you with your dressmaker.'

'That explains it,' she said as they entered the shop and were immediately shown to a table.

'I'm decidedly peckish,' Susan announced. 'What about you, Winnie?'

'Now you mention it I am rather.'

'What it is to be young,' Mrs MacFarlane sighed as they waited to be served. 'We'll see what they have to offer but I must refrain.'

'Why, Mrs MacFarlane?'

'Because, Winnie, dear, when my new gown arrives I should like it to fit and at my age it is extremely easy to put on weight and very difficult to lose it.'

'Very trim and stylish is how my papa describes you,' Winnie said mischievously, 'his words exactly.'

'Coming from your papa that is quite something, he was never one for flowery speeches.'

The tables in the Willow Teashop were covered with snowy white damask tablecloths. Fashionably dressed matrons and a sprinkling of younger women were engaged in whispered conversations as they sipped tea from the fragile china cups. A waitress in a stiffly starched white square of apron arrived at their table and took their order.

Teapot, sugar and milk arrived on a silver tray followed by a plate of sandwiches cut in dainty triangles. There were two kinds of cake, seed and fruit, sponges filled with jam and cream and a selection of biscuits.

'That should take the edge off your appetite,' Mrs MacFarlane said gushingly as she weakened and reached for a sandwich. Halfway to her mouth it was arrested by a voice and she swung round.

'Caroline, my dear, it's you!' Putting down her sandwich she said, 'Do come and join us.'

'Yes, do, Caroline,' Susan joined in.

'I'd love to but I can't. My friend was just paying the bill when I caught sight of you, Mrs MacFarlane. How are you keeping?'

'I have my good days and my bad days but this is one of my good days I am happy to say. But let me introduce you to Winnie. Winnie, this is Caroline, a friend of Matthew's. Miss Caroline Beverley – Miss Winifred Clapperton,' she said formally.

As they shook hands Winnie managed a smile but Susan saw the sparkle leave her eyes as she looked at the newcomer. The contrast could not have been greater. Caroline was small made and perfectly proportioned. Her luxuriant blue-black hair fell in tumbled curls to her shoulders. Long silky eyelashes fringed the deep blue of her eyes and she had a dazzling smile.

'Did Matthew tell you I've been in Bournemouth with Mama?'

'Yes, he did. I hope she benefited from the change.'

Caroline made a face. 'Difficult to know with my mother but I'll tell you this,' she said gaily, 'I certainly didn't. It was deadly dull just taking Mama for walks and keeping her company in the hotel in the evenings. Oh, that's Kirsty looking for me, I'll have to go. Heavenly to have seen you both and to meet you, Miss Clapperton. Be sure to give my love to Matthew, Mrs MacFarlane.' Then she was gone in a whirl of skirts with a few heads turning to watch her departure.

Mrs MacFarlane bit into her sandwich, took a sip of tea then shook her head in mock relief. 'Like a whirlwind, Winnie, a little of Caroline and I'm exhausted.'

'And the only one of Matthew's friends who can charm Papa,' Susan added then wished she hadn't.

'Mr MacFarlane sees a very shrewd young woman behind all that excitable chatter. Matthew needs a steadying influence and he thinks Caroline could give him that.'

CHAPTER SEVEN

In those weeks since Dr Sullivan had warned Susan about her father's health she had done everything possible to protect him from petty annoyances, smoothing over difficulties wherever she could. It had helped and Hamish seemed much more relaxed of late.

'Papa is much improved isn't he, Dr Sullivan?'

'He is that, my dear. Could be the man's getting some sense at last and what is this I'm hearing?' he said, raising his bushy eyebrows.

'What have you heard?' She smiled.

'Learning the business no less and why not? Told Hamish it was a sensible move having you brought in.'

'I'm not acceptable in the mill.'

'No matter, lass. That doesn't have to be such a drawback. It's not where the work is carried out it's how that counts. Quite a turn-up for the books if you'll excuse the expression. It's not only times that are changing – it's Hamish too!' He went off shaking his head and chuckling.

Those same weeks had established a routine. David Cameron arrived at ten o'clock on Tuesdays and Thursdays for two hours and so often in that time Susan blessed her good fortune that Sarah had never caught a glimpse of the handsome young man.

Confident in the belief that her daughter's tutor could only be one of the elderly clerks, Sarah had dismissed the whole tiresome business from her mind.

On this, his last morning at Aran Heights, David greeted Susan with quiet courtesy as he took his customary seat.

61

'You probably know, Miss MacFarlane, that this is to be my final visit,' he said, turning his dark eyes on her.

'Yes, Papa told me,' she said, feeling absurdly close to tears.

'I knew it couldn't go on much longer. After all you do have a good understanding of the financial side of the business.'

'And you to thank for it.' Her eyes were over-bright and the smile she gave him held such sweetness that his heart turned over.

What had started out as an attraction was so much more now. Susan MacFarlane was constantly in his mind. That she was lovely enough to disturb any man he knew, but for him it was so much more than that. He was in love with his employer's daughter and had been, he supposed, ever since that first morning when she had been so proud and aloof. Only then he had been too annoyed at her haughtiness to recognise it.

Whatever the future held for him he knew with absolute certainty that Susan MacFarlane would be the only woman he could ever truly love.

Through the corner of her eye Susan glanced at David surreptitiously while arranging and rearranging the papers. What were his feelings now? she wondered. Was he too feeling regret that their time together was to end?

'I'm going to miss this – miss you,' she said simply.

'I too,' he said gravely. He mustn't show his real feelings, at all costs he must avoid that.

Their eyes met and held. For the first time Susan saw that his eyes were blue but so dark that they appeared black. For him he saw something else that tore at his heart. For all the proud haughtiness she sometimes displayed there was an innocence and a curious vulnerability about her that moved him deeply.

Before he could stop himself he reached out and took her hand bringing it to his lips then, realising what he had done, he dropped it, and his blood rushed to his face.

'I'm – I'm sorry,' he stammered. 'I shouldn't have done that.'

The feel of his lips on her hand, the unexpectedness of it made Susan catch her breath.

'It – it's all right, I'm not angry,' she said unsteadily.

They stared at each other.

'It was unforgivable of me, Miss MacFarlane, and my only excuse is that I couldn't help myself. You are very beautiful,' he said softly.

His dark, charismatic eyes were on her and she half turned to hide her confusion. For all those weeks she had lived only for the precious hours spent together in the library and she couldn't bear the thought that they were to end. Guilt and longing struggled for control. Papa had trusted her with this young man and she hated to deceive him but this agony of longing was proving too strong.

She swallowed. 'We are both in Aranvale, perhaps we may see each other.'

'There's nothing I'd like better but I think it unlikely.'

'Oh, I don't know. You like walking?'

'Very much, I do a great deal of it.'

'Then we could arrange to meet by chance.'

'Accidentally on purpose,' he said laughing.

'My aunt lives at the Old Mill House and I do visit her from time to time.' She bit her lip. 'If I left her house earlier than usual you could accompany me part of the way back to Aran Heights.' Not wishing to hurt his feelings but knowing he must be made to understand she added hastily, 'We would have to leave each other before I reached home in case – '

'We were seen together?'

She lowered her eyes but not before she had seen the glint of anger in his. 'Try to understand,' she pleaded. 'I don't have a great deal of freedom and if my parents got to know . . .' her voice trailed off.

'A sharp reprimand for you and the end of my career at the Aranvale Papermill,' he said with an attempt at humour.

'I'm sure my father wouldn't go to that length but he would make sure I was closely chaperoned with even less freedom than I enjoy now.'

A chill of fear hit David. That it would be instant dismissal and probably without a reference he was in no doubt. For himself the risk was one he was prepared to take but there was his mother.

Something of his misgivings must have shown on his face as he became conscious that she was looking at him far too intently.

'Perhaps you consider my company not worth the risk?' she said coldly.

'I'd risk a great deal more.'

Reassured, she gave him a brilliant smile. 'Then from today and only when we are alone together we'll dispense with formality. I shall call you David and you may use my Christian name.'

'Thank you – Susan.'

Warning bells were ringing in Susan's head but she ignored them. What she couldn't ignore was the delicious new excitement surging through her.

That first arranged meeting had posed no problems. Mrs MacFarlane had given her permission to visit Aunt Rachel. Though she, herself, was seldom in her sister-in-law's company she had never raised objections to her family visiting their aunt.

The drawing-room of the Old Mill House where Susan and her aunt were sitting was filled with an assortment of chairs, sofas and little tables crowded with ornaments and family photographs. A huge oil painting of the first Master of Aranvale had pride of place above the wooden mantelpiece. No drastic changes had been made since the death of Susan's grandparents and only in the last few years had the dark green wall covering been changed for an embossed paper in sky blue with patterned curtains of the same shade hanging at the windows.

'Susan! I've never seen you so anxious to escape,' Aunt Rachel said reproachfully. 'That must be at least the fourth time you've looked at the clock in the last half hour.'

Susan flushed at the rebuke. 'How rude of me and I do apologise,' she said guiltily.

'Are you so anxious to be away?'

'No, of course not, at least – ' She stopped. There was no use trying to hoodwink Aunt Rachel. 'I've arranged to meet someone that's all.'

'Meet someone?' Her lined face was thoughtful and her eyes questioning as she saw that her niece was covered in confusion. 'Only a young man could put you in this state and most certainly he isn't Edward Brodie. Child, what is it you're getting yourself involved in?'

'Nothing Aunt Rachel, honestly it's nothing like that at all. He's just someone – someone – '

'Yes, I'm sure he's that,' her aunt said tartly.

'Listen, please just listen.' She took a deep breath before continuing. 'Papa had an accountant come to Aran Heights,' Susan began desperately as the clock struck the half hour.

'Yes, I do know about that, your papa told me. Very sensible since Matthew is not shaping up. But not quite so sensible, my dear, if you are having clandestine meetings with this young man.'

'I'm not,' Susan said indignantly. 'This is the first time and my interest in Mr Cameron is purely business. Papa terminated the lessons too soon, I have a lot to learn.'

'Certainly I would endorse that last bit. You do have a lot to learn. No doubt he is an excellent accountant and you have enjoyed his tuition – '

'That's it exactly,' she said eagerly. 'I have enjoyed his tuition and if we've become friends there's nothing wrong with that.'

'Susan, my dearest, you have been protected all your nineteen years. This young man of whom you think so highly may have hopes and ambitions above his station. Hopes centred around you. Far better to discourage him now before it gets out of hand. You will both recover if you avoid each other and whatever the attraction it will die a natural death.'

'It's not like that at all,' Susan protested.

'It's always like that, Susan. I may be an old spinster but I can still recognise the signs.'

Susan smiled at that. 'Aunt Rachel, why didn't you marry? You were pretty, I've seen photographs of you.'

'Passably pretty! Yes I suppose I was and had I wished I could have married.' She hesitated. 'Marriage isn't for everyone, Susan. I never wanted a husband though I confess I would have liked children.' She laughed. 'Since one is undesirable without the other I content myself with my niece and nephew, both of whom I love dearly.'

'You're a darling, Aunt Rachel,' Susan said impulsively. Then with another despairing look at the clock she got up, collected her cloak from where it lay on the sofa and pulled it around her.

Aunt Rachel got up too. She was tall and straight and scraggily thin.

'Take care,' she said worriedly as Susan hugged her.

'You won't say anything to Papa?' Susan said fearfully.

'No, I won't, though I'm not at all happy; in fact I'm worried.'

'No need to be, I'm not a child you know.'

No, she thought after Susan had departed. You're not a child and that is what worries me. What you are is a lovely warm-hearted girl who doesn't know the dangers. Maybe I'm wrong not to warn Hamish. She sighed as she went to the table for her book.

Not until she was well clear of the Old Mill House did Susan allow herself to search the long winding lane. Seeing it deserted her heart plummeted, disappointment flooded through her and her footsteps faltered. Had he waited then gone away, thinking she wasn't going to honour their arrangement or had he decided the risk was too great and hadn't turned up at all? Just as she was deciding that that was the more likely she saw his dark head appear in the dip in the road and disappointment and hurt swiftly changed to relief and happiness and only by a supreme effort did she keep to a ladylike walk. With David's long strides they were soon drawing level.

'Good evening, Miss MacFarlane,' he said gravely but there was a smile lurking at the corner of his mouth.

'Good evening, Mr Cameron,' she said demurely. 'How strange that we should meet.'

'Just what I was thinking and if you would allow me it would be a privilege to escort you to Aran Heights. I take it that is where you are heading?'

As they fell into step she said hurriedly, 'Did I keep you waiting very long? It was difficult to get away.'

'I was prepared to wait a good deal longer.'

'My aunt knows.'

David looked startled.

'I'm afraid glancing at the clock too often gave me away but you are not to worry. Aunt Rachel may not approve, indeed she doesn't, but our secret is safe with her.'

David certainly hoped so, then his misgivings evaporated, her sudden smile was so enchanting.

'All we are doing is walking side by side. What could anyone have to say about that?'

'You'd be surprised,' he said drily as his brooding eyes sought hers. 'I'd be a lot more comfortable if we could meet openly.'

'So would I but we both know that is impossible.' She looked at him wistfully. 'David, surely we can just be friends, enjoy each other's company and forget the difference in our backgrounds?'

He thought that impossible but nodded.

'I know nothing about you,' she said lightly, 'even to where you live.'

'That is easily remedied,' he said, taking her arm and pointing to a cluster of cottages, tiny specks at that distance. 'The far end one is my home.'

'Your parents live there?'

'Just my mother,' he said abruptly, then added after a pause, 'You might as well know now that my mother is unmarried and I know nothing of my father.'

All the time he was speaking she knew he was watching her face, studying its expression and she lowered her head, but even so she was quite unable to disguise the shudder or hide the shock his words had evoked.

'Excuse me, David,' she faltered. 'I'm sorry, I shouldn't have asked.'

'Why not?' he demanded harshly. 'It was a perfectly natural question to ask and surely it is better that I should answer it truthfully. Strangely enough I had expected better from you,' he said bitterly, 'though I should have known with your upbringing that was impossible. Without knowing anything of the circumstances you are prepared to condemn my mother.'

'That is not true, how dare you say that to me,' she said hotly, coming to a standstill. Facing him her colour had risen and her eyes flashed. 'You are the one who is drawing conclusions and though I cannot deny the surprise the rest is only in your imagination.'

'Is it, Susan?' he said quietly. His eyes were bleak but there was a proud lift to his head. 'You might as well hear the rest.'

His sensitive face had set in a grim mask as he continued: 'Some of your so-called gentry consider girls in their employ to be fair game and don't try telling me the girls have a choice because it is no choice at all. Either she satisfies her master's desires or she finds herself thrown out in the street, bag, baggage and penniless. You've never gone hungry so you don't know what that means.'

'Is that what happened to your mother?' Susan asked in a small strained voice.

'Something of the sort,' he said heavily. 'My mother is tight-lipped. For a few gold coins she gave her vow of silence and, knowing her, she'll go to the grave with her secret.'

Susan felt a clammy coldness. Though not well informed on the subject she did know enough to recognise that what David was saying could be the truth. They were within sight of Aran Heights but she was reluctant to let him go like this. Her fingers touched the sleeve of his jacket.

'There's enough time to go round by the churchyard.' He turned with her. 'Please, David, don't look like that. I do understand about the wickedness that goes on. Your mother must have been a very brave woman.'

'Hardly a woman, Susan, she was only seventeen when she had me.'

'How dreadful!' She drew in her breath sharply. 'How ever did she manage? Was her family supportive?'

'Supportive!' He gave a short, humourless laugh. 'My grandparents disowned her but her married sister was more charitable. Her house was overcrowded with her own family but they managed somehow and that's where I was born. Later, we, that is my mother and I, came to Aranvale and until recently she was scrubbing and cleaning and taking in washing. Thankfully there is no need for that now though had I not insisted she would be slaving yet. A very independent woman, my mother.'

'And you a son to be proud of,' Susan said gently.

There was a white, pinched look about his face as he turned to her.

'What I am I owe to her.'

Leaving the grassy slopes for the narrow cinder path they were both silent until David gave a rueful smile.

'Blurting out all this was the last thing I intended. Now you know my history you won't want anything to do with me.'

She tucked her arm in his and he looked at it in surprise.

'How little you know me, David Cameron, if you think that. My first reaction was inexcusable but it was the unexpectedness of it, that was all. Neither you nor your mother has anything to be ashamed of.'

'My mother would agree with you there. She has always held her head high. In a strange way she is proud that I should be the son of a gentleman. Don't ask me why, it is quite beyond me.'

As a farmhand approached she withdrew her arm but unhurriedly.

'This is where we must part,' she said.

'I suppose this is the end?'

'It doesn't have to be.'

'You mean I can see you again?'

'Yes.'

'Not if it is out of misplaced pity,' he said savagely.

'Don't be so tiresome, David,' she said, sounding like her mother. 'Why should I pity you? You seem to be doing quite well. Papa has a high opinion of your work and he is not given to idle praise. Just stop being so prickly.'

'That's me put in my place.' He laughed. 'When will it be possible?'

'My parents are leaving after church on Sunday to visit friends which should mean I'll be free all afternoon.'

'Where shall I meet you?'

'Oh, David, I don't know. Beside the bridge would be best, I think. Make it three o'clock but don't wait any longer than half an hour. Mama may have arranged something for me.' The words came out staccato and she seemed flustered.

'Susan, I've been honest with you and I'm not stupid. You have no intention of being there, admit it. This is just your way of letting me down lightly and I don't need it.'

'Then you're wrong again, Mr Smart Alec.' But he wasn't, she thought with a rush of shame, it had been her intention. She was remembering Aunt Rachel's warning and her own heart told her that it was dangerous to go on seeing David.

'Are you quite sure, Susan?' he said quietly.

He's giving me every chance, she thought desperately, but I can't just let it end like this, I can't. She took a deep breath.

'David,' she said slowly, 'if I'm not there beside the bridge between three and three thirty it will be because I have been unable to get away. You can believe that or not as you please,' she said as a parting shot, then she was running through the wide open gates and across the lawn. He stood watching until she was out of sight and for a long time afterwards.

Would she come? David couldn't be sure and wondered if it would not be better if she did not show up. After all, why keep tormenting himself? Better that it should end now before it had properly begun. She was not for him, never could be and to think otherwise would be foolish.

Even so he was standing before the mirror, pleased with his appearance. The cut-away coat and dark check trousers fitted comfortably. His mother had been right as usual. It wasn't enough to sound like a gentleman, one had to dress the part too was her excuse for what he considered until that moment to be an unnecessary extravagance.

'Don't know when I'll be home, Mother,' David said as he stood tall and straight in the doorway.

Eliza Cameron felt the familiar pride. 'That's all right, son. It's a lovely day and I'll mebbe take mysel' over to see Mrs Johnson. She's been that poorly of late.'

David frowned. 'Let that lazy good-for-nothing husband of hers lift a hand to help, you're not to, Mother.'

'I'm only goin' tae see the body,' Eliza said mildly.

'So you say. Anyway I'm off.'

The door closed and Eliza smiled to herself. That there was a lass in David's life she was sure but she would never ask. In his own good time he would tell her. Of one thing she was sure: it wasn't anyone from around here. David was ambitious. He would choose well.

Those loitering about the street, an area of the decayed dwellings that drew them, watched the well-groomed young man shut the door and move smartly away. Those who shouted a greeting he acknowledged with one of his own, well aware of the sneers that would follow his progress. But it was a matter of indifference to him. They had nothing in common. And it was this very indifference that angered and irked some. Eliza Cameron's bastard son had no right to such airs and graces.

The June day was just as Susan had laughingly forecast. The sky was a clear blue without a cloud in sight, the air was deliciously warm and the ground below baked hard in the sun. Well before he reached the bridge he reduced his pace. He didn't want to linger and draw attention to himself but found there was no fear of that. Smiling foolishly he watched her coming. Even at that distance he could recognise the proud tilt to the head and the youthful spring to her step. In a blue and white polkadot gown and a lightweight cape on top she looked like a breath of summer. Her hair, that he had only seen swept up and secured with combs, now hung in soft curls to her shoulders.

She waved happily and as they walked towards each other he saw that her face was flushed and her eyes sparkling.

'You didn't expect to see me? Be honest, you didn't?'

'Then why am I here?'

'Why are you?' she teased.

'There was hope in my heart when I set out.'

She thrust a package into his hands. 'In case we get peckish.'

'What is it?'

'Apples. Mrs Dunbar won't notice. Anyway there's always plenty.'

'Where would you like to go?' he asked.

'Had you anywhere in mind?'

He shook his head. 'You decide and it'll suit me.'

'I do know a lovely spot; it's over at the other side of the reservoir then a climb after that. Matthew and I used to have poor Nanny puffing and blowing long before she reached the top. Later on we came by ourselves and Matthew found a sheltered heavenly spot.'

He was smiling as she rattled on. 'I know this walk, I've done it many times.'

'I'm sure you have but I bet you missed our little hideaway.' The sun caressed the soft curves of her face as she chatted animatedly. Her voice had a lovely lilting quality and he felt he could have gone on listening for ever. A little tentatively, he took her arm to help her across a rough stony patch.

'How much further?' he asked, pretending to wilt in the heat.

'Almost there, lazybones.' She laughed as she ran ahead to an area of short grass almost hidden by the trees. By her expression he knew that she was waiting for him to say something.

'Now why is it I missed a paradise like this?'

Looking pleased, she discarded her cape and spread it out

on the grass before sitting down on it and leaning her back against the tree trunk.

'David,' she said patting the place beside her.

'Not on your cloak!'

'Of course on my cape, why not?'

She opened the paper bag while he settled himself then handed him an apple. In a companionable silence they ate their apples down to the core then, smiling to each other, they leaned back, squinting through the branches into the strong sunshine.

'Isn't this heavenly?' Susan said dreamily. 'We could be alone in a little world of our own.'

'That's because few people have the energy to come this far,' he teased.

'But you are glad I brought you here?'

'Very glad,' he said softly.

She turned her face to him and a tremulous smile touched her lips. He was so dark and good-looking but there was so much more to David than a good appearance. She could sense the restlessness that spoke of ambition but how could that ever be satisfied? The right family background could open so many doors but for someone like David they would remain firmly shut.

His eyes flickered and she became aware that he had been watching her through eyes only half closed and two spots of colour stained her cheeks. Hastily she moved her back to a more comfortable position and stared straight ahead.

'That must be painful through your thin gown.' He hesitated. 'Lean against my arm if you would be more comfortable.'

'Yes, David, thank you, I'll use you as a pillow.' She managed to say it lightly as she moved into the curve of his arm but her heart was racing. She was so aware of him.

'Is that better?' He gave her a smile that made her heart hammer and lurch.

'Lovely.' Few people frequented these hills and she prayed that no one would come and spoil the delicious thrill of being alone with him. Was he as acutely aware of her as she was

73

of him? Surely he must feel something too. 'David, if you had a wish what would it be?'

'To be rich and successful,' he said without hesitation.

'More than anything else?' she asked, feeling let down.

'If I were rich and successful we could be together without all this secrecy,' David said quietly, 'and it is possible to rise from humble beginnings you know.'

'Of course it is,' she said stoutly and watched his face as he moved. Something in the angle of his head reminded her of someone but like that other occasion it remained just long enough to tantalise her then was completely lost.

'One day I may go to London to try my luck.'

'Would you leave Aranvale?' she asked in a low voice.

'Not as long as my mother needs me.'

A kind of desolation swept over her. Aranvale without David? She didn't want to think about it. 'It's perfectly ridiculous that I have to steal out this way to meet you.' She pouted like a spoilt child.

'No, it isn't, Susan. I can quite understand your parents wishing to protect you.' He paused and there was a sinking feeling at the pit of his stomach. 'No doubt they have a suitable young man in mind.'

She thought of Edward. 'If they do and I don't want to marry him then I won't.' She paused and her voice softened. 'I want to marry for love.'

'Even if that person were totally unsuitable, someone like me?' He sighed. 'No beautiful home, Susan, no servants.' Lightly he touched the hem of her gown. 'I very much doubt if my year's salary would stretch to the cost of your gown and cloak.'

They were playing but he was giving her a strong warning of what it would be like.

For a long time her fingers pulled at the grass. 'It's a great deal to give up, David, and I know I couldn't do it.' Then she brightened. 'If you did go to London would it take you a very long time to get rich? I'm being silly, of course it would.'

'Yes, I'm afraid so. A very long time if ever.' He frowned. 'No, that isn't what I believe. Given the chance and that is

74

all I need then I would be a success. Money grows, Susan, once you have some you make it work for you.'

'And we'd be old before that time. I'm not brave, David,' she whispered. 'I love my family and I love Aran Heights.' Her blue eyes were swimming with tears and with a hoarse cry he gathered her to him.

'Oh, God, I have no right to say it but I can't help it. I love you, Susan, more than I thought possible to love anyone,' he said shakily.

'David! Oh, David!' She clung to him and as their lips met she could feel the rapid beating of his heart. Hardly aware of what she was doing her arms tightened round his neck and encouraged by her response his kisses became more urgent, more demanding. Time stood still. All about them was the fragrance of summer and a faint breeze whispered through the beech leaves. Somewhere a bee hummed and a flock of birds, alarmed at some noise rose as one and with a frenzied flapping of wings flew into the sky.

What was wrong with her? Why didn't she push David away? Her upbringing, everything she had been taught, screamed that what was in danger of happening was wrong and all it needed to save it going any further was a small show of resistance. It would give her the chance to show her disgust and blame it all on his lack of control then she could end the relationship and they need never meet again.

Her unbuttoned gown was falling from her shoulders, she could feel it, yet her only move was to slip her hands beneath David's shirt to touch the smooth skin. She heard his quick indrawn breath, felt his warm hand close round her breast and was totally unprepared for the flame of desire that took hold of her.

There was a confusion of pain and ecstasy then in the moment that David's weight shifted from her, it changed to an agony of terror. She must be bad, she must be wicked or how else could she have allowed this awful, dreadful thing to happen to her? She was trying to adjust her clothes, fumbling with the buttons, uncaring that they were incorrectly fastened and all the time she hadn't looked at him.

75

They sat well apart. David had his elbows on his knees, his face hidden in his hands, appalled at what had happened.

'Susan,' he whispered unsteadily, 'I'm so sorry, so very, very sorry.'

She gave no sign that she had heard. Her back was to him and she kept staring ahead like someone in shock. Desperately he wanted to reach out and comfort her but the archness of her back warned him against that and at last he got up and began brushing the grass from his trousers. Some of it was in her hair and with a dogged persistence he picked out each one. Still she didn't move.

'Susan,' he said helplessly.

She got up, her back still to him and he bent down for her cape, shaking it clear of grass and it was then that he saw her expression. It would live with him for a long time. Her eyes were huge in a chalk white face and she looked like a terrified child.

'Susan, please – ' The choking feeling in his throat made it difficult to speak. 'Oh, God! I shouldn't have let it happen.'

'Don't say anything, just don't speak about it,' she said harshly, then she was running ahead, falling and stumbling through the bracken in her need to escape.

With his long strides he drew level with her while she kept up the same punishing pace until her breath was coming in painful gasps. Only then did she slow down. The despairing silence lasted until Aran Heights came into view.

'Goodbye, David.' Susan tossed the words over her shoulder and in those words he heard the finality.

Sick at heart he watched her go.

In a panic and desperate to reach her own room before anyone saw her, Susan raced round to the back of the house, almost knocking to the ground a startled Polly.

'I'm sorry – '

'Miss Susan! Miss Susan! Don't go. I was comin' to look for you. When you wasn't in the library or your own room Mr Brodie thought you might be in the garden.'

'Mr Brodie,' Susan said faintly.

'Mr Edward Brodie, he's in the mornin' room, Miss Susan, least that's where I left him.'

Susan took a deep, shaky breath. 'Tell Mr Brodie I'll be down once I've changed.'

Polly's brown eyes were full of concern. 'Miss Susan, you not comin' down with somethin'. You look all white.'

'Too much sun that's all it is, Polly, I've been silly.' Then as Polly made to go she gripped her arm. 'After you tell Mr Brodie bring water, plenty of hot water to my room and be quick, please.'

'Ever so quick I'll be,' Polly said as she hurried away.

Once in her room Susan stripped naked and put on her robe then went over to her wardrobe. Fiercely she held other thoughts at bay, concentrating solely on what she would wear for Edward. In the end she decided on a salmon pink gown and had it off its hanger when Polly arrived out of breath and carrying two jugs of hot water which she put on the marble top.

'Mr Brodie is quite happy, Miss Susan. He said to take your time.' Her eyes fell on the bundle of clothes on the floor. 'These for washing, Miss Susan?'

'Yes. No.' She swallowed. 'What I mean is yes they are to be laundered. Polly – '

'Yes, Miss Susan.'

'Are you handy with a needle?'

'Oh, yes, ever so neat I am.'

'Then you could alter that gown for yourself couldn't you? It's not a particular favourite of mine,' she lied 'so you're welcome to it.'

Her brown eyes widened in her pointed little face. 'You wants me to have it?' she said in wonderment.

'Yes, take it away and you may as well have the cape to go with it.'

'Thanks ever so, Miss Susan, I've never ever had anythin' that pretty.'

'Off you go then,' Susan said impatiently. 'You can come back later and tidy up.'

'Yes, Miss Susan,' Polly said, sweeping up the bundle and making for the door.

Alone again, Susan began washing herself with thorough-
ness as though she could wash away the memory of the
afternoon. After towelling herself dry she slipped into fresh
undergarments and pulled the salmon pink gown over her
head. Carefully she examined her face, not knowing why but
expecting to find some difference there. Reassured that she
looked much as usual apart from being paler she took a tip
from her mother and pinched at her cheeks with her fingers
to bring some colour into them.

The earlier events crowded in again and she had to bite her
knuckles to stop crying out. Somehow she had to act normally.
Stiffening her shoulders and taking a shaky breath she went
down to meet Edward. A touch of welcome normality greeted
her. Edward was reclining in a deep armchair and looking very
much at ease. At the sound of the door opening he sprang up
and looked at her admiringly.

'A long wait but definitely worth it.' He grinned.

'My apologies, Edward, for taking so long but this heat
doesn't encourage hurrying.' She held up her cheek for
his kiss.

'Where were you? The maid had almost given up.'

'In the garden,' she lied. 'Stupid of me but I stayed too long
in the sun and no doubt I'll pay the price.' To her own ears the
words sounded ominous and an icy shiver went through her.

'It doesn't seem to affect your skin so think yourself lucky.
A little of it and I go like a beetroot.' He looked at her
quizzically. 'I take it you don't feel like a walk?'

'To be honest, Edward, I don't.'

'The carriage – a drive somewhere, does that appeal?'

'No, but I could do with something to eat.'

'I'll keep you company. A little sustenance would be
welcome and we can't have you falling apart.'

Already normality was returning, thanks to Edward. If she
didn't think about it, refused to allow herself to think about
it, then maybe she could make herself believe it had never
happened.

'I'll just go and see Mrs Carson. Excuse me, Edward.'

*   *   *

78

Two places were very quickly set in the small dining-room and Polly brought in a selection of cold meats, crusty bread and a salad. Food had been the last thing on Susan's mind but she felt that conversation with Edward over a meal would be easier than sitting together when every expression could be analysed and remarked on. Nothing much missed Edward.

To her surprise she enjoyed the meal and felt the better for it. After they had finished Edward suggested a stroll in the garden and she agreed.

'Get yourself a hat, one with a brim.'

She laughed. There was something very solid and reliable about Edward. 'You're beginning to sound like Mama and incidentally what brought you here?'

'Charming,' he said drily. 'Just a whim, Susan, and the need to see a pretty face. And let me hasten to add that I didn't know that you'd be on your own.' He smiled. 'That was a bit of luck.'

'Well, I'm glad you came,' and surprised herself by meaning it. 'Just let me get that hat.'

She made no objection when he took her arm and put it through his. They walked the paths admiring the colourful borders, stopping to smell the honeysuckle and chatting comfortably.

'By the way I had a long chat with Matthew's lady love.'

'Who? Oh, you mean Caroline. I'm not sure how that relationship stands, it blows hot and cold. Matthew doesn't say much but I do know that she hasn't been near Aran Heights for some time.'

'Then all I can say is that Matthew had better look out. Caroline is a strikingly beautiful young woman and not the type a chap can afford to be careless about.' He grinned and looked pointedly at Susan. 'If a certain young woman of my acquaintance keeps me waiting too long then I may try my charms with the very delectable Caroline.'

'I don't think she is your type, Edward,' Susan said a little sourly then was immediately ashamed.

There was a satisfied smirk on Edward's face as he took

out his pocket watch. 'I'd love to stay longer but I have your reputation to think of. Since your parents are not here and Matthew isn't around they may consider this not quite proper.'

Susan stiffened at the word reputation but she managed to smile as she accompanied him to the courtyard where Donald was tending the horses.

Edward sprang up and gathered the reins. 'Give my regards to Mr and Mrs MacFarlane. See you sometime,' he said carelessly.

She raised her hand in farewell and wondered why she should be disappointed at his cavalier departure. Exasperated with herself she went back into the house.

It was a long, long, day. Would it never end! She was tired, her brain wouldn't even function properly. If only she could lie down, let sleep claim her but her parents would expect her to wait up for them.

It was to be a very long time indeed before any of them got to bed that night.

CHAPTER EIGHT

Her needlework was on her lap when the carriage bringing her parents passed the window and drew up at the entrance. As soon as she heard voices in the hall Susan picked up the work and began stitching. Minutes later Mrs MacFarlane bustled in and Susan raised her head to smile.

'I didn't expect you for another hour, Mama. Did you have a pleasant day?'

'Very pleasant but your papa looked so tired that I made our excuses and came away.' Her voice dropped to a warning whisper. 'Not a word to your papa, you know what he's like.' Then as if suddenly becoming aware of Susan's busy fingers she said in a shocked voice, 'On the Sabbath day, Susan! Put that sewing away at once.'

'I'm sorry,' she faltered. 'I forgot what day this is.' Hastily she folded up the cloth and put it and the threads in the work basket.

Hamish came in, grunted a greeting to Susan and sank down gratefully into his chair.

'Getting too old for all this gallivanting, not that I ever had much time for these social affairs. Inane gossip and poor quality port is about the strength of it,' he added peevishly.

'There was a heavy shower of rain in Airdrie just before we left.'

'Not here, Mama, it's been lovely.'

'How did you spend your day, Susan?' She looked over to her husband and frowned. 'You could so easily have been with us. Beatrice Wakeham was there with her parents. Such a plain girl with nothing to say for herself yet she's managed

81

to get herself engaged to some army captain in the – what was it, Hamish?'

'Artillery.'

'Edward was here, Mama.'

'Edward! Now that was nice,' her mother said, visibly brightening. What did you do, go for a walk?'

'No, we had a meal together. Mrs Carson prepared something cold and Polly served it.' She stopped when she heard the outside door shut, heavy footsteps across the hall then Matthew came in. Susan saw the suppressed excitement and some nervousness and wondered. Like most twins they were attuned to each other's moods.

'Matthew, dear, this is early for you,' his mother exclaimed. 'We just got in ahead of you.'

'I know, I saw Donald putting the carriage down the drive. I – um – have something to tell you – an announcement actually.' He remained standing with his hands on the back of a chair.

'An announcement,' Sarah repeated wonderingly. 'You make it sound like an engagement. Have you and Caroline –' she began.

'No, Mother, not Caroline.' He paused and put his weight on the other foot as all eyes settled on him. 'After getting Mr Clapperton's approval I proposed to Winnie and she has honoured me by accepting,' he said stiltedly.

There was a moment's stunned silence then Hamish spoke.

'All right, Matthew, let's hear the rest of it. There's more to come, isn't there?' he said bitingly.

'Yes, Father, I was coming to that,' Matthew said quietly, swallowing nervously. 'Once we are married I shall be taking up farming. I'm sorry I'm disappointing you, Father, but I've never hidden from you my dislike of working in the mill.'

'Instead you are prepared to marry that plain, dull daughter of Euan Clapperton to get your hands on Moorend. You are despicable, do you know that?'

Matthew's face was flushed and he was scowling. 'Whom

I decide to marry is a matter for me and I'm not prepared to let you or anyone else dictate.'

'That is no way to speak to your father, Matthew, and you, Hamish,' she said angrily, 'have no right to speak so disparagingly about Winnie. I'm just as surprised as you at the news but there was no call for that remark, it was most unkind.'

'Oh, of course,' Hamish sneered, 'Winnie is special to you; she'd have to be, she's Euan Clapperton's daughter after all.'

Sarah's face went pale then a dull red.

'You used the word despicable to Matthew and it is exactly what this is, Hamish.' She was breathing hard and Susan and Matthew exchanged startled glances.

Raising a shaking finger to his son Hamish shouted, 'Loyalty, you don't know the meaning of the word.'

Matthew started to speak but Sarah's voice cut short the words.

'Enough has been said, we will not discuss this any further if you please.'

'Why not?' Hamish roared as he got up from his chair. 'Have you no loyalty to the mill either? Let me tell you this, Sarah, it's what my grandfather began all those years ago that has allowed you the extravagances that you think of as your due, if you bother to think about it at all – '

They saw him stagger, his face turn an alarming shade of grey, a hand clutch at his chest then he collapsed on to the floor.

Susan screamed, 'Papa! Papa!' as she leapt out of her seat but Sarah was over and thrusting her roughly out of the way.

'Matthew, get Dr Sullivan.'

With an agonised look at the still figure, his own face as white as a sheet, Matthew ran out of the room and they could hear him shouting for the coachman. Donald must have been at hand for they heard the sounds of the horses and the crunch of the wheels as the carriage tore down the drive.

A calmness had come over Mrs MacFarlane as she took complete control.

'Susan, get Mrs Dunbar then get Polly to help you bring a pillow and blankets.'

'Mama – '

'Do it, don't waste time.'

Mrs Dunbar was quickly on the scene. Sarah had loosened Hamish's necktie and unfastened the buttons of his shirt. Carefully, with Mrs Dunbar's help, she lifted her husband's head on to the pillow and tucked the blankets around him.

''Tis better to leave him, m'am, until the doctor gets here.'

'If only he were here now; it's dreadful to feel so helpless.' She looked at Susan in mute appeal and with a sob Susan went into her mother's arms.

For those who waited it seemed an eternity before Dr Sullivan was kneeling beside Hamish. With an impatient movement of his arm he indicated that he wanted everybody out of the room. Sarah was reluctant to obey but after another look at the figure on the floor she followed the others into the morning-room. Polly had already poured out cups of tea and with Mrs Dunbar's coaxing they each reached for a cup.

'It was my fault,' Matthew said, clattering down his cup and spilling some of it. 'If he dies – ' He gulped.

'He won't, not Papa,' Susan sobbed as she put her arms around her twin. 'Dr Sullivan will pull him through.'

'We must all be brave,' Sarah said unsteadily, 'and blaming yourself isn't going to help, Matthew.' She smiled. 'Your father is a fighter, he's going to get well, he must.' Her hands were clenched.

Dr Sullivan's face was grave as he beckoned to Sarah. He lowered his voice but they could all hear what he said.

'An upstairs bedroom is out of the question. A bed will have to be brought down here and put in a couch or something for me. I'll remain with him.'

'Is he – ' Sarah said fearfully then, pulling herself together, said in a normal voice, 'How is my husband?'

He shook his head. 'The next few hours – all we can do is wait and hope,' he said quietly then he addressed Matthew: 'Once the room is ready you can help me move your father.'

Matthew nodded. 'Please, I want to sit with him.'

'No, lad.' Something in the young man's drawn face and anguished eyes made him change his mind. 'Yes, well perhaps that would be helpful. That way I can snatch a little sleep and you can waken me the moment there is any change.'

'Thank you.'

'May I – is there anything I can do?' Susan wavered.

'Prayer, my dear, you could try that,' he said. It was surprising coming from Dr Sullivan who was not renowned for his appearances at the kirk.

'We'll all be doing that,' Sarah said quietly before going with Mrs Dunbar to supervise the transfer of bed and bedding.

Afterwards Susan was to remember how they were all drawn together, family and servants, as if together they could will the master to recover.

Sleep for anyone that night was fitful if at all. Susan prayed as she never had before. Everything else was banished from her mind. Her only thoughts were of her beloved papa and how desperately ill he was.

'Mama, have you had any rest at all?'

'Yes, I had a few hours.' She smiled sadly. 'Sleep seems so unimportant just now but I have promised Dr Sullivan to try and get some rest.

'You must, Mama. Is there anything – '

'No, dear, there is nothing you can do.'

Aunt Rachel arrived and any coldness between the sisters-in-law was forgotten in their shared anxiety. Later in the day Edward and his parents arrived and were shown into the drawing-room. Tall and well built, John Brodie held himself very stiffly erect and was a fine-looking man though there was the beginning of a paunch. His dark hair was peppered with grey and the long sideburns nearly white. Lilian, his wife, was small and stout and being pear-shaped was the despair of a succession of dressmakers. Her auburn hair had faded to a dull blonde and weak blue eyes blinked frequently. Susan liked them both.

'Sarah, my dear.' Lilian kissed her friend and her voice was full of concern. 'We were so terribly distressed to hear – how is Hamish?'

'Holding his own according to Dr Sullivan.' Sarah bit her lip to stop its trembling and Lilian patted her hand.

'There! There! He's in good hands and Hamish will put up a fight.'

'No doubt about that.' John Brodie came from behind his wife to take both Sarah's hands in his own. 'By God! If anyone can put up a fight it's Hamish. Mark my words, lass,' he said with a brusque kindliness, 'he'll be all right.'

Susan turned from the window and seeing the stark misery in the young face Lilian went over to take the girl in her arms, clucking soothingly as if to a child.

'Susan, my dear, your papa has always declared you to be a true MacFarlane. He wouldn't like to see you giving way like this. Now would he?'

Susan raised eyes bright with unshed tears and tried to smile.

'I know, Mrs Brodie,' she said unsteadily. 'I haven't been much help and Matthew and Mama have been wonderful.'

'When it's needed, dear, we all get that extra strength.' Her voice dropped to a whisper. 'Your mama has always been capable but like most women she has kept it hidden until something like this happens.' Her eyes moved to watch her son go over and say a few words to Sarah. Then she turned her attention back to Susan. 'The young are ill at ease where there is illness and Edward is no exception. He's deeply upset, Susan, and wanted to call and see you before going on to the distillery.' She gave Susan a small push. 'Let him take you outside for a breath of air, it will do you good.'

Edward had overheard. 'Mother's right, Susan. Why don't you come outside for a few minutes?'

Like an obedient child she went with him and once they were down the steps he asked about Matthew.

'He was up all night sitting with Papa to let Dr Sullivan snatch a short rest. Then this morning he went to the village to bring the nurse. She's with Papa.' The lump in her throat was almost choking her. 'Poor Matthew was almost sleeping on his feet and we had a job persuading him to get some rest.'

'He's in bed now?'

'Yes, Mama looked in and he's dead to the world.'

'What brought on the attack or don't you know?'

She hesitated then said evasively, 'Mama said they shouldn't have gone visiting yesterday. She didn't like his colour but he was adamant he was all right. Mama did make some excuse to leave early and we were just together talking – when it happened.'

'Think how much worse it would have been if he had collapsed away from home,' Edward said, putting a comforting arm round her shoulders.

'That's just what Mama said. He was warned to take things easier but you know Papa.'

He nodded. 'Doesn't take too kindly to that kind of advice.'

'He should have, it was foolish of him. This coming on top of his bronchitis, he'll just have to resign himself to a shorter working day.'

'Probably will. Once he gets over this he won't want a repeat performance.'

She looked at him gratefully. He really was a dear. Sensing that she didn't want to talk he lapsed into silence.

In the house, in the atmosphere, she had found it difficult to think but out here it was easier. That Matthew's announcement had triggered off her papa's collapse she was in no doubt though that ugly scene between her parents must have contributed. It had been so out of character. Like all married couples they had their differences but there had never been anything like that. Maybe she was more to blame than Matthew or Mama. Had she agreed to become engaged to

Edward none of this need have happened. Matthew was no asset to the mill, Papa knew that better than anyone. He would have been little more than a figurehead and someone to sign papers. Her thoughts were becoming feverish. She could still – maybe it wasn't too late.

'Edward – '

'Mmmm.'

'Edward, your proposal, I mean, if you still want – ' she stammered and looked at him helplessly.

'Was there ever a time I didn't? Of course I want you. I love you and I want to marry you.' Surprise and something more shone out of his eyes. 'You're trying to tell me you've changed your mind?'

'Yes.'

'We can be married just as soon as you wish,' he said softly.

'Thank you, Edward.' Her nails were digging into the palms of her hand.

Turning her to him and uncaring whether they could be seen his lips brushed her cheek then moved to her mouth in a kiss that would have lingered had she not moved her head away. More than anything else she wanted to escape, to get away. It was all wrong that they should be kissing at a time like this, she thought resentfully.

'Susan, I'll never give you cause to regret it and I promise to make you happy,' he said huskily, then, almost in the same breath, 'When shall we make the announcement, make it official?'

Her startled eyes told him that he was going too fast for her.

'Not yet, Edward. When Mama is alone I'll tell her and you can inform your parents later, can't you? It seems so out of place just now.'

'I think you're wrong but I bow to your wishes.'

'Once Papa is well enough to hear the news then we'll make it official.'

'Mr MacFarlane won't object to me as a son-in-law.'

'No, you'll be welcomed into this family.'

Her eyes strayed to the courtyard where another carriage was drawing up. In a moment she saw Euan Clapperton help Winnie down, then together they walked to the door.

'That's Winnie Clapperton and her papa just arrived, Edward. Matthew must have gone over last night to tell them. You will excuse me but I must be on hand to help Mama.'

'Of course, my dearest, and I imagine the parents will be ready to leave now. Chin up, darling, our news might just help your papa's recovery.'

Once Edward and his parents had departed Susan went in to find Euan Clapperton and her mother in earnest conversation. Winnie was sitting a little apart but sprang up when she saw Susan.

'Susan,' she said urgently, 'is there some place where we can talk privately?'

Susan looked at her unsmilingly. 'I suppose so,' she said ungraciously and, turning her back, left Winnie to follow. She stopped at the door of what had once been the schoolroom but was now little more than a storeroom for unwanted furniture. Being at the back of the house the sun only reached there in the late afternoon and at this time it was chilly and cheerless. Engaged in moving two chairs in order that they could face each other, Susan was struck by the other's appearance. Winnie had dressed with care and she was wearing her hair in a softer and more flattering style.

'This will have to do, I'm afraid,' Susan said with a wave of her hand. 'Most of the downstairs rooms are in use, three of them are being used as temporary bedrooms.'

'I understand and this is quite satisfactory. What I have to say won't take long.' She appeared composed but her voice was jerky.

'Very well, I'm waiting,' Susan said coldly.

'When Matthew came to tell us about Mr MacFarlane, Susan, he was in a terrible state. He blames himself for what happened and of course I must share some of that blame.' Her eyes didn't waver as they met Susan's. 'Matthew has given

89

up all thought of going into farming,' she said very quietly. 'He sees now that his place is in the papermill.' She paused to moisten her lips with the tip of her tongue. 'All this has changed Matthew, Susan. Given time I'm sure he'll acquire whatever qualities it needs to control the mill.'

It was a long speech for Winnie and one which had obviously been prepared. Susan didn't take it in, not at first. Then she grasped it. Matthew was to remain in the mill. Matthew had had a change of heart, a belated loyalty to the mill. That was what Winnie was telling her. She closed her eyes. There had been no need to tie herself to Edward, no need to enter into a marriage she didn't want. But it was too late. She had offered herself and been accepted. There was no going back.

Winnie was looking at her strangely. 'Susan, are you all right? Oh, I see what is worrying you,' she said with a strangled laugh. 'Well, you needn't worry any longer, I won't hold your brother to his promise of marriage.'

Susan saw the hurt. 'I'm sorry, Winnie, so much is happening you must excuse me.' Then as Winnie's sacrifice got through to her she shook her head. 'We all seem to be trying to do the right thing but your sacrifice and Matthew's turn-about have come too late for me.' Without another word she ran out of the room leaving a stricken Winnie to find her own way to the drawing-room.

Aran Heights was quiet, the late hour making it beyond the likelihood of callers and Mrs MacFarlane sighed with relief. The genuine concern shown by friends and acquaintances was comforting but the constant need to repeat oneself to each caller became more wearisome as the day dragged on.

Seeing the tiredness in her daughter's face she put it down to the same reason and smiled sympathetically.

'It becomes quite a strain doesn't it, dear?'

'Yes. Mama, there's something I want to tell you.'

Her tired smile turned to Susan.

'I've agreed to marry Edward.'

'That is quite splendid, my dear,' Sarah said, her tiredness temporarily forgotten. She kissed Susan warmly. 'I'm so delighted and I know how pleased your papa will be.' Then she frowned. 'You don't look very happy and the word agreed seems a peculiar choice.'

'Not really, I'm marrying Edward to please you both but mostly in the hope that it will help Papa get well.'

'No, Susan, don't go,' as Susan made to get up. 'I want you to sit down and listen to me.' She took a deep breath. 'First, I must explain about your papa's outburst and his mention of Mr Clapperton,' she said, the colour coming and going in her face. 'You are entitled to an explanation.'

'There's nothing to explain, Papa wasn't himself.'

'I have nothing to hide and nothing to be ashamed of but you may as well hear the facts now.' She paused. 'There was a time when I might have married Mr Clapperton and your papa hasn't forgotten it.'

Susan smiled in spite of herself. 'I find it hard to see you as a farmer's wife.'

'That was the problem, I couldn't either. Moorend then was nothing like it is today.'

'Then Papa came on the scene, you fell in love with him and married him. Was that how it was?'

She didn't give a direct answer and there was an odd look on her face.

'Love can grow out of liking, my dear, and it is possible to love more than once.' She paused and there was a look of regret on her face. 'We have never been close you and I and that was my fault. A mother gets wrapped up in her sons but that is no excuse. I should have been more sensitive to your needs.'

'It doesn't matter now,' Susan said awkwardly.

'You weren't entirely blameless but I'm straying,' she said, putting a hand to her brow. 'What I wanted to say was that in time you will learn that the secret of a successful marriage is to work at it and that very much depends upon the woman.'

'Yes, I suppose so.'

'Believe me, my dear, if we hadn't thought Edward to be right for you we would never have encouraged the union.' She looked steadily at Susan but Susan's face was expressionless.

'You like Edward and liking will blossom into love and the marriage all the stronger for it.' She smiled. 'Tomorrow morning, Susan, you must tell Papa yourself and after that I'll see about the announcement of your forthcoming marriage going into the newspapers.'

'Surely there is no need for all this rush,' Susan said, alarmed at the way everything was being speeded up.

'Nonsense, it is what your papa would want.'

Everything was crowding in on her and with a mumbled excuse Susan almost ran from the room.

When she did eventually sleep Susan dreamed of David Cameron, a confused dream that made her blush but by the time she was fully awake her thoughts were only of her papa.

The morning was dull, not like a June morning. There was hardly a movement in the trees. The air was clammy inside and out and the maids looked fatigued as they went about their duties. Matthew had left the house early and Susan and her mother were breakfasting together.

'What about Papa?'

'Dr Sullivan is quite pleased and now that we have a night nurse he feels he no longer requires to remain overnight.'

'But he'll come each day?'

'Of course. Papa is still a very sick man.'

Susan was outside the sickroom and waiting for Dr Sullivan when he came out.

His brows shot up. 'There you are, Susan. Your papa has taken some nourishment and there's a wee improvement.'

'If I promise not to tire him may I see Papa for a few minutes?'

'Can't see why not. Keep it short, he's very weak.' He turned back, opened the door and beckoned Susan to follow him. Tiptoeing in she was shocked at the change in her papa. His cheeks were sunken, his face grey and propped up with pillows he looked an old man. Her distress must have shown on her face.

'Don't look like that, Susan, I'm still in the land of the living and not ready to leave it just yet,' he said in a voice she had to strain to hear.

'Five minutes, Susan,' Dr Sullivan gave as his parting shot.

Hamish muttered something under his breath as she bent down to kiss his brow.

'Papa, you're some better,' she said unsteadily but it was hard to believe by looking at him.

'Up and about in no time,' he whispered.

'Here's something to cheer you. I'm going to marry Edward.'

She saw relief in the sunken eyes as his hand fastened on hers.

'He'll make you a good husband.' The effort of speech had cost him and he closed his eyes but his grip on her hand tightened. The nurse, out of earshot but watching, came to her patient and rearranged the pillows. Her starched uniform seemed to crackle with professional annoyance.

'The patient is not to be encouraged to talk,' she admonished severely but moved away at Hamish's ferocious glower.

'Old battleaxe,' Hamish grunted and it was so like her papa that Susan had to stifle a giggle. His speech became telegraphic.

'Matthew – misjudged him – says he'll stay on in the mill.'

'You must be pleased about that?'

'Lying here – time to think – no good, Susan – with the best will in the world he'd be no good. Better he should go into farming.'

'Don't tire yourself, Papa,' Susan said, alarmed.

'Don't you start. Edward now – capable – good head for business.'

He lay back exhausted and she was about to go but he held on to her hand.

'Get married quickly – let me get my affairs in order.'

Bristling with annoyance, the nurse almost propelled Susan from the room.

*   *   *

93

Matthew had slept his exhaustion away and even after a full day in the papermill he looked remarkably fresh. Sarah had felt one of her headaches coming on and had returned to her room leaving brother and sister together.

'Matthew, I had a few minutes with Papa and he was saying you are prepared to stay on in the mill.'

'What choice had I after what happened? Mind you, come to think about it, he wasn't as relieved as I would have expected. Still, that could be attributed to the way he is just now.'

'I've decided to marry Edward,' she said quietly.

He looked at her sharply. 'When did this come about?'

'Yesterday.'

'Nothing would please him more. How did he take it?'

'As you would expect. It came as a great relief and Matthew, he appreciates your offer but he said as much to me that it isn't necessary. Edward will take on much of the responsibility and presumably I'll be allowed to make some contribution.'

His relief was almost comical. 'You're sure about that, I mean really sure?'

'That's what Papa said, Matthew.'

'Look, Susan,' he said awkwardly, 'I know what I said before but I wouldn't like to think of you marrying Edward just for the sake of the mill.'

'Rest assured, Matthew, there was no pressure, the decision was mine. And if you want over to Moorend hadn't you better get a move on?'

'You're right. She's a good sort, Winnie is, wasn't going to hold me to the marriage.'

'How about you, would you have gone through with it?' she asked him as he prepared to go but he made no answer.

Susan knocked first then went into the darkened bedroom.

'No, you're not disturbing me. I was just about to get up,' her mother said as she removed the net cap from her head. 'Is Matthew still downstairs?'

'No, he left for Moorend a few minutes ago.'

She smiled. 'Now that he has Papa's blessing to go

into farming everything is working out after all. Mind you, Matthew and Winnie making a match of it takes some getting used to.'

'Wasn't she looking smart?'

'Just what I thought. The sudden interest in clothes must have been for Matthew's benefit. Quite a dark horse our Winnie.'

Susan wandered over to the window to open the curtains a fraction then turned back to the bed. 'Mama, I'd much prefer to wait until Papa's a lot stronger but he wants the marriage to take place as soon as possible.'

'Then we must fall in with his wishes.' Her brow puckered. 'There's such a lot to arrange,' she said worriedly. 'Edward and his parents must come over to let us get started. And I must see Hamish,' she said, swinging her legs out of bed. 'Miss Beattie, I must get in touch with Miss Beattie and persuade her to stop everything else and do a rush order. But of course she will, after all we are valued customers.'

Susan could almost see her mind dart from one thing to another. There was a feverishness about her and Susan saw life becoming very difficult from now on. She would have to try and act the part of the happy bride yet all she could feel was a dreadful reluctance to tie herself to Edward Brodie. Leaving her mother, she went outside across the lawn and sought refuge in the summer house which Mrs MacFarlane had had built for her but seldom used. No one would worry her here and she had a great need to be alone with her thoughts. Gazing ahead without really seeing, Susan shivered and tried to banish the memory of those dark anguished eyes and her own panic-stricken flight. Shame mingled with guilt as she remembered her own conduct. David hadn't forced her. Her own body had betrayed her with its sudden, shameful, urgent desire and she knew her nearness had aroused him.

Well, it had happened and there was no turning back the clock. She had been foolish but now she must forget all about David Cameron. And in time she would, she must.

CHAPTER NINE

'Don't be wishing her back, lad,' the doctor said as he sat down with a weariness that had nothing to do with age. 'Your mother had only pain ahead of her. This way, going in her sleep, she is spared that.'

Dr Archibald Anderson was thin-faced and wore waxed moustaches. Years ago he had come to this practice in Aranvale with all the energy and optimism of the newly qualified doctor only to find that the fashionable Dr Sullivan had creamed off the top families leaving him to take his patients from those families on the poverty line and under, who could ill afford his fees and a fair number who could but preferred to keep the publicans in business. The constant battle to make ends meet had soured and prematurely aged him.

'I pleaded with her to see you,' David said brokenly.

'And so she did, a long time ago and I only told her what she already knew.'

David's hands moved in a gesture of hopelessness. 'Why didn't she tell me? Why didn't she?'

'Her way, David, she wouldn't want to upset you.' Sighing, he took out a watch dangling from a chain across his middle and frowned. 'I'll need to be getting on my way,' he said, getting up. 'Do you have someone to stay with you, help you through this?'

'I've sent word to an aunt; she'll be over. Don't worry about me, Dr Anderson, I'll manage.'

'I dare say. You were a good son to her and now you must look to yourself,' he said kindly. 'You have your whole life ahead of you.'

'Yes.' From the dresser David picked up some coins and handed them over.

'This is more than my fee,' Dr Anderson grunted.

'Take it, you've been very kind.'

'Very good of you, lad,' he said, pocketing the money. 'Not many about here would do that.'

They shook hands. The door closed. David was alone, yet not alone. Behind the curtain lay the cold, still body of the mother who had suffered slights and cruel jibes yet had managed to hold her head high and devote her life to the son she had loved so dearly.

His eyes went to the empty chair which had always been hers. The sagging cushion was askew and automatically he went over to right it. On a corner of the table, neatly folded and ready to put away in the drawer, was his laundry, the shirts carefully ironed as she had once done for the gentry. She had been so particular about his clothes, so anxious that he should always be well turned out.

'Oh, Mother,' he whispered brokenly. The pain of loss was indescribable and for the only time in his adult life he gave in to his grief with great racking sobs that shook his body.

Tears were unmanly. He could imagine her reproachful eyes and he half smiled. Unmanly perhaps but the storm of weeping had left him calm and more able to face what had to be done.

The water in the big, black kettle was still warm and he used it to wash at the sink. The fire was low and he added some kindling then once it caught he rearranged the hot cinders and put on more coal. The chill of death was in the house and he shivered.

He couldn't eat but he made himself tea and drank it then went next door to the McDonalds. He could leave it to them to inform the neighbours. Those in the mill would know there would be a good reason for his lateness. Time off would be no problem. Though Mr MacFarlane lay ill at Aran Heights his rules regarding illness and bereavement would be carried out to the letter. There would be offers of help, he knew that and it comforted him.

Aunt Meg, his mother's sister, was in the cottage when he got back. She had the table set and the kettle on the boil.

Neither were demonstrative but they hugged each other. She made him eat a meat pie she had brought with her and he surprised himself by enjoying it. Like his mother Aunt Meg knew when to be silent. Later they would talk but the time wasn't right. He felt restless, not knowing what to do with himself.

'David, lad, take yourself for a long walk, you'll feel the better for it.'

'I can't leave you alone with – '

She knew what he meant and smiled sadly. 'We loved them in life, why should we fear them in death is what I always say.'

David walked with long strides until he was out of the village and following the burn which wound its tortuous way through the countryside until it flowed into the River Clyde. From Clapperton's farm he could hear the pigs squealing for food and the sounds of carts rattling up the farm track. The sun had slunk behind a cloud and in the distance the hills looked like purple shadows. The lonely figure of a shepherd could be seen with his flock and on other slopes the cattle grazed. Aranvale could pull at the heart, David thought with a pang, yet all he wanted was to get away from it, far away. There was nothing for him here.

In the short space of a week he had been dealt two crushing blows. The death of his mother was a devastating and unexpected loss. The other had not been altogether a surprise but it had left him low-spirited and depressed. The local newspaper had made a big splash of the forthcoming marriage of Susan MacFarlane to Edward Brodie, the younger son of John Brodie, owner of the Granton Distillery.

Thinking back to that Sunday David had only self-disgust for his behaviour and the guilt weighed upon him heavily. That she had done nothing to discourage him was no excuse. She was young, four years his junior and so vulnerable, so in need of protection and instead – he shut his eyes to blot out the memory. The past was dead. Very soon he would leave Aranvale never to return.

* * *

Only a handful of mourners stood in the drizzling rain to see Eliza Cameron laid to rest in the graveyard behind the kirk. At the end of the short service one or two mourners shook hands with David, offering sympathy but with a clumsy awkwardness. David Cameron was something of a mystery. He had always preferred his own company to hanging around with others his own age.

Leaving them to find his own way back to the cottage, David wondered what was expected of him. Should he invite any of the neighbours in? Perhaps it was the custom yet he recoiled from it. How many had shown kindness to his mother during her lifetime?

He only wanted Aunt Meg and she was waiting for him, looking worried.

'I should have been asking if you'd be bringing anyone for a bite.'

'No, I don't want any of them.'

'Get a good send-off, did she?'

'A few turned up and it was a nice service.' There was a catch in his voice and she busied herself at the fire.

'There's broth and bannocks, we'll both be the better of something.'

'I'm not hungry.'

'Nor am I but we have to eat.' She was a small, stout woman not a bit like his mother. Only when she smiled did the resemblance show.

David ate to please her and she to encourage him.

'What are your plans, lad?'

'Once I've settled everything I'm going to London.'

Her eyebrows rose in perplexity. 'Don't rush into anything, lad, think on it well.' She shook her head. 'So many of the young seek their fortune in London and a lot of them find only loneliness and heartbreak. Besides which you'd be givin' up a good job.'

'I have a friend there, Aunt Meg, and accountants don't have too much trouble finding work.'

'If your mind's made up then that's that.'

'As long as Mother was in Aranvale I would have stayed

but now I want a change.' He smiled. 'A suitcase is all I need so please take anything from the house you want.'

She was on the verge of weeping. 'I wish you'd just bide here.'

David put his arms around her. 'Mother would have wanted you to have her things and if you have no use for them then give them to someone.'

'Oh, I'll find a home for them, never fear.'

There was something he had to ask, he'd been waiting for an opportunity and perhaps this was it.

'Aunt Meg, you were always closest to Mother and you were the one who came to her rescue when she was in trouble.'

Her face darkened. 'Your grandparents, good livin' by their way of thinkin' but hard as nails. They were the sinners not Eliza.'

He swallowed hard. 'You must know who my father is?'

She was silent for a long time. 'She told you nothin',' she said at last.

'Nothing.'

'Gave her word and being Eliza she wouldn't break it.'

'You could tell me,' he persisted.

'I didn't take an oath on it but I don't know – ' she said slowly.

'I believe I have a right to know, Aunt Meg.'

'Maybe you do at that.' She moved her flabby body in its too tight black gown and settled into a more comfortable position.

'See if you can squeeze another cup out of that pot, there's a lad.'

David got up to make a fresh pot of tea, taking glances at his aunt while he waited for the kettle to boil. She was looking straight ahead and David tensed with excitement. At long last he was to hear who had fathered him and abandoned his mother.

Taking the cup gratefully she drank from it then put it down.

'I'll tell you as much as I remember but mind, my memory isn't what it used to be.'

'Please, Aunt Meg, you remember very well and I must know.'

'She wouldn't want you taking your revenge. Whatever it was between them there was no hatred in her heart. He was a gentleman, she said to me as if that explained it all.' She paused. 'I'll be needin' your word, David, that you'll cause no mischief.'

'How could I? Haven't I just told you that I'm off to London?'

'Now then, where do I start?'

'At the beginning and leave nothing out.'

She sighed. 'I hope I'm doin' the right thing.'

June became July and with the wedding day coming ever closer Aran Heights was thrown into a frenzy of preparation. Ever fearful of another attack and anxious that his affairs should be in order, Hamish MacFarlane had shamelessly used his poor health to insist that the young couple be married within the month. And under the watchful eye of Dr Sullivan Mrs MacFarlane had had to agree. All the while she was frantic, wondering how an important occasion such as their only daughter's wedding could be arranged in such a short time. In the end she had gained one week and the date was firmly fixed for five weeks ahead.

Susan carried out the tasks allotted to her and tried to show some enthusiasm when the bride and bridesmaid's gowns were discussed but it was all such an effort. Nothing seemed real, they could have been discussing someone else's wedding.

She had always enjoyed good health but now it had deserted her and she seemed drained of energy. Then there was that awful nausea and the retching. Pre-wedding nerves her mother would put it down to. Thankfully the nausea was easing a little but at breakfast all she could face was dry toast, even the weak tea she could not stomach.

No one noticed. Mama had a tray in her room and Matthew had gone before she came down.

In the early days of his illness the life of the household had kept pace with the faltering strength of the master but as he gradually grew stronger the services of the night nurse were considered no longer necessary. Scorning the help of the day nurse he would get up and stand at the window looking over at Aranvale.

Lilian Brodie was a great help to Sarah at this time and the two friends, equally delighted at the coming union of their children, were frequently closeted together.

Today, Susan, Edward, Sarah and Lilian were seated in the small sitting-room. Lilian was having difficulty in containing her excitement as she turned her head to face her future daughter-in-law.

'Susan, dear, I think I have come up with the perfect solution and Edward agrees but only,' she added hastily, 'if it meets with your approval.'

Susan smiled politely. 'I'd like to hear it.'

'The matter of a home for you – to find one of your own in the short time available and have it furnished is quite, quite out of the question. I think we are agreed on that. But,' she paused, 'the Templetons, I hear, are going down south for six months and closing up their house.' She stopped, looked at Edward and he took over.

'Mother feels, Susan, that she could persuade the Templetons to let us occupy Hillview, rent it furnished – '

'How perfectly splendid,' Sarah interrupted. 'Susan! Edward! That would give you breathing space to look around for what you want and Hillview though small is quite charming.'

'That sounds fine and I'm perfectly agreeable,' Susan said, trying to infuse some enthusiasm into her voice.

'Are you sure, Lilian, that the Templetons would agree to this?' Sarah said doubtfully.

Lilian pursed her lips, nodded and dropped her voice. 'The business term, I believe, is financially embarrassed. John knows something of the circumstances and thinks they will be glad of the money and of course the staff can be retained.'

'Splendid! That takes care of that,' Sarah said briskly.

The carriage left with Mrs Brodie and her son and Susan and her mother returned to the drawing-room.

'Wasn't that just a little bit thoughtless of you, dear? I'm sure Edward would have appreciated some time with his bride-to-be. There must be things you wish to discuss in private.'

'Sorry, Mama, I didn't think about that, it was just that I didn't feel like a walk.'

'You're not unwell are you?' she asked anxiously.

'No, just tired.'

'Oh, well, just one of your difficult days I expect,' Sarah said in a hushed voice as she sat down at the Regency desk with pen and paper and a worried expression.

'This is all very awkward for me, Susan. Some of our friends are going to be greatly offended not to receive an invitation, particularly those who have invited us to weddings in their families.'

'Surely not, Mama. With Papa ill they must realise the position.'

'They will, my dear, they will, just until they find out that someone close to them is invited then jealousies arise and the whole thing becomes difficult, very difficult indeed.'

Susan looked over her mother's shoulder. 'Mama!' she burst out. 'That can't be the final list of guests, it's supposed to be a quiet wedding.'

'Mrs Brodie can't reduce her list and I'm not doing any further trimming of ours,' her mother said with a finality that brooked no argument.

Headaches were a thing of the past, Mrs MacFarlane had no time to suffer from one. Every minute of every day was occupied. Top priority were the visits to Miss Beattie who had given over her entire staff to the making of Susan's wedding gown, her trousseau, the bridesmaid's dress and the outfit for the mother of the bride. An ever more excitable Sarah had Susan shunted here and there and Susan did as she was bid without complaint, hiding her tiredness and lethargy as best she could. She marvelled at the amount of energy her mother was displaying while she herself had never felt so low-spirited and drained.

With his days in the mill numbered, Matthew was spending more time there than had ever been his custom and those who had previously written him off as lazy and virtually useless were now admitting, albeit grudgingly, that he was putting his back into the work in his father's absence.

'Matthew's very quiet these days, have you noticed, Susan?'

'Yes, I have. Papa's collapse was a terrible shock and it affected him dreadfully. Winnie has noticed the difference too.'

'Mmmmm.' Mrs MacFarlane gave a deep sigh. 'Once you and Edward are married I must see Mr Clapperton and his sister. Neither will have a clue as to how to go about arranging a wedding and I rather think the bulk of the work will fall to me. Not that I mind but I would like time to draw my breath after yours.'

'Winnie would hate fuss.'

'Even so her father will want to do the right thing by his only child and that reminds me of the shopping trip the three of us had,' she said, flitting to another subject. 'How very fortunate that your buttercup yellow gown hasn't been worn.'

'There was no occasion to wear it.'

'True. Entertaining has been far from our minds these last few weeks. Of them all that gown remains my favourite, the colour is perfect for you and I'm sure Edward will be quite dazzled when he sees you in it on your honeymoon.'

At the mention of honeymoon Susan felt her throat constrict. Until now she had managed to block from her mind that she wasn't going to Edward as an innocent young bride but as a woman who had shamelessly sinned. Busy with her own thoughts, Mrs MacFarlane noticed nothing amiss as she poured tea from the silver teapot.

'Susan, we really must spare an hour to visit Moorend. Winnie will have received her gowns from Miss Beattie and may want our opinion as to which to wear for your wedding.'

'Perhaps she's had something else made up. After all Winnie is taking more care over her appearance.'

'And about time. Still, we must go over before Hannah descends on us, then truly we won't have a minute.'

Susan laughed. 'Hannah's a darling, I'm looking forward to her coming.'

'Apparently she's over the moon about being your brides-maid but the child is such a chatterbox.'

'Hardly a child, Hannah's seventeen.'

'She doesn't act it. Maybe I made a mistake asking your aunt and uncle to bring her here a week before the wedding.'

'No, mama, she'll be a great help and don't worry she'll be quiet enough when Papa is around.' She raised her eyes to the clock. 'Papa should have had his rest by now?'

'Yes, off you go.'

Hamish was sitting up in bed propped up with pillows and with papers strewn over the bedcover when Susan went in.

'Well, you do look more like yourself.' Susan smiled and kissed his cheek.

'Rarin' to be up and about, Susan.'

'Just don't be overdoing it. In fact,' she said severely, 'we are all going to make sure you don't.'

With her nursing duties about to end the stern-looking nurse – Hatchet Face, Hamish nicknamed her – was busy tidying bottles and stacking them neatly into a medicine cabinet. Looking up she muttered something and left father and daughter together.

'Got her trained now that she's leaving,' Hamish said, catching Susan's eye and grinning wickedly.

'Be fair, Papa,' Susan reproached. 'Nurse Robertson has looked after you very well.'

'So she has,' he agreed quietly. He raised himself and pointed to a porcelain figure of a crinoline lady. 'Fancies that thing, I'm sure she does, seen her looking at it often enough. In case I forget to tell your mother see that she gets it along with her wages and get yourself a chair, you can't stand there

106

and I'm not having you sitting on the bed,' he said irritably. 'We have things to discuss.'

'Yes, Papa,' Susan replied as she brought a chair across to the bed and sat down.

'Preparations well in hand?'

'Mama is doing everything almost single-handed.' She laughed.

'In her element she'll be.' He smiled and sobered. 'Susan, I'm having my solicitor draw up a new will.'

Feeling uncomfortable at this turn in the conversation Susan bit her lip and looked away then turned back to face her father.

'Matthew shall have his inheritance now. I have no wish to have a son of mine dependent for his living on Euan Clapperton and this way Matthew can buy additional land, land which will belong to him and in time to his family.'

'He'll appreciate that, Papa.'

'So he should,' he grunted.

'He'll make a good farmer,' Susan said gently.

'But will he make a good husband?' His eyes were bleak. 'Matthew's getting married for all the wrong reasons. Still, that's his problem.' He sighed. 'Thankfully I've no such fears for you and Edward but that is not what I want to discuss.' He paused and looked at her searchingly. 'The mill, does it still mean as much to you?'

'The mill is a part of me, Papa, and I'm hoping you will allow me a share in its management.'

He smiled and there was a hint of moisture in the blue eyes as he patted her hand.

'I hoped you'd say that, lass.' He coughed and took a short rest. 'Lying here with time to think I'm seeing things much more clearly. What I'm saying or about to say is no disrespect to Edward. He is a fine lad with a good brain and a great hankering after responsibility but we have to be careful. Edward must never have total responsibility. He has a touch of his father's ruthlessness which some would admire but it isn't my way. John and I respect each other but his ways are not mine and what is tolerated in the distillery would not be in my mill.' He paused and moved his position. 'Workers are human beings, never lose sight of that, Susan. There could come a time when their loyalty could be crucial to survival.'

He was deadly serious, she could see that.

'Don't misunderstand me, my dear, this marriage is very important to me. When your marriage to Edward was being considered we had quite a talk. At that time I expected Matthew to become the eventual owner of the mill and Edward to be second in command and that seemed to satisfy him.'

'By refusing Edward I upset your carefully laid plans.'

'Not at all. Your mother and I never doubted but that you would change your mind and in the event we were proved right. Now where was I – oh, yes! Don't be alarmed but we must face facts. Heaven forbid that I should suffer another attack like this one but should it happen I'm well aware it could be fatal.'

'Papa!' Susan cried in distress. 'Don't talk like that, please.'

'Tch! Tch! Come, Susan, you are no longer a child and I'm in no hurry to leave this world but I do want to be prepared.'

'I wish you wouldn't – '

'I am treating you like an adult, kindly act as one,' he said sternly.

'I'm sorry.'

He glowered and continued. 'When I do go the papermill will become your responsibility,' he said, his eyes on her face.

'Papa!' She stared at him.

'You heard correctly. I am leaving the mill to you in the firm belief that you are capable of its management,' he said quietly.

'I can't believe this.'

'Let me go on. Many, perhaps your husband-to-be among them, will resent taking orders from a woman and to deal with the situation you will need both tact and firmness.'

She made to speak but he silenced her with an impatient move of his arm.

'Once I'm no longer here Edward may decide that my methods are old-fashioned and be anxious to make sweeping changes. You must decide their worth, Susan, and if you have doubts be strong enough to voice them. He cannot act without your authority. Remember that, Susan. *You* have the final say.' He smiled then. 'Edward is not likely to be difficult and one day, God willing, you will bear Edward's child and the mill shall pass to my grandson.' He lay back exhausted.

'You've tired yourself.'

'Talking tires me but I needed this conversation.'

She swallowed painfully and gave herself a few moments before speaking.

'Whatever lies ahead you have my promise that I shall carry on the way you taught me.'

'I know that. If I hadn't been so sure I would have held on to Matthew.'

'He was prepared to stay in the mill.'

'Yes, I know I was too hard on the lad.' He frowned. 'Perhaps I haven't explained myself very well. Don't think I'm against change – far from it. Change is healthy when the tried and trusted is replaced by something better but not when it is just for change itself.' He broke off for a drink from the covered glass and after a few sips pulled a face. 'Something a bit stronger than water would be welcome but I suppose I'll be denied it until I'm on my feet and can get it for myself.'

'You're not allowed it so don't look at me.' Susan laughed.

'All right, back to what I was saying. You must decide, Susan, what changes would be to the mill's advantage and not be talked into something that goes against your better judgment.'

'I do understand that.'

'Make time to read the journals, find out what is new and if it would be profitable in the long term. A time will come when you will need to install new machinery, nothing stands still. Occasionally, Susan, a calculated gamble is necessary to keep ahead of one's competitors. All this you will learn in time.' He sounded weary. 'Go now, Susan, I'll have a rest.'

Susan got to her feet, kissed her papa and left the room quietly.

So much was going through her head that she felt quite

dazed by it all. The need to be by herself, to go over in her own mind what Papa had said, was strong and taking a lightweight cape from the hallstand she went out into the warmth of the day. The old gardener, turning over the soil, raised his cap while the simple-looking youth with him watched Susan with his mouth hanging slack. She turned away hurriedly towards the tree-lined path with her head down. She was barely able to grasp at the enormity of the responsibility that would one day be hers. Everything was happening too quickly and it worried her. Such a short time ago she had been fighting to gain a small foothold in the mill and now she was to prepare to be at its head one day. Fervently she prayed that that day was far off. And of course it would be. Wasn't Papa getting stronger every day and just so long as he was there to advise – strange that he should feel this way about Edward, she mused. She, herself, had felt a bit apprehensive recently, in fact since Matthew had made his decision to become a farmer. Her stomach lurched. Hadn't she just of late had the distinct impression that Edward was smugly satisfied? And why not? With Matthew out of the way he must see himself as the future Master of Aranvale Papermill.

Dressed in a gown of pale green silk trimmed with gold thread, Susan looked both fresh and pretty. An unbroken night's sleep had left her refreshed, her colour was back and she was looking forward to the arrival of her cousin, Hannah, and her aunt and uncle.

When the carriage arrived with Mr and Mrs Forrester and their daughter, Hannah was first to fling herself into Susan's outstretched arms before Uncle George and Aunt Millie stepped into the hall and looked on with the amused indulgence of parents of an only child. Hannah was as tall as Susan but thin, shapeless and deeply concerned that her figure had failed to fill out despite repeated assurances from her mother that in time it would do so.

'Oh, it isn't fair,' Hannah wailed. 'Every time I see Susan I'm green with envy. Mama, how did you manage to produce such an ugly duckling?'

'Not an ugly duckling just a silly goose.' Susan laughed as she greeted her aunt and uncle. 'And just wait until you see your bridesmaid's dress, it's lovely and you may well steal the show.'

'Your Miss Beattie managed with the measurements?' Aunt Millie asked as she turned to embrace her sister who had just come into the hall.

'My apologies,' Sarah said as she moved from Millie's arms to turn her cheek for George's kiss. 'A small emergency in the kitchen which needed my personal attention. Come along to the sitting-room, it gets the sun at this time and while the meal is being prepared we can catch up on each other's news. The maid has just put a tray in and I'm sure a cup of tea will refresh you after your journey.' Gracefully she led the way and after the ladies were seated George sat down.

'Mama, Aunt Millie was asking about Hannah's measurements.'

'Miss Beattie managed with them. Incidentally she is coming with one of her assistants to Aran Heights for the final fittings. That is tomorrow but if Hannah needs more than one that can be arranged,' she said indulgently and with an upward glance as she poured tea and Susan handed it round.

'How is Hamish?'

'Very much better, Millie, I'm thankful to say, though nothing like his old self.' She sighed. 'One tries to be optimistic but I very much doubt if he ever will get his health fully back.'

'Rest and freedom from worry can work wonders,' George said in his kindly way then turned to Susan. 'Getting a bit nervous are you, Susan, now that the big day draws near?'

'I'm being kept so busy that I haven't time to be nervous.' She smiled.

'Really it's all been so sudden I don't know how you are managing, Sarah. I mean between the worry about Hamish and the preparations for the wedding. Even thinking about it and I'm exhausted.'

'It hasn't been easy but it was the only way to keep Hamish

111

calm. He worries about the mill you see, George,' she said, bringing her brother-in-law into the conversation, 'and he wants Edward as family as soon as possible.'

'What about cousin Matthew?' Hannah piped in.

'Yes, well, Hannah my dear, things don't always work out as we would like. Of course your Uncle Hamish would have preferred his own son in the mill but he has come to accept that Matthew would only be happy in farming.'

'It's decided then?' Millie enquired as she replaced her cup and declined a fill-up.

'Yes, Matthew is – oh, dear, this isn't quite official but there is the likelihood of an announcement soon and you are family – '

'That delightful girl, Caroline – '

'No, Millie, there was no serious attachment there,' Sarah said firmly. 'The young lady is Euan Clapperton's daughter, Winnie.'

'Never!' Millie's eyes widened with shock, then seeing Sarah's frown she hastened in with, 'I mean, Sarah, Matthew is such a good-looking and sophisticated young man and Winnie is – well – homely and hardly his type I would have thought.'

'Matthew's gorgeous,' Hannah said dreamily, 'and if I'd thought he would fall for someone plain like Winnie Clapperton I would have set my cap at him ages ago.'

They all laughed. 'Sarah, what am I to do with this child of mine, the outrageous things she comes away with?'

The arrival of the maid to announce that the meal was ready saved a reply.

Following her aunt, Susan thought how attractive she looked yet she must only spend a fraction of the money her mother spent on clothes. She was much slimmer, which gave her an immediate advantage but in colouring the sisters were alike and each had neat features. Hannah to her disgust had inherited her father's blunt features but this was in part compensated for by a bubbling personality.

George left most of the talking to the women but the way

his eyes rested on his wife and child it was easy to see he adored them.

With his sister-in-law George was never completely at ease, knowing that she had always considered him a poor match for her sister. Perhaps sensing this, Hamish was at pains to put him at his ease on the rare occasions the two met but even so George felt a bit out of his depth.

A snowy white damask cloth covered the long dining-room table and each place was set with the heavy silver cutlery which had been kept for special occasions in Hamish's parents' time but was now in daily use at Aran Heights. The empty chair at the head of the table emphasised the absence of the master of the house and all eyes went to it as they sat down.

'Hamish sends his apologies. Though getting up for longer periods each day he prefers to have lunch in his own room but you'll see him before you go,' Sarah explained as Polly and another maid began serving from the silver dishes.

'Will he be well enough to take Susan down the aisle?'

Sarah smiled. 'In his own words he'll be there to give his daughter in marriage as long as he can put one foot in front of the other.'

'Sounds as if he's anxious to get you married and off his hands, Susan,' George joked but the remark didn't bring forth laughter and Hannah's questioning eyes went to her cousin. In an unguarded moment she saw the bleakness in Susan's face and something like resignation.

'I can just imagine Hamish saying it in his dry way and Hannah, dear, you will remember Uncle Hamish tires easily and be on your best behaviour?'

Hannah looked outraged. 'I'm not a child, I know how to behave.'

'Of course you do,' Sarah said soothingly, 'and I know you're going to be a great help to Susan. With gifts coming in all the time it's so important not to get the cards mixed. You can write out the names and the gifts alongside and that way we'll have a double check.'

'All those thank-you letters,' Aunt Millie said feelingly. 'You have my sympathy, Susan. Lovely though it is to receive

113

so many gifts, penning a note to each and trying to think of something new to say is bound to be a trial.'

'I'm afraid they will be all more or less the same.' Susan smiled.

'Men get it easy every time,' Hannah butted in. 'About all they have to do is put in an appearance at the wedding.'

'Shows how much you have to learn, young lady,' her father answered.

Later, when Hannah's parents departed, Susan accompanied her cousin to the guest bedroom nearest to her own and helped her unpack.

'Polly would have done this.'

'And have her see my wardrobe!'

'What's wrong with your wardrobe?'

'What's right with it?'

'Aunt Millie has excellent dress sense.'

'For herself but when it comes to buying for me,' she raised her eyes to heaven, 'you would think I was still in the schoolroom.'

Looking at the woebegone expression Susan wanted to giggle. Poor Hannah had such swings of moods. 'Tell you what, my gift to you for being bridesmaid and helping will be a new gown from Miss Beattie.'

'No!' Hannah was scandalised. 'You can't do that. Whatever would Aunt Sarah and my mama have to say and who would pay for it?'

'I will, otherwise it wouldn't be a gift from me, would it. I do have some money of my own. Aunt Rachel encouraged us to save so we got money for Christmas and birthdays with instructions that it was to go into the bank.'

'Lucky you.'

'That's not your real gift of course. Edward will have the pleasure of seeing to that and the bridesmaid's gift is usually a piece of jewellery.'

Hannah's eyes shone. 'Really, I had no idea.'

'And the gown, it will give me a lot of pleasure, so please no arguments.'

'You're a darling and I'm going to miss you, Susan,' she said, dangerously close to tears. 'Aran Heights won't be the same without you. I mean we're more than cousins – '

'I know,' Susan said gently, 'more like sisters.'

'And friends – '

'But not for long,' Susan joked, 'if you don't lift your idle hands and hang up your gowns while I put this underwear in the drawer.'

They got the job completed. 'Better put in an appearance downstairs.'

'Not yet, Susan, I want to ask you something.'

'Ask away then.'

'Everyone expected you and Edward to make a match of it one day.'

'But not you, Hannah?'

'Don't get me wrong,' she said hastily, 'Edward is nice and good husband material as Mama once said.' She caught Susan's eye and they both giggled. 'But I thought you would fall in love with someone new who would be gorgeous and exciting.'

'Edward can be very entertaining,' she said lamely.

'Hardly the same.' The freckles stood out on her pale skin and her face was deadly serious. 'Edward loves you, no doubt about that but then who wouldn't, you're so lovely. You're not in love with him and I'm so afraid for you.' She paused and whispered, 'What happens if one day you fall in love, deeply in love and you're married to Edward?'

'That won't happen and the only reason I'm not dancing about with excitement is because Papa has been so desperately ill.'

'And desperate to see you married to Edward,' she said quietly. 'You're marrying Edward to please Uncle Hamish and you can't deny that, not to me.'

To change the conversation Susan said, 'Edward's cousin is to be best man.'

'What's he like?'

'I don't know, I haven't met him but Edward is bringing Samuel – Samuel Hargreaves is his name – to Aran Heights tomorrow evening to meet everybody and you in particular. All I can tell you is he's two years younger than Edward, very shy and apprehensive about his duties as best man. Edward, I may say, is looking to you to bring him out of his shell.'

'He won't like me, young men don't because I haven't got a bosom.'

'Hannah! For goodness sake!' she exploded. 'Whatever will you come away with next?'

'It's all right for you saying that but I'm as flat as a pancake.'

'Nonsense! You do have a little. Don't you?'

'Hardly any.'

'There's still time to develop, you're only seventeen.'

'All my friends have bosoms. Katie, you know Katie, she's quite magnificent.'

'I don't agree. Last time I saw her I thought she looked top-heavy.'

Hannah let our a squeal of laughter. 'If she fell flat on her face she'd bounce back, is that what you mean?'

'It is not, you horrible creature.' Arm-in-arm they went downstairs to find Sarah ordering the servants to be careful how they carried the wedding gifts through to the room made over for that purpose.

'At last! I was beginning to wonder when you two were to show face. Now that you are here you can open these gifts carefully and take a note of the senders.'

'We'll do that, Mama and we'll be very careful. Matthew's late isn't he?'

'No, he told me he'd be delayed. There are a few acres of land adjoining Moorend that have just come on the market. Euan had his eye on it and the farmhouse. It was to be his wedding present but your papa will have none of it. Apparently Matthew is to get his inheritance now so that he can offer for it himself.'

'I think Papa's right and Matthew will be happier about it too. He'll want to stand on his own feet rather than have everything handed to him from his in-laws-to-be.'

A touch of anger crossed Sarah's face. 'Euan is not blind

to that, Susan, though why any of this should be a problem I can't understand. It is no different from John Brodie giving Thomas and his wife the Laurels as a wedding gift and I imagine Edward will be treated with the same generosity.'

'You're wrong there, Mama. As the younger son Edward will get a lot less.'

She looked surprised. 'Perhaps you're right. Your papa wouldn't have differentiated between Ralph and Matthew but then John has his own ways and maybe feels the younger son is not entitled to the same amount,' she said vaguely.

'Edward resents it, I do know that.'

'Hardly surprising but with all this talk you nearly put it out of my mind.'

'What?'

'Rumour has it that the Templetons will have to sell.'

'That won't alter anything, it's only temporary as far as we are concerned.'

'I shouldn't bank on that.'

'I haven't even seen the house,' Susan said indignantly, 'and I think I should have some say in the matter.'

'Don't be silly, of course you've seen it.'

'From the outside and I've always thought it very low-lying and there can't be many rooms.'

'Compared to what Edward and you have been used to of course it is small,' Sarah said patiently, 'but adequate to start off with. In any case Edward and you can come to your own decision.'

'He's coming over tomorrow so we can see over Hillview then.' Susan turned to Hannah. 'You must come too and meet the best man. Edward is bringing Samuel.'

'I'd love to come.'

The following day was packed with activity, everyone dashing around and getting in each other's way. Miss Beattie and her assistant set to with a will and, satisfied that the bridal gown and the mother-of-the-bride's outfit were perfect in every detail, turned their attention to the bridesmaid.

Standing before the mirror with Miss Beattie rearranging

the bodice to add fullness and a nimble-fingered assistant undoing the tacking thread where it failed to please the critical eye of Miss Beattie, Hannah was turned this way and that.

Susan had chosen her favourite shade of blue for the bridesmaid's dress. The material was a fine taffeta with a delicately raised flower pattern decorating the skirt. Appreciating Hannah's shortcomings, Miss Beattie had deftly added darts to the ruched bodice and a suggestion of a bustle to give her a new shapeliness.

'Is that quite comfortable?' Miss Beattie mumbled, her mouth full of pins.

'Yes, thank you, but even if it weren't I'd suffer gladly to look like this.' Then turning to the bride, 'Susan, it really looks as if there is a bosom under all this.'

'You look lovely,' Susan said gently.

'I do, don't I? Mama won't recognise her daughter and from now on I'm going to refuse to wear those ghastly girlish gowns she buys me.'

'Now! Now! Hannah, I heard that,' her aunt said as she returned to the fitting-room.

'Well, it's true, Aunt Sarah and you should have a word with my mama. She may listen to you.'

The assistant's mouth quirked and Miss Beattie, her mouth now free of pins gave her tinkle of a laugh.

'Don't ever think of yourself as thin. You are slim which is a much more attractive description. Stout and heavy-hipped young ladies have difficulty in camouflaging their figure faults and never totally succeed. You, on the other hand, require no more than a stiffener in the bodice and some padding at the hips.'

'That's an expert's opinion, Hannah, so stop complaining.'

'No more complaints, Susan, I promise,' she said with a faint flush on her usually pale cheeks.

Earlier in the day Susan had spoken to her mother about her wish to give Hannah a gown from Miss Beattie's collection and was rewarded with a smile.

'How very thoughtful of you, dear. Hannah does have a genuine grievance and Millie is not good at selecting clothes for her. Once you're on your honeymoon I'll arrange a visit to Miss Beattie and if Millie doesn't get on her high horse I'll chose a day gown for Hannah as well. Millie most certainly won't accept anything for herself.'

'She doesn't need to, Mama, she dresses beautifully,'

'And fortunate for her that she can get away with buying from the cheaper stores. Your Uncle George doesn't have the money to allow for the small luxuries we take for granted.' She sniffed. 'If I live to be a hundred I'll never know why she married George Forrester.'

'Mama, they are very happy and it shows.'

'Happy! She could have been rich and happy. Your aunt had looks, still has and she could so easily have been the wife of a very distinguished gentleman instead of throwing herself away. There was plenty of opposition to George from your grandparents but she just went ahead and married him.'

'That must have taken a lot of courage.'

'Stupidity more like.'

Susan said no more but she wondered if her mother had switched her affections to the son and heir of the Aranvale Papermill and had chosen for greater security. That she had been a good and faithful wife was not in dispute but there had been that uncharacteristic outburst from her papa that had shown all too clearly that Euan Clapperton was still a shadow between them.

Like her father, Susan had a great love of the stark, almost savage beauty of Aran Heights and though she found Hillview a pleasant enough house and the gardens attractive she was by no means taken with it. The others were loud in its praise and she smiled and nodded as the elderly housekeeper took them on an inspection of the house. Susan and Edward went ahead, leaving Hannah and Samuel to follow.

Samuel was a slight, very young-looking man with fairish, wispy hair, skin that flushed easily and eyelashes so fair that one had to look closely to discover if he had any at all. For Hannah it had been an uphill job getting through his painful shyness but she was getting there and

119

discovering behind it an interesting and intelligent young man.

After a thorough inspection of the rooms and a look in at the servants' quarters, Edward declared himself satisfied and looked to Susan for agreement.

'As a temporary home it seems perfectly suitable and it has the advantage of not being too far from the mill.'

'Just what I thought,' he said eagerly, then becoming aware of the housekeeper hovering nearby he gave her a dismissive nod and a murmured 'thank you.'

She inclined her head, opened the vestibule door, waited for them to enter, closed it then crossed the floor to the main door. With it open she stood stiffly. Susan smiled her thanks as did Hannah. Samuel for all his shyness said, 'Thank you for all the trouble you've taken.' Edward gave another nod then they were all outside and into the fresh air. As they walked down the stone steps to the gravel drive they heard the bolts being shot into place.

'Hannah and Samuel, would you mind making yourselves scarce? Susan and I have matters to discuss.'

'Delighted to oblige,' Hannah said pertly. 'We shall inspect the gardens and don't hurry on our behalf,' she called back as Samuel, greatly daring, touched her elbow, hesitated and immediately Hannah slipped her arm in his.

'Wonders will never cease, we've all but despaired of Samuel but then possibly he's never met anyone like Hannah.'

'Interesting to see if it develops.' Susan smiled.

Reaching the summer house Edward flicked his handkerchief over the seat before allowing Susan to sit down, then joined her. 'I'm glad you like Hillview,' he smiled, taking her hand in his and separating her fingers with his own.

'As a temporary home.'

'Only as a temporary home?'

Her tone sharpened. 'Edward, is there something I should know?'

He nodded uncomfortably. 'Susan, there are some decisions that have to be made quickly without time for discussion.' Her eyes didn't move from his face. 'The thing is the

Templetons have decided to let Hillview go and a quick sale without the trouble and expense of putting it on the market would suit them very well.'

'I see.'

'Our solicitor got the price down provided it was an immediate acceptance.'

'So Hillview is ours whether I like it or not.'

'But you've just said you like it.'

'Only because I assumed it to be a temporary dwelling.'

'What don't you like about it?' She could hear the barely suppressed anger.

'It's too small and it has no character.'

'No doubt we could make alterations, add another wing but I fail to see how that would be necessary until we start a family.'

'Perhaps this is the time to tell you, Edward, that I intend continuing to assist Papa with the paperwork and that means I shall require a room where I can work undisturbed and my desk and other necessary working equipment will have to be brought from Aran Heights.'

'What nonsense you do talk, Susan.' His eyes glittered with anger and he was having difficulty in hiding his impatience. 'Foolishly, in my opinion, very foolishly, your father weakened and gave in to your whim but that ceases now. There will be no question of you continuing in any capacity whatsoever. My future father-in-law has already expressed his confidence in me – indeed Matthew being permitted to follow his own inclinations bears proof to that.' The ready colour suffused his face as he went on. 'I am not disputing your ability, far from it, but for a woman and a young woman at that to be involved in business is ludicrous.'

He had made an attempt to laugh it off but one look at her set face and his laugh took on a hollow sound.

'Edward,' Susan said in a dangerously quiet voice, 'you are quite mistaken. Papa made it clear to me as recently as two days ago that it was his wish that I continue to take a part in the management of the mill.'

'Management! Really, Susan, I gave you credit for some

121

sense. Your father is ill and rambling on. It takes some people that way and later they have no recollection of saying any such thing. What do you know about management? You've never as much as stepped inside the mill.'

'That isn't to say I won't one day,' she said spiritedly.

A little alarmed at the way things were going, Edward put his arm round her waist drawing her near but she kept her back rigidly straight.

'I see I'm going to have quite a time taming you, my love, but I'm rather looking forward to the experience. Nothing more do I enjoy than a challenge and two await me.'

She looked at him quickly.

'The smooth running and greater prosperity of the mill will be my first aim then taming the lovely creature very soon to be mine will be second.'

Susan shivered and thinking it was caused by the cooler breeze which had sprung up his hold tightened.

'If you're getting cold we'll go in a few minutes but we came here to discuss Hillview and we've rather strayed from that. Truly I do regret that it had to be a snap decision but I was awkwardly placed.' He frowned. 'Instead of the cheque I expected, my parents decided that Hillview would be their wedding gift to us.'

'I didn't know that, Edward, and I do apologise. Indeed there was little else you could do and of course it is extremely generous of them.'

'I'm glad you think so, I certainly don't,' he said bitterly. 'Compared to the Laurels I would say Hillview is modest in the extreme but of course good enough for the younger son.'

'Edward,' she said gently, 'try to think of it this way. If you had been the elder son would you have expected an equal share with Thomas?'

'Maybe not but Thomas is not a natural leader.'

'Whereas you are?'

'Yes, I am and Father, if he weren't so blind, would see that.'

Feeling sorry for him but sorry too for Thomas who must find it difficult to give orders to someone so unwilling to take them, her eyes softened. 'We'll be quite comfortable at Hillview and I'm sorry that I was so awkward.'

'Understandable,' he said generously, 'and to be honest I had thought with a decent cheque from both families we could have bought something superior.'

'My parents haven't said what their gift will be but in all likelihood it will be money and with it we can furnish Hillview.' She smiled. 'Once we have our own choice of furnishings the house will look very different.'

'You'll see to that side of things and you know, Susan, when we are married your days will be completely occupied with your wifely duties.' He paused and smiled. 'That means doing all you can to give comfort and pleasure to your husband.' It was said teasingly but there was no doubt that he meant what he said.

Susan swallowed hard and held herself in check. Now wasn't the time but later Edward must be made to understand. In fact it might be better coming from Papa. Edward would not dare raise objections if it was voiced by Papa that she was to have a hand in the management of the mill. She shook her head. No, Papa must not be worried, this was something she had to do herself. With shrewd insight she knew that if anything happened to Papa Edward would do all in his power to shut her out, keep her away from the mill.

Just then Hannah, accompanied by a more relaxed-looking Samuel, strolled into view and stood on the terrace facing the summer house. They had been intending to descend the steps but at sight of Susan and Edward, their heads close together and apparently deep in conversation, checked themselves and turned away.

Susan sprang up, anxious to be gone. 'Let's go, Edward. Hannah and Samuel have been very patient but we should be getting back to Aran Heights.'

He rose but reluctantly and tucked her arm into his. 'Very well, but we do have more to discuss.'

'Such as?'

'Our honeymoon.'

'That was the last thing on Susan's mind. 'Edward, just a

123

few days, please; the way Papa is I don't want to be away any longer.'

'I can understand that, my dear, and since it is to be just a few days what about Edinburgh?'

'Or Helensburgh? When we were children we had lovely holidays there.'

'Then Helensburgh it is.'

'Thank you, Edward.'

A warm breeze wafted in the open bedroom window and caressed Susan's face. Leaning over the sill she watched the moon peeking out from between the dark sombre hills and felt the tears sting the back of her eyes. Tonight she would sleep in this room for the last time, the room that had been hers for all the years she could remember. Slowly she turned, went over to the bed and undressed. Between the cool sheets she lay with her hands behind her head and looked across to the wardrobe. On top was her collection of dolls looking at her with their beady eyes and on the shelf the little knick-knacks, inexpensive gifts from Ralph and Matthew, chosen so carefully and paid for out of their pocket money. Poor, poor Ralph, once so full of life and now lying in the family burial ground behind the kirk where tomorrow she would take the solemn vows of marriage – to love, honour and obey.

Oh, Ralph, Susan wept silently, if only you had been spared none of this would be necessary. Below the sheet her hand clenched and unclenched. Soon her body would belong to Edward and she felt herself recoiling from what that meant. Yet maybe Mama was right and love would grow out of liking. But if it didn't – she closed her eyes and drifted into an uneasy sleep.

She awoke as the house began to stir and, throwing back the bedcovers, padded over to the window and parted the curtains. Down in the courtyard the horses were being groomed and she could hear the mingled sounds of men and beasts. With her head resting against the cool windowpane Susan looked up at the sky and the dark, ominous clouds and wondered if it were an omen. Happy the bride the sun shines on.

After a freshen-up Susan put on her clothes, pulling over her head the gown lying to hand. That she was expected to breakfast in bed she knew but she wasn't hungry. She would go down for tea and toast. When she reached the breakfast-room Matthew was alone. The porridge plate was empty and he was tucking into eggs and crispy bacon.

'Susan! Good morning!' he said, springing up to give his sister a bear-like hug. 'Surely you're breaking with tradition. The bride should be breakfasting in bed, her every whim catered for.'

'I couldn't lie any longer.'

'Then allow me to do the honours,' he said, standing to attention, a white napkin draped over his arm. 'Pray what is her ladyship's pleasure?'

Susan gave a nervous giggle. 'Stop fooling, Matthew, I'm not in the mood and if you want to be helpful, toast please but nothing cooked.'

'Never get through the day on that. Bet Edward's enjoying a hearty breakfast,' he leered.

Levelling a dark look at him she stretched over for a few fingers of toast. 'You can pour me some tea.'

'Certainly.' They both turned as the door opened and Mrs MacFarlane came in followed by Hannah, her hair hanging limp though she had pinned it up the previous night.

'Good morning, Mother and cousin Hannah,' Matthew said with exaggerated formality.

'Susan,' her mother said severely, 'you should be in bed taking all the rest you can.'

'No, really, I'm better up.' She looked over to the window. 'Not a blink of sunshine.'

'I know, it's very disappointing.' Mrs MacFarlane sighed.

'That was the one thing Mother was unable to organise,' Matthew said cheekily.

The mother of the bride knew that there would be great excitement in Aranvale and disappointment at the dullness

125

of the day. The MacFarlanes were Aranvale and the entire village and beyond would be lining the route to the kirk. The outfit of every guest would be remarked upon and discussed while the bride's gown would be remembered and talked about for a long time. None would be disappointed, Mrs MacFarlane had been determined upon that.

'Polly's on her way up to you with a tray, Susan,' her cousin stated.

'Hannah, dear, you go up and tell her.'

'All right, Aunt Sarah,' Hannah said, darting out of the door.

'Has Susan eaten, Matthew? She seems to be just picking these days.'

'Mama, I'm quite capable of speaking for myself.' She shot Matthew a warning look. 'I've had a good breakfast.'

'I'm very glad to hear it. Ah! there you are, Hannah.'

'She's taking it back to the kitchen and I suggested she bring fresh toast and replenish the bacon. I'm famished.'

'Can't have the bridesmaid fainting for lack of sustenance.' Matthew grinned.

'Aunt Sarah, you'll have to do something about that boy,' Hannah said primly as the maid arrived with more bacon and a basket of toast.

'Rather late for that, dear,' her aunt said absently as she studied Hannah's hair. 'A session with the tongs for you. As soon as you've had breakfast see the hairdresser and have yours done first.'

'Goodness is she here already?'

'Yes, Susan, she's here and so is Miss Beattie's assistant to help us dress.'

'That include me?'

'Matthew, will you stop it.'

'Bet he won't be so chirpy when it's his big day.'

'Men have fewer worries on these occasions, Hannah, and yes, please, I'll have a finger of toast though I doubt if I can eat anything.' She put a hand to her head. 'Did someone mention the weather?'

'Mother, we've already dealt with that subject.'

She took a drink of tea and clattered the cup back on the saucer. 'I never closed an eye last night for going over everything and I just know there is something I've forgotten,' she said worriedly.

'Not much you can do about it now,' Matthew said cheerfully.

'I get sick when I'm excited,' Hannah announced as she carefully put down her knife and fork on the empty plate.

'You're not going to be – '

'No, no, it doesn't always happen, thought I'd just mention it.'

Matthew got up. 'This is all getting too much for me, I'll go and see how Father is bearing up.'

'You'll do no such thing. I'll go up presently.'

'Mama, I hope all this excitement isn't going to put him back.'

'It won't. He's had a sharp lesson and with Dr Sullivan at the wedding we can all relax.'

'I've had a peep into the dining-room and it looks absolutely gorgeous.'

'Thank you, Hannah. The hotel will do the main catering but relatives and close friends will end up here.'

Hannah was over at the window. 'There's a glimmer of sun.'

'I'm quite sure it'll clear up to a fine day and now, Hannah, please, see about that hair of yours.'

'Goodness, yes.' She bolted.

'That child is in a state of nerves and you are far too composed, Susan. It is your wedding day.'

As if I didn't know, Susan thought resentfully. 'Better to stay calm, surely.'

'Yes, I'm sure it is but few brides manage it. While Hannah gets her hair seen to we'll go along to the sitting-room and have a little talk.' Suddenly her mother looked uncomfortable. 'This is all such a dreadful rush and so different from what I would have wanted for you. Has Papa mentioned our gift to you and Edward?'

'Not exactly – '

'Our reason for delaying,' she interrupted, 'was because we thought both families would share the cost of buying and furnishing a home for you. Your papa was most upset about the purchase of Hillview. Like you he thought it suitable until something larger and more prestigious came on the market.'

'You were in favour of Hillview.'

'That's true, I find it quite charming but then I don't see any advantage in a huge barn of a place. Your father had Aran Heights built and I had no say in the matter. Something smaller and cosier would have suited me; however that is beside the point. Our wedding gift to you is to be money, a substantial sum. Your papa has been very generous but he'll tell you about it himself.'

Susan swallowed the lump in her throat. 'Everyone has been so good and as for Aunt Rachel – ' She shook her head and her eyes misted.

'Matthew and you are all she has and she wanted you to have the benefit of the money before she is kicking up the daisies – her words, I need hardly tell you.'

'And as for you, Mama, you've done so much and I am very grateful.'

Her mother's eyes swam.

'What have I said? What is the matter?'

'Nothing, I'm just being silly.' She sniffed into a wisp of handkerchief. 'I didn't think it would affect me so much – you getting married then Matthew so soon after. Aran Heights is going to be so quiet, just your papa and – and he isn't always the best of company.' She blew her nose and managed to look both aggrieved and sorrowful. 'I'll be virtually alone, he'll take himself off to the library or hide behind his newspaper.'

'Mama, I'll need you,' she said gently, 'You've reminded me often enough about how little I know about supervising the housekeeping.'

'With cause.' She brightened. 'I'd enjoy that and I must say the staff at Hillview are not acceptable now that it is to be your permanent home. That dour-faced housekeeper has to go.'

'I entirely agree.' Susan breathed a sigh of relief. 'May I leave it to you?'

'Yes.'

'I'd very much like to take Polly with me. It would be one known face and I like her.'

'That could be arranged I'm sure. Mrs Dunbar will train one of the others to replace her.'

'Thank you.'

Mrs MacFarlane looked at the clock. 'We still have a few minutes. Susan, there are things I haven't mentioned, not forgotten, just that I considered it unnecessary.' She paused and her eyes went beyond Susan as if she were addressing the wall. 'Don't worry too much about what will take place, you understand what I mean. Before I married your papa I knew nothing at all and I don't believe it mattered. Just accept that it is something you have to put up with.'

Susan felt her colour rising and wished she could escape but her mother was still addressing the wall. 'To begin with you may experience – embarrassment, awkwardness but that is quite normal.' She frowned. 'I'm not making a very good job of this but I wanted to put your mind at rest and free from worry.' At last she removed her eyes from the wall and settled them on Susan's face.

'It's all right, Mama,' Susan mumbled.

Glad to have that out of the way, Mrs MacFarlane picked up a sheet of paper, neatly ruled off at various points, put on her spectacles and studied the writing.

'This is my timetable which I do need if things are to run smoothly.'

'Don't worry, Mama, they will.'

'I sincerely hope so.' She smiled. 'Off you go, dear and lie down for half an hour. I'll get my hair done next and let's hope the tongs have made some difference to Hannah's locks.'

CHAPTER TEN

The rain, never far away, had kept off and a weak sun showed behind the clouds as carriage after carriage drew up at the Aranvale kirk where that morning professional hands had arranged the magnificent floral display. The guests, smiling and murmuring among themselves, were shown into the pews by the ushers.

His music in place, the organist began playing a selection of church music while fashionably dressed ladies and handsomely attired gentlemen nodded to acquaintances before carefully seating themselves.

At a hidden signal the organist ended his recital, flexed his fingers and crashed into the rousing tune of the Bridal March. Susan, pale and lovely, walked slowly down the aisle on her father's arm while the bridesmaid, pretty in blue, showed her nervousness in the way her teeth caught at her lower lip.

Holding himself stiffly erect Hamish looked straight ahead. Susan could hear the wheeziness from his chest and unconsciously she tightened her hold on his arm as they walked down the red-carpeted aisle to where the minister in his robes and holding the bible watched their progress. The groom stood easily, a smile on his lips, as he watched the bridal procession in the mirror above the organ. The best man was beside him standing rigidly to attention.

That she felt so calm amazed Susan. It was almost as though she were a spectator at her own wedding. At every stage of the way villagers craned their necks for a better view of the bride. Rather than the traditional white Miss Beattie had suggested a cream shade would be more flattering with Susan's fairness. The rich material had an embossed pattern of roses and the style had been kept simple. As always

131

Miss Beattie's creations were understated, depending for their elegance almost completely on the cut of the material. Her advice had also been taken on what would be the most suitable hairstyle and the hairdresser, working to a sketch, had swept Susan's hair high on her head with tendrils of curls escaping at the brow and at her ears to soften the effect. Firmly set into the thick fair hair nestled a silver and pearl headdress and flowing from it the long veil in exquisite lace which had been handed down to brides on her mother's side of the family.

As Hamish MacFarlane moved away to join his wife in the first pew Edward turned to get his first proper look at his bride. She smiled and she saw him swallow as if the sight of such loveliness had momentarily affected him.

Clearing his throat the minister began the solemn task of joining the two young people in holy matrimony. In a break in the sing-song voice he raised an eyebrow to Samuel who hastily reached into his pocket for the ring.

She was married! She was Mrs Edward Brodie and suddenly the uncertainties and anguish of the last few weeks were swept away in a flurry of excitement. Edward loved her and suddenly she felt a rush of real affection, perhaps it was even love, for the man who was now her husband.

In the large reception room at the Grand Hotel in Airdrie, the market town nearest to Aranvale, bride and groom stood together to receive the good wishes and congratulations from the long line of guests while waitresses circulated with trays of glasses and discreet enquiries as to the preferred drink. Hamish MacFarlane, without a flicker of annoyance, obeyed Dr Sullivan and sat down in one of the red plush chairs carried over by a waiter. That the occasion was taking a lot out of him was noticed and later remarked upon.

'Papa, are you quite sure that you're all right?'

'Just fine, Susan. Don't worry about me.' He took her hand in his and she saw that his eyes were moist. 'There was never a bonnier bride,' he said unsteadily, 'and no father could be prouder than I am this day.'

She kissed him. Then it was mother and daughter hugging

each other in an unusual display of affection. All the while Edward was smilingly accepting congratulations on winning such a prize. After her new in-laws it was Matthew's turn with a quietly radiant Winnie at his side.

'Be happy, Susan,' Matthew said huskily, 'and Edward, you look after my sister or you'll have me to reckon with.' There was banter but seriousness behind it.

'Your sister is in safe hands, Matthew,' he said, putting his arm around his wife and drawing her close.

Winnie hugged her. 'You look beautiful and I know you are going to be very happy.' Then she turned to Hannah. 'You're looking very pretty.'

'Thank you.' Her eyes went to Winnie in her lovely rose pink gown, her hair softly waved and a tell-tale flush on her cheeks. 'You look quite marvellous yourself.' Then she grinned. 'Just shows what we plain ones can do when we try.'

Mrs MacFarlane had heard and said in a shocked voice, 'Hannah, that was a dreadful thing to say.'

'I'm sorry, have I offended you, Winnie?'

'Not in the least.' Winnie laughed good-naturedly. 'Being outspoken myself I can hardly complain about it in others.'

After the wedding feast where champagne flowed like water the best man rose to his feet and amid much laughter stood silently until the noise stopped.

With the help of a few notes and an encouraging smile from the bridesmaid, Samuel delivered a well-prepared and fitting speech before sitting down to a storm of applause. Then the bride's father rose and there was a stillness in the room. All eyes were on the man who had aged so suddenly in the last months. An excellent speaker, it came as a shock to those seated away from the top table that they had to strain to hear his words.

He spoke without notes. First he welcomed the guests then went on to describe incidents in his daughter's early life which had obviously amused him at the time though he had been at pains to disguise it. Susan's lips twitched; she was remembering being severely chastised along with Matthew and in the shared memory brother and sister caught each other's eye and grinned.

After the laughter Mr MacFarlane bent down to take a sip from his glass then turned to Edward. 'My wife and I feel we are not losing a daughter, Edward, but rather gaining another son.' There was some clapping and he waited until it had died down. 'Our daughter is very precious to us and now she belongs to you, Edward and I know that you will love and protect her. May God bless you both and give you many years of happiness together.' He picked up his glass. 'Ladies and gentlemen, will you be upstanding and join me in a toast.'

The guests rose. The murmur went round. 'Susan and Edward.'

After the applause Edward got to his feet and in a firm and clear voice began, 'On behalf of my wife and . . .'

It was all over. A good many of the guests had driven to Aran Heights and were now on the lawn as the newlyweds made their escape through a shower of rice and rose petals. Edward had changed from his formal wedding suit into a perfectly tailored lightweight grey. For her going-away outfit Susan had favoured a peacock blue skirt and jacket and under the jacket a cream lacy-patterned blouse with a plain neckline and a double string of cultured pearls. Perched on her head was a saucy feathered hat in the same shade of blue. The maids were clustered at an upstairs window and seeing them Susan gave a wave.

The bride and groom were in the coach taking them to the station. Looking frail and tired Mr MacFarlane lifted his hand in farewell with his wife protectively by his side.

Edward frowned. 'You look worried.'

'I am, Edward, Papa looked exhausted.'

'Hardly surprising, it was quite an occasion after all, but a good night's sleep and I'm sure he'll be all right.' He paused and added, 'Regarding the mill your father can stop worrying. After all I have a lot more to offer than Matthew.'

Susan was nettled at his high-handed dismissal of Matthew.

'Matthew has worked very hard since Papa's illness,' she said sharply.

His mouth touched hers in a light kiss. 'He did what he could but I intend increasing profits,'

'My father won't want changes.'

'Don't worry your pretty head, I'll do nothing to upset your father.'

Susan was becoming increasingly uneasy. 'As long as my father draws breath he'll make the decisions and he means me to be involved.'

'I hadn't forgotten but a sick man does not always make wise decisions and that is when the business is most at risk, but I intend minimising those risks. Anyway this is us,' he said briskly as they stopped outside the station.

The newlyweds and those others travelling first class enjoyed a comfortable journey with soft leather seats to cushion the jolts and jerks, but for the third-class passengers huddled together in the overcrowded wooden-seated compartments it was a different story, though judging by the hilarity they didn't seem to mind.

A horse and carriage belonging to the Imperial Hotel stood outside the station awaiting Susan and Edward and on their approach the coachman lifted his hat and opened the door for them to climb in. Susan arranged herself in a corner and Edward moved up beside her. The luggage was put in beside the driver and then they were off.

Earlier Susan had wondered if she'd made a mistake suggesting Helensburgh. The resort on the north bank of the Clyde offered little more than pleasant walks and beautiful scenery whereas in Edinburgh, as Edward had suggested, the evenings could have been filled with a visit to the theatre or a concert.

Soon they joined the procession of coaches heading towards the seafront and at one point the coach lurched perilously over a deep rut in the road and Edward muttered a string of mild expletives.

Susan turned to him and burst out laughing. 'That was naughty, Edward.'

'I know. My humble – ' but he didn't finish. Instead he cupped his hands around her face and gently, oh, so gently, kissed her mouth. The moment was so tender, so unexpected that it brought the hot stinging tears to her eyes.

'Tears, Susan, surely not?'

'Tears of happiness, Edward,' Susan said tremulously. 'We are going to be happy, aren't we?'

'How else could it be?'

She nodded, her spirits lifting more by the minute. Edward was a dear, at least most of the time he was. If only he would be more understanding about the mill and her place in it. Still, she wasn't going to think about that and spoil their honeymoon.

Perched on a rocky hill overlooking the Gareloch the Imperial Hotel enjoyed the finest view in Helensburgh but the steep hill put a strain on horse and coachman. Inwardly relieved that they had made it to the top, Susan got out and inhaled the fresh, clean air. The porters busied themselves with the baggage but Susan was in no hurry to go indoors. There was a pleasant cooling breeze and tucking her arm in Edward's she looked about her with interest.

'Edward, do you know how Helensburgh got its name?'

'No, but then I was never curious enough to ask.'

'Then let me complete your education. Sir James Colquhoun designed Helensburgh and named it after his wife. Wasn't that lovely?'

'Who gave you that gem of information?' he teased.

'Papa. Matthew used to complain that no matter where we went Papa always made a history lesson of it.'

The room they were to share was large with a four-poster bed and immediately they were on their own Edward settled his weight on it and declared himself satisfied. Susan was embarrassed and to hide it she admired the bowl of flowers on the dressing-table. Mingling with their scent was a faint aroma of beeswax coming from the polished furniture.

Edward opened the communicating door to a dressing-room. 'I'll make use of this, Susan. Do you want a maid to help you unpack?'

'No, thank you, that won't be necessary. Incidentally what time do we go down for dinner?'

'Just as soon as we are ready. Feeling peckish, are you?'

'Yes, I ate very little at the reception.'

Susan hung up her gowns and was grateful to Edward for respecting her privacy. He was to change in the dressing-room. She had already decided what to wear and had spread out on the bed the pale blue gown with the tiny sprigs of white flowers decorating the skirt.

Edward's eyes rested on his wife approvingly as they went down the graceful stairway and across the panelled hall to the dining-room. Soft music was playing and there was a quiet elegance everywhere from the delicate, wrought-iron chandeliers to the large gilt-framed mirrors on each wall.

'You look beautiful, my darling,' Edward whispered. 'In fact I think that we look a really handsome couple.'

'I saw you admiring yourself in the mirror,' she teased.

'Wrong, I was admiring us, my dear.'

Some guests were already dining and eyes were briefly raised from the food to follow the attractive couple who were being shown to a window table. The service was pleasantly unhurried to allow time between courses and the appreciation of good food.

After a delicious meal which they both enjoyed they rose and went outside for a breath of fresh air. When it grew too cold for comfort they went in and sat in the lounge until Edward looked pointedly at the clock.

'Yes, it is getting late,' Susan agreed and wished her colour hadn't risen. She was all but sure by the quiet smiles on the faces of the few remaining guests that they realised they were on their honeymoon.

Edward was undressing in the adjoining room and giving her ample time to be in the big four-poster bed. In her lovely, lace-trimmed, shell pink nightdress Susan looked like a bride.

137

Only she didn't feel like one. How could she? She should have been coming to her husband as a virgin and what if he suspected? After all he would be looking for the proof of her innocence and when there was none what would be his thoughts? That some violent exercise when she was young or something of the sort was responsible? Yes, of course Edward would think that. She shivered. What if he ever found out the truth? But how could he? David Cameron was no longer in Aranvale, she had found that out, and there was no chance of their paths crossing.

The door opened and Edward came through in his silk dressing-gown. Susan smiled from her side of the bed, successfully hiding her nervousness.

Her fears were unfounded. Edward was gentle with her, taking no more than she was prepared to give and she was caught in conflicting emotions. She didn't want to remember David Cameron but couldn't stop herself. Though she looked back on that day with self-loathing she remembered how natural it had seemed, a drawing together of two people caught up in a passion that was too strong for them. She wondered if it had been David's first time.

With Edward there had been no gaucheness, indeed she supposed him a skilful lover and only experience, she decided, could have made him that. It made her realise how little she knew of the real Edward. The boy she had partnered on so many occasions was far removed from the sophisticated and worldly man to whom she was married. The thought of those other women did disturb her, then she tried to dismiss them. Young men were expected to sow their wild oats before they married and settled down and Edward was a man of the world but now that he had a wife all that would stop. Susan vowed to herself there and then that she would do all in her power to make Edward happy, be a good wife to him and by doing so make up for her wrongdoing.

On the evening before their departure a charity ball was being held in the hotel and for the occasion Susan decided to wear her golden yellow gown. As she began her preparations she was smiling happily. Helensburgh had been a good choice after all. Edward had said so and he had enjoyed the walks as much as she had. Best of all had been the tramp over the moors, an easy tramp, and at the end of it the unbelievable beauty of Loch Lomond. Her colour heightened as she remembered how Edward had folded his arms around her and she had leaned into him. In those moments surrounded by such beauty she had wanted Edward as much as he wanted her and only the sound of distant voices had prevented them making love in the soft grass near the banks of the loch.

'What are you smiling about?' Edward asked as he came through from his dressing-room.

'Pleasant thoughts, Edward, that's all,' she said as she made another attempt with the hooks. 'Do me up, please, dear, I can't get them in.' She held in her breath until he had the last one in place.

'My darling wife, your dressmaker hasn't left much room for manoeuvre. Not that I'm complaining; it accentuates your curves and I'm sure every male in the ballroom will wish himself in my shoes.'

'Flatterer,' she said, but as she said it she felt the first twinge of unease. The gown had fitted comfortably. Miss Beattie wouldn't have let it pass otherwise. Forcing the uneasiness to the back of her mind she whirled round, eager for his approval. 'This is Mama's favourite.'

'Mine too I think. You look ravishing,' he said softly.

The ball was an occasion that brought out the top families. Away from the dance floor and fanning themselves, the more elderly ladies eyed the young, perhaps remembering with nostalgia when they too had danced the night away before age and its accompanying weaknesses had taken over their bodies. Ruby and diamond necklaces gleamed and glistened between the fleshy folds of their aristocratic necks or hung disconsolately from a scrawny stem.

It was a colourful scene with so many beautiful gowns. Susan and Edward made a handsome couple as they circled the floor in time to the orchestra playing from a raised platform. Having danced together on many occasions their steps fitted perfectly and many eyes followed their progress. Though her gown came in for a lot of admiration it was the girl herself who caused something of a sensation. Her facial beauty may have been equalled but not her hair. The silver fairness was unique and she wore it piled high in the way her hairdresser had taught her.

As the evening wore on Susan put a cloak over her gown and they strolled arm-in-arm along the paths circling the rose gardens. It was a still evening with the lingering scents of summer. An evening for lovers and Edward drew her closer.

'Happy?'

'Very,' she said softly.

'A perfect honeymoon would you say?'

'Quite perfect.'

From where they were walking they could hear the strains of music, hauntingly beautiful. The moonlight threw the lawn in shadow and suddenly, without warning, Edward stopped and swung her to him then with a bruising fierceness brought his mouth down on hers. 'Blame that on looking so desirable,' he said thickly as she tried to draw away.

'Edward,' she faltered, 'the – the ball isn't over –'

'For us it is,' he said, steering her through the entrance and over to the stairway. Their rooms were on the first floor and he almost pushed her in. Suddenly she was afraid, afraid of the stranger he had become. He was breathing heavily and was the worse for drink. She had lost count of the number of times his glass had been replenished.

He was asleep, his breathing regular but Susan had never felt more awake. Looking down at his face flushed in sleep she thought back to when they were children. Edward had a quick temper but he always apologised afterwards. His charm and good manners were never more in evidence than when adults were present. She remembered Ralph grinning knowingly. 'Trust Edward,' he'd said, 'he knows when to turn it on.'

The bed moved and, alarmed that he was about to waken, Susan kept quite still. But he merely grunted, mumbled something and flung an arm across her. Carefully, so as not to waken him, she moved herself as far over to her own side as she could. Then she lay with her eyes wide open.

There was a cruel streak in Edward and last night or rather this morning he had been brutal, ignoring her protests, her unwillingness. She had been sickened and humiliated by what she had been made to endure. At the memory her lips curled in disgust. And on top of that the nagging worry had returned and was refusing to go away.

Was it two months since – why hadn't she taken a note? But she'd never been regular and she was panicking needlessly. Once she'd approached her mother on the subject but Mrs MacFarlane had been dismissive, the mention of such matters distasteful to her fastidious nature. 'Being irregular is of no consequence,' she'd said, 'I was like that myself.'

Susan grasped at the straw then found it giving way. Mama had meant a week, two at the outside but she was well beyond that. Her head ached. If only she weren't so ignorant, but all she knew was from girlish chatter and her friends knew little more than she did.

What were the symptoms? More tired than usual? That had passed; she cheered up. Goodness hadn't she danced the hours away without feeling in the least exhausted? Mentally she deleted the tiredness and lethargy. Morning sickness? A sinking feeling – she had been troubled with nausea. And the yellow gown, measured for her some months ago and now too tight. Girls put on weight for other reasons – other reasons than pregnancy.

There it was out! She was actually considering the possibility. She crammed a knuckle into her mouth to stifle her cry. No! No! No! she screamed inside. It can't be, no one conceives the first time. She'd heard that somewhere or was it that it was not impossible just unlikely? Going hot and cold with fear she tried to get a grip on herself. Drawing the bedcovers to her chin and staying as far away from Edward as possible she prayed that her fears were unfounded. Then she fell into a troubled sleep.

*   *   *

141

In the morning Edward looked haggard and she saw him eyeing her uncertainly as she folded her clothes. Her lovely yellow gown was torn where he had ripped it and she had it already in the trunk. Keeping her face averted she continued with her task.

'Susan?'

'Yes, Edward,' she said coldly.

'Was I – um – objectionable last night?'

She didn't answer, just took a blouse off its hanger and began fastening the buttons.

'Your silence speaks for itself. I was. Was I?'

'Yes.'

'I'm sorry, you have my humble apologies and, Susan, you must know it was completely out of character.'

'How should I know that?'

'Don't be so damned ridiculous,' he said, moving his head and the action causing him to grimace. 'Haven't I always been considerate?'

'Yes.'

'Your trouble is that you don't like that side of marriage.'

She stopped packing and looked across at him. 'That isn't true. When you were gentle – '

'You enjoyed it,' he smirked.

'Perhaps I did.'

'Then what has changed?'

'You know perfectly well,' she said, giving a small shiver. 'Drink played its part but you were disgusting and to me it is very obvious that you have experience of women – a certain type of woman.'

'What exactly do you mean by that remark?' he said, deadly quiet.

For a moment she faltered, thinking she had gone too far then she held up her head proudly. 'I meant what I said, Edward. Perhaps you don't know me as well as you think. Being your wife does not give you the right to abuse me.'

'Drink was the cause of my lack of control but your attitude is all wrong. Believe me, my dear, you have a lot of growing up to do.'

She returned his gaze but remained silent.

'You belong to me, Susan, and what gives me pleasure should be pleasurable for you. In time you'll find it true.'

'No, I won't.'

'We'll see.' Suddenly he grinned and his manner changed. 'Drink may be the curse of the working classes,' he groaned loudly, 'but it has a pretty devastating effect on management too. My tongue feels like leather and my head is thumping.'

'Serves you right,' she said but she was laughing. 'You look awful.'

'Forgiven?' he begged, holding out his hand.

'This time, yes.' She ignored his outstretched hand.

'Thank God I'm out of the dog-house.'

'You'll be in trouble with someone else if you're not careful. Didn't I hear you arrange for our trunks to be collected after breakfast?'

He got up and reached for his dressing-gown. 'I'll dress, pack my trunks and settle the account.' He sat down heavily on the bed. 'Can you face breakfast?'

'Very easily,' she said sweetly, 'I wasn't drinking.'

'You'll have to go down on your own.'

Most of the guests had already breakfasted, their tables cleared and fresh tablecloths in place for luncheon. One elderly gentleman looked above his newspaper and nodded a greeting as she passed his table. Susan felt conspicuously alone. The waiter was already behind her chair and saw to it that she was comfortably seated before opening out a starched linen napkin and placing it across her knees. In the mirror she could see herself in her navy two-piece costume with its white piping round the collar.

'My husband won't be coming down.'

'Would the gentleman like something sent up to his room, madam?'

'No, thank you.' She paused. 'I'll have a lightly boiled egg, toast and tea.'

Breakfasting alone Susan thought of the previous night and Edward's behaviour, his roughness. He had apologised and obviously remembered little of what happened. But she did and she was uncomfortably aware that she hadn't been entirely honest. Certainly she had been disgusted but there had been some of the time when she had been roused and it shamed her to remember that.

She glanced out of the window, thinking how quickly the weather changed. Large raindrops splattered on the pane sending rivulets down the wide sill. Soon they would be on their way home yet she couldn't bring herself to think of Hillview as home. It was comfortable enough but home was Aran Heights.

Edward kept up a brooding silence for much of the journey to Aranvale and she didn't try to engage him in conversation. That his stomach was upset was all too evident by the greyness of his face. Eventually he smiled. 'I think the worst is past.'

'Maybe talking will take your mind off it.'

'Then let us talk about Hillview.'

'Yes, all right. There is money from my parents and Aunt Rachel to buy furniture.'

'That is your department.'

'We should choose together or maybe I'll get something you don't like.'

'Then I'll have to live with it.'

'What about the removal of the Templetons' furniture?'

'No problem. Once you have a delivery date I'll have them remove their belongings or failing that have it put in store.'

'With our own furniture around us and our lovely gifts Hillview will seem much more like home.'

'What else is there to arrange?'

'Neither Mama nor I like the housekeeper so I want her replaced and new staff engaged.'

He looked alarmed. 'You had better stop your mother from overdoing it. Hillview isn't Croft House or Aran Heights.'

'Even so it needs adequate staffing,' Susan said firmly. 'To hear you, Edward, one would think we had to look to every penny. Papa is very much against extravagance but he wouldn't think a well-run house an extravagance.'

'Duties properly allocated, that's what is needed. It applies in business as well as the home and as mistress of my house it will be your duty to see that the maids are fully occupied and money not frittered away.'

Susan was shocked into silence. Edward, she could see now, would be driven by a need to accumulate wealth and if he ever got his hands on the mill his first undertaking would be to reduce the workforce yet expect the same output at the end of the day.

'If I didn't know you better I'd think you had a mean streak.' She kept her voice light and smiled into his face.

'Not mean, my dearest Susan, just careful.' He paused. 'The mill has marvellous potential you know but it needs someone with drive to get it out of the rut.' He saw her scandalised expression and hastened in with, 'That was an unfortunate choice of expression, your father has done wonders but it needs a younger man to take control. My father is doing that, leaving more and more to Thomas but unfortunately Thomas is totally out of his depth.'

'What works in the distillery would not be acceptable in our mill.'

'Why not?'

'Our business methods are very different.'

'The distillery makes a greater profit.'

'Not in dispute. It is a bigger concern.'

'The papermill could grow, expansion is the way forward.'

'You overlook one important thing, Edward. We have a contented workforce and the same can't be said for the Brodie concern. There are always rumblings of discontent from the distillery workers.'

'They don't voice them where it matters.'

'They wouldn't dare but the discontent is just below the surface.'

'That type spend their entire life grumbling, it is second nature to them.' He smiled. 'What are we arguing about? We are on the same side and all my energies will be devoted to

145

the papermill. Indeed one day I fully intend us to have a profit greater than the distillery.'

Edward's colour had improved and he looked much his normal self when the train reached Aranvale. The carriage was waiting and soon Hillview was in sight. As they drew nearer Edward groaned. 'Oh, God! A reception committee – I could have done without that.'

Susan craned for a better view then looked daggers at him. 'Don't be so disagreeable, Edward, our parents have got together to welcome us home and I think that was a lovely thought.'

She needn't have worried. Edward took her arm and was all smiles as both sets of parents waited to greet them.

'Papa, you look so much better.' Susan smiled. His face was less hollow-cheeked and he looked stronger.

'I'm just fine.'

Susan looked about her. The vestibule had been dull and drab but now pots of healthy-looking geraniums covered the octagonal table and on the broad window ledge there were small pots of African violets and yellow primroses. Decorating one wall was a hanging basket with greenery cascading almost to the floor.

'Mama, this is simply lovely.'

Mrs MacFarlane looked pleased. 'Flowers, I always think, bring life to a house and I got our gardener to raid the greenhouse for these.'

'Very thoughtful of you,' Edward said as he ushered the ladies out first.

'How was the weather?' John Brodie asked. 'Or didn't you notice?' he added with a wink to Edward.

'We did notice.' Susan laughed. 'It was fine and warm and the hotel was excellent.'

'Susan, I wondered what to do about the wedding gifts then decided not to have them brought over until I knew your plans.' She turned to Edward. 'Once the Templetons get their furniture away you'll want the decorators in?'

'That is Susan's department.'

'Quite right, son, that way you can't be blamed. I left all that to your mother.'

Hamish MacFarlane spoke quietly, his eyes on his daughter. 'Susan will manage but she has other qualities that shouldn't be overlooked, Edward. Since my illness she has been a great help to me, in fact I don't know what I would have done without her.'

'Brains and beauty,' John Brodie barked. 'Don't know how lucky you are, my boy.'

They were comfortably seated in the drawing-room before Edward answered. 'You are wrong there, sir, I do appreciate my luck.' Then, showing a smiling face to his father-in-law he spoke firmly. 'Susan has been a wonderful help to you, sir, but she can safely step aside now knowing that I am in a position to give you every assistance.'

Lilian Brodie beamed over to her son. 'There you are, Susan, you have nothing to worry about. Edward will be on hand to see that your papa doesn't overdo it. And you are a married woman with responsibilities in the home.'

'Mrs Brodie,' Susan said quietly but firmly, 'Edward and I have already discussed this and he knows that I have no intention of stepping aside.' She saw Edward's mouth harden and her own mother gave her a reproachful look.

'Mama, what about the meal?' Susan whispered. 'shall I go and see – '

'No, dear, everything is in hand.' She excused herself and returned to announce that the meal was ready to be served. They trooped into the dining-room, the one room that Susan found acceptable. It was a good size with a large bay window and two smaller ones overlooking the lawn and beyond to the flowering shrubs.

'That was a very enjoyable meal, Mama.'

'Can't fault the cook,' Edward said as he leaned back.

'Will she stay on, Mama?'

'Yes and we'll discuss the housekeeper once the gentlemen remove themselves for a glass of port.'

'Finding a good housekeeper is not easy, Susan,' her mother-in-law said. 'Anyone not already engaged must be viewed with suspicion but I feel sure you will be satisfied with Miss Wilson. She is very refined and kept house for her father until his death. Now she is alone she must earn a living.'

Susan nodded politely.

'I have every confidence that she will meet with your approval but not having been in service before she is understandably nervous so do make allowances.'

'Yes, of course, but if she doesn't meet my requirements I take it I can look around for an experienced housekeeper?' Susan said, nettled at having everything arranged for her.

'I don't think it will come to that and she is a decided improvement on her predecessor,' Lilian Brodie said, sounding both hurt and peeved.

'You've been very kind,' Susan said, feeling ashamed and to make amends rushed in with, 'Mama is helping me to choose furniture and I'd be happy if you could come along too.'

'I'd be delighted and Susan, my dear, we can't have you calling me Mrs Brodie.'

'I know, but what do I call you?'

'Vexing question.'

'How does Elizabeth address you?'

'Before the children I don't recall her addressing me as anything. Now I'm Grandmama to them all.'

'What about Mama Brodie?'

'That'll do very nicely.' They all looked over at the door as John Brodie poked his head around.

'Lilian, we should be getting on our way and in any case these two young people will be anxious to be on their own.'

'We won't be long behind you but I want to introduce Miss Wilson to Susan.'

'She's here?'

'Yes, we thought it better that you saw her right away.'

The Brodies departed and Susan accompanied her mother to interview Miss Wilson.

'I feel most inadequate, Mama,' Susan said worriedly.

'And whose fault is that? You would occupy yourself with

other things instead of what would prove useful to you in the future.'

'I'm ready to learn now.'

'If you do decide to engage this Miss Wilson make it clear from the start what her duties are to be.'

'Do I do the interviewing?' Susan asked nervously.

'Of course and for goodness sake be dignified, you are the mistress.' She smiled to take the sting out of the words before opening the door to the morning-room. A woman had been sitting at the window and got up hurriedly.

Mrs MacFarlane sat down and Susan did too. 'Do sit down, Miss Wilson.' She indicated a chair facing them. The woman was very tall, exceptionally so for a woman and there was a proud lift to her head. She may have come down in the world, Susan thought, but she was accepting her new status with dignity. Her tired grey eyes didn't blink under Susan's scrutiny.

'If you should decide to engage me, m'am I shall do my utmost to give satisfaction,' she said in a quiet well-modulated voice.

Susan inclined her head. I like her, she thought. She's nervous under that calm look and she needs the position. 'My own duties as mistress are new to me and if you were to be housekeeper at Hillview much of the smooth running of the house would rest on you.'

Miss Wilson bit her lip. 'I prefer to be completely open with you, m'am. My only experience of housekeeping has been on a very small scale. I kept house for my father until his death.'

'In the circumstances, Miss Wilson, I am prepared to give you a trial period. We'll say three months.'

'Thank you, m'am.'

Mrs MacFarlane gave a dismissive nod and Miss Wilson went out quickly.

'You handled that very well, Susan.'

'I liked her.'

'Someone with more experience would have been preferable.'

'At the end of three months we'll see.'

'Don't let your heart rule your head, Susan. If Miss Wilson doesn't meet your requirements get rid of her at the end of the trial period. No doubt by then I will have heard of someone.'

'Mama, I've a feeling she's going to be perfectly suitable,' Susan said and swiftly changed the subject. 'I worried about Papa when I was away but he does look so much better.'

'What is it?' Susan asked fearfully when the silence lasted too long.

'This goes no further, my dear, not even to Edward.' Her voice dropped. 'Dr Sullivan saw me and said that I wasn't to bear the burden alone, that Matthew and you had a right to know.'

Susan felt her chest tighten. 'Know what?'

'Susan, you must learn to hide your feelings,' she said gently, 'and remember it is very much worse for me, I have to hide my concern all the time.' She took hold of Susan's cold hands. 'Your papa's heart is very weak and the bronchitis is causing breathing difficulties. God willing, we could have him with us for a long time but we have to be prepared. His heart could give out at any time.'

'Oh, Mama,' Susan said brokenly, 'I can't bear it, I can't bear the thought of – of – '

'You must be brave, we all must.' Her mouth pursed in a disapproving line but there were tears in her voice. 'Dr Sullivan is making a serious mistake agreeing to Hamish going into the mill even for an hour or two.'

Susan shook her head. 'No, Mama, I don't agree with you. I think Dr Sullivan is right and he understands Papa so well. Keeping an active interest in the mill, going in for a short time, an hour or two, will keep him from fretting and worrying at home.'

'Well, I suppose I expected you to take that attitude but I hadn't expected it from Matthew.' She paused. 'Maybe I am wrong but I'm certainly not happy about it.' She looked about her as if anxious to get away from any further discussion of her husband's failing health and said too brightly, 'This room is shabby and depressing, Susan, but once it is freshened

150

up and your own possessions in place it should be quite charming.'

Susan murmured her agreement but her mind was on this fresh worry about her papa.

She and Edward went out to the carriage.

'Thank you for all you've done, Mama.' She smiled to them both and waved until the carriage was out of sight.

CHAPTER ELEVEN

Those first few days at Hillview were pleasant and Edward, though not very forthcoming about his time spent in the mill, seemed well content.

'How did the shopping spree go?' he asked as they sat together in the dying hours of the evening.

'Come out from behind that newspaper and I'll tell you.'

She heard the sigh but he obliged by folding his paper and dropping it at his feet. 'I'm waiting.' He smiled indulgently like an uncle with a favourite niece and she wanted to laugh.

'Hectic, exhausting but successful I think and I was thankful to have both mothers with me.' She grinned mischievously. 'That way we were guaranteed a majority verdict.'

'So you're quite happy?'

'Yes, I am and I'm sure you'll approve. Incidentally in case you don't know, your mother heard that the Templetons intend selling their furniture rather than have it sent on and have instructed their solicitor to get what he can for it.'

Edward frowned. 'Knowing that you went ahead and spent my – our money on new furniture?'

'Most certainly I did. Surely you do not expect me to start my married life with second-hand furniture?' Amazement was written on her face.

'If it is good and most of it is, whyever not? We are paying rental for it already.'

'That doesn't matter.' Her arm waved round the room. 'None of this is my choice and in any case our wedding cheques will more than cover the bills.' None of it, she added silently, is coming out of your pocket.

'Can't you get it into your head that that money could have been set aside and used for some other purpose? Really, for someone who saw herself as a budding business woman you are quite hopeless. Not your fault.' He gave her a quick smile. 'Women don't have the right mentality or quick-wittedness so necessary to succeed in the cut-throat world. Well-known fact, my dearest.'

'Some of us lack ruthlessness, I would agree with that, but ruthlessness isn't necessarily a recipe for success. Papa's dealings with everyone have always been fair and honest.'

'And he is losing hand over fist.'

'That is absolute nonsense,' she shouted angrily. 'Until quite recently I was doing the books with my father and there was no cause for concern. Quite the reverse in fact.'

'That could change tomorrow. What is needed is a whole new approach and for a start I'd turf out that doddering old fool – '

'To whom are you referring?'

'McNeil – Murdoch McNeil.'

'Mr McNeil is a trusted employee, my father holds him in high esteem and, Edward, if I were you, I wouldn't make your opinion known – '

'Give me credit for some sense.' He put his hand up. 'That is enough, we were discussing furniture. Have you refurnished completely?'

'No, the servants' quarters need to be inspected to find out what is required.'

'Without an inspection I can tell you that whatever is there will remain. Anything else?'

'The guest rooms I hadn't decided on the colour scheme,' she said stiffly.

'I have a feeling your extravagance is getting completely out of hand.'

His eyes narrowed into slits. 'For your own good I have decided from this moment to monitor the household expenses until such time as I can trust you to be moderate in your outlay.'

She got to her feet and she was shaking with anger.

'How dare you! Just whom do you think you are addressing?' she said haughtily, her blue eyes flashing dangerously.

'I am addressing my wife,' he said calmly, 'and just you remember, my dear Susan, that I am master in my own house and you will do as you are told.'

She sat down. 'And if I don't?' she said quietly, the nails digging into the palms of her hands.

'But you will.' He paused. 'Think how upsetting it would be, fatal even, if things were seen to be awkward between us. Your father needs me and was quite desperate to have me as a son-in-law.'

'What has happened to you, Edward?' You were never like this.'

'I'm still the same person.'

'Not to me.'

'All right,' he said grimly. 'I intend being successful.' His eyes glittered. 'All my life I've had to play second fiddle and do you know what that is like? To know that you have a superior brain but by an accident of birth Thomas takes over the distillery when Father dies.'

'Your father isn't a fool. He must have confidence in Thomas.'

'The old fool sees what he wants to see.'

'You care about the distillery, don't you?' Susan said gently.

He shrugged. 'Waste and inefficiency in any form distress me. However, Thomas can sink or swim, it is nothing to me.' He seemed to have forgotten her. 'One day the mill will be mine, mine to control and when that day comes I'll double the profits and expand the premises.' He gave an embarrassed laugh. 'Susan, my love, I have great plans. I'm not criticising your father, he's a shrewd enough business man but his methods are old-fashioned and his outlook out of date. The mill is stagnating.'

Only by taking a deep breath did she keep her temper in check.

'My father is a shrewd business man and because of that he is wise enough not to overstretch. He considers he has a duty to his workforce as well as to his family and he wouldn't gamble with the well-being of either. It distresses me to say

155

this but I have a feeling that all you care about is power and you won't care who suffers just so long as you get what you want.'

'Power!' He repeated the word, savouring the sound. 'Yes, you are absolutely right. I want power and I mean to get it.' He paused. 'I haven't changed, Susan, you didn't know me as well as you thought, that's all.'

'I'm just beginning to realise that.'

'All I want is to prove to my father how wrong he was.'

'Bitterness only brings unhappiness and if you carry on in this way all you will be doing is building up misery for everyone and destroying yourself into the bargain.'

'As if you cared?'

'Of course I care, Edward. I care very much.'

'Then help me. Together we can do so much but if you attempt to thwart me,' he said threateningly then laughed. 'You wouldn't do that; after all, my success is yours.' He opened the newspaper and folded it ready to read, but changed his mind. 'There is one area where you can't but shine.'

'I'm glad to hear it,' she said, not hiding her sarcasm. 'You are going to tell me I suppose?'

'Entertaining our friends and business associates. You are blessed with charm when you choose to exercise it and you have beauty and intelligence. No one could ask for more in a hostess. Thomas is less fortunate. Elizabeth comes from a good family but she is an empty-headed chatterbox.'

'I don't know Elizabeth all that well but she struck me as a pleasant, friendly girl.'

'Oh, she's that,' he conceded, 'but she never has anything of interest to say.'

'With your tight hold on the purse-strings how could we possibly afford the lavish entertainment you appear to have in mind?'

'That is a necessary expense and one that is likely to pay a dividend. A lot of contracts are secured over a glass of port after a good dinner.' He smiled. 'You won't find me stingy there nor with your dress allowance. Be lavish to those who may be useful and don't look so disapproving. The end result will be a healthier order book.'

'You are infuriating and insulting. Anyone listening to you would think the mill a second-rate business. And another thing, if you have such a low opinion of the mill why were you so anxious to get a foot in?'

'That's the spirit. You look magnificent when you're roused. Now to answer your question. I didn't see Matthew as a major stumbling block. He would have left the decision-making to me and with clever marketing the money would be there for expansion.'

'My father would be appalled to hear all this. He believes that by putting too much emphasis on quantity, quality invariably suffers.'

'Rubbish and typical of his old-fashioned thinking.'

'He doesn't use people.'

'Your mother does though,' he said, raising an eyebrow.

'What do you mean?' she asked sharply but she had a horrid suspicion of what was coming.

'My mother has never been blind to the fact that her friendship was cultivated to improve your dear mama's social standing. As it happens they have become good friends.'

When she made no reply he rustled the paper. 'Now, maybe, I'll get a chance to read this.'

After Edward left for the mill Susan rang the hand-bell. It was answered by Mary, a pretty, dark-haired maid with a curvaceous figure who had worked for the Templetons.

'You rang, m'am?'

There was a touch of insolence in the voice.

'Tell Polly I want to see her and straighten your cap.'

An anxious-looking Polly arrived. 'Is there somethin' wrong, Miss Susan – I mean m'am?' she said, flustered.

'What makes you think there is something wrong?'

'Mary said – '

'What did Mary say?'

'Nothin', m'am, it was just the way – ' She bit her bottom lip and worked it with her teeth.

'Sit down, Polly.' She gestured to a chair and Polly sat down on the edge of the seat.

'How would you like to be my personal maid?'

Polly's eyes widened incredulously. 'Oh, m'am!'

'Then I take it you would?'

'Ever so pleased I'd be.' She was flushed and her eyes were shining like twin stars.

'I'll see Miss Wilson about relieving you of some of your duties. Sewing is going to take up a lot of your time and I know you are good with a needle. A few of my gowns are uncomfortably tight.'

'If the material is there the seams can be let out a wee thing or – '

'Yes, yes, I'm sure you'll manage. There's a small room presently used as a store I'm told. That can be cleared and you must consider it your workroom.'

'That's ever so kind, m'am.'

'Did you mind leaving Aran Heights?'

'Not when I was to be with you, Miss Susan.' She blushed. 'Beggin' your pardon, m'am, I keep forgettin'.'

'Don't worry about it,' Susan said kindly. 'There are times when I forget myself. Off you go then.'

For a long time Susan sat staring ahead and seeing nothing but her mind was working feverishly. This uncertainty had to end before she went mad. She shrank from consulting Dr Sullivan or Edward's doctor. No, it had to be someone unknown to her and she had the glimmer of an idea of how she could go about it. Tomorrow morning immediately after the coachman had driven Edward to the mill she would be dressed and waiting, then she would get him to take her to the station. And if everything worked to plan there would be ample time to catch the train to Glasgow. Never before had Susan gone anywhere alone except in Aranvale but she was a matron, she reminded herself, and Glasgow was not unknown to her. With it being so near to Aranvale there had been frequent trips to the city to see the sights when they were young and then more recently the journeys to Miss Beattie's salon. And it was on one of those journeys with her mother that she had seen it. Not long after leaving Queen Street station the coach had been held up and with nothing to do but gaze about her Susan recalled seeing the big brass plate belonging to a doctor's surgery. Apart from Buchanan Street and Sauchiehall Street she had never paid attention to the street names and without the name and address of the doctor she could hardly take a cab. Anyway the short walk was the least of her worries.

With that planned Susan felt calmer and, taking a book, went out to the garden. The first blooms had gone from the roses and some of the petals lay untidily on the black earth. Summer was slipping away, soon it would be autumn with the leaves fluttering from the trees. The seasons had a pattern, nothing changed, everything predictable – well, apart from the weather. But in life nothing was predictable. She closed her eyes. If only – if only David Cameron hadn't come into her life but it was too late for thoughts like that. Of one thing she was sure, David Cameron wouldn't be suffering, the David she remembered would be too busy trying to make his fortune.

After the first bewildering two weeks David Cameron settled happily in London. True to his promise his friend from student days had fixed up temporary accommodation. Young qualified accountants were in demand and David was overjoyed to gain a position with Hamilton & Hargreave, an established company with an excellent reputation and with offices in all the major English cities. One of his colleagues was leaving at the end of the month and David was fortunate to get the room he was vacating which was walking distance from the office.

Morning seemed a long time coming. She both welcomed and dreaded it. Like her father Edward disliked conversation so early in the morning and recently she had been glad of it. She saw him to the door, held up her face for his kiss and went indoors only after the carriage moved off. In an agony of impatience she awaited the return of the carriage and hearing it in the courtyard she went out quickly. Ramsay had already jumped down.

'Good mornin', m'am,' he said, taking off his cap and twisting it in his hands.

'Good morning, Ramsay,' Susan said crisply. 'I want taking to the station and there is little enough time to catch the Glasgow train.'

Without wasting time on words Ramsay saw his mistress seated then set the horses to a spanking pace. There had been a gradual change in the weather. The early morning had been sunny but now there was a slow hazing of the sky and the hills were shrowded in mist. At the entrance to the station Ramsay brought the coach to a halt. He seemed anxious to speak but hesitated.

'What is it?' Susan said impatiently.

'Beggin' your pardon, m'am, but I wouldnae be venturin' far in this. That mist's goin' tae thicken, tak' my word for it.' He was sturdily built, had fathered six healthy youngsters and had a kindly way with him.

Susan glanced at the sky. 'You may well be right but I have only a very short journey at the other end. Expect me back on the late afternoon train and now I must hurry.'

'Ye've time enough.'

She began to walk away then stopped. 'Ramsay.' She forced a smile and a light tone. 'Don't mention this journey to my husband, he would only worry.'

'Can't say as I blame him but I'll say nothin'.'

She left him shaking his head and looking perplexed. A real nice lady she was that, but her and her kind were none too keen on taking advice.

He had been with John Brodie for many years, employed in the main for odd jobs but he was capable of taking the place of the coachman when necessary. It had been Lilian who had suggested to her husband that Edward should have the second coach as part of their wedding settlement and Ramsay had been only too delighted to take over the new position of coachman at Hillview.

Passengers were few at this time of day and Susan found

herself sharing a compartment with one other lady. After a brief smile and a remark about the weather, her fellow passenger buried her face in a book and was engrossed in it for the rest of the journey. Thankful that polite conversation wasn't called for, Susan closed her eyes and by concentrating on one thing at a time was managing to remain calm. She had the route pictured in her mind. Left coming out of the station and then not too far on, it was left again. At the corner was a double-fronted shop with fruit and vegetables piled high in one window and the other was a hatter. The incongruity of it had struck her at the time.

As the train steamed and puffed into the station the woman closed her book and put it in her bag. She was ready when it pulled up with a squealing of brakes. Doors up and down the train opened and people spilled out on to the platform.

'I hate fog and one doesn't expect it at this time of year,' the woman remarked as she hastened away and was soon lost from sight.

Other trains had arrived in Queen Street station and Susan was caught up in a mass of moving bodies impatient to reach the exit. Some had baggage and were none too careful of the comfort of others as they jostled for position.

Susan held back until the worst of the crush was over then she too was outside and without warning enveloped in a fog that slopped over the high buildings, successfully obliterating those landmarks on which she was depending.

In Aranvale Susan had experienced fog but she had never been alone in it and this was Glasgow. She shivered with fear. This was smog – a mixture of thick smoke and fog – and it caught at her throat, almost choking her. Stupid to rush out until her eyes became accustomed to the greyness. She waited until she imagined the fog to be less thick and stepped out, thinking that if others could cope then so could she.

Far away she heard the barking of a dog, a lonely sound, then coming closer the eerie clanging of trams. She let out a thin scream as she felt a violent push at her back. She would have lost her balance had a hand not steadied her.

161

'Sorry, hen. Cannae see sae weel in this pea-souper. I hevnae hurt ye, yer a'richt are ye?'

'Yes, thank you,' she whispered. She was trembling with fright and near to tears but not at the voice. It had been couthy, holding concern not malice.

Clutching her bag to her Susan strained her eyes, finding it marginally easier to make progress. Had she gone too far? It was so difficult to judge, she could make out nothing in this swirling mist. Then just as she thought she would scream she saw it, the shop, the double-fronted shop. Hats of all descriptions sat on their stands like disembodied ghostly apparitions in the blurred light. Almost sobbing with relief she quickened her pace. The fog was less dense here as though there were pockets of fog and this part had escaped the worst.

And there it was – the big brass plate and she had so nearly missed it. Going closer she looked at the lettering. Dr E. R. Skinner. There was more but she had seen all she needed.

With her heart beating like a sledgehammer, Susan pulled at the bell sharply. An echoing sound reached her followed by light footsteps, then the door opened.

'Yes?'

'May I see the doctor, please?' Susan asked, her voice wobbling with nervousness.

'There's plenty waitin' but if you've a mind to you can wait.'

'Thank you.' Susan stepped in gratefully, aware that the woman was eyeing her curiously but she said nothing more and Susan followed her along a passage with worn brown waxcloth. Stopping at a door she opened it and ushered Susan in.

'Move up and make way for this lady,' she said in a no-nonsense voice. There was a shuffling of feet and a space was made for Susan.

It was a square-shaped room with green painted walls chipped in places and a long wooden bench down two walls. The stench of unclean bodies and stale perspiration mingled with the smell of disinfectant. With the first onslaught Susan thought she was to be physically sick. She took out her handkerchief and held it to her nose. Around her were people with dry, racking coughs and one with the same kind of wheeziness as her papa. He was struggling for breath but holding on to an empty pipe in his gnarled hand. One old man hunched forward, his eyes fixed on one spot in the worn waxcloth. So still was he that he might have been carved in stone.

The patients were thinning out; no one was getting much time from the doctor. A whimper broke out and Susan looked at the boy in sympathy. He could have been no more than seven years of age. A woollen scarf was wound round his head and under his chin and Susan could see a huge swelling on his face. Gently the woman drew him towards her and it was her eyes that were filled with pain.

'He's tae get it lanced,' she said, seeing the sympathy in Susan's face.

They were from very different walks of life but as the woman and her child went out the two women exchanged sad smiles and Susan touched the boy as he went by.

A little later there was a piercing scream followed by another, then silence. Later still came the murmur of voices then the receptionist was telling her that she was next.

'Is the little boy all right?' she found herself asking.

'Right as rain. You've to be cruel to be kind and the doctor had a sweetie for him. He's good with bairns.'

The smell of disinfectant was stronger in the surgery. It was a small room with a desk, three chairs, a sofa covered with a blanket and a set of drawers.

The man behind the desk had his head bent and he was writing on a pad.

'Sit down.' The head didn't rise but an arm indicated the chair opposite.

Even in her worry and distress Susan still felt outraged at this appalling display of bad manners. She didn't move and his head went up slowly. In those moments when they looked at each other she saw that he was a man perhaps in his late thirties. He was clean-shaven, heavy featured and with smudges of tiredness under the grey eyes.

'Sit down,' he repeated then added, 'I haven't all day.'

She sat down.

Susan had dressed in the most sober outfit she could find in her wardrobe but it was still obvious that she was out of place in this surgery.

If he was surprised by her appearance he concealed it admirably.

'What can I do for you?' It was a pleasant voice with a hint of impatience as if already he had wasted enough time.

'I think I may be pregnant,' she said quietly.

'If this is an unwanted pregnancy,' he said harshly, 'you've come to the wrong place.'

She stared at him and moved her hands as if at a loss for words.

'You do wear a ring so perhaps I misjudged.'

She swallowed nervously. 'I want to have it confirmed or otherwise.'

'Very well,' he said brusquely, 'you had better answer a few questions before I examine you.' He leaned forward placing the palms of his well-shaped hands together. 'When was your last . . .'

Embarrassed at all the personal questions, she stammered out the answers while he kept nodding.

'Remove your jacket and blouse and undo the rest.'

Susan put her bag against the leg of the chair and her gloves with it. He was watching her and it made her clumsy and slow but at last she was ready. It was an impersonal, professional examination and he engaged himself elsewhere while she dressed. She bent down for her handbag and gloves and wished he would put her out of her misery.

Her eyes were huge in her white face. 'Please tell me,' she whispered.

'The signs all point to the fact that you are pregnant, Mrs . . .' He waited for her to fill in the name but she ignored it and with a slight shrug he picked up a pen, dipped it into an inkwell and did a swift calculation on his pad. 'Middle

March give or take a week either way. Difficult to be more precise, particularly with a first baby.'

He saw the panic in her eyes and he looked at her kindly. 'For God's sake don't believe all the stories you hear. You're a healthy young woman so there should be no problems. Just remember it is a natural function of the body. Is there anything else you want to ask?'

She saw his impatience. 'No, nothing else.' She opened her bag. 'What is your fee?'

'My receptionist deals with that,' he said curtly.

I'm going to have a baby, she thought wildly as she got up. The room swam then steadied. He was holding the door open, the receptionist was ushering in another patient.

'Good day,' he said politely then the door was closed. She paid the receptionist, amazed how little was asked, but had she known it was more than double the usual fee.

Then she was outside with no conscious thought of where she was going. Visibility had improved though fog still lingered. The air was warm and clammy and there was a film of moisture on her forehead yet Susan felt icy cold and dreadfully afraid.

What was she to do? Dear God, please help me but she didn't expect her prayers to be answered. She had sinned and now she had to pay the price. And what would that price be? Disowned by her husband; Edward would show no mercy, of that she was sure. But worst of all what would it do to Papa? Her heart filled with black despair and death would have been welcome. She didn't deserve to live but somehow she had to face what lay ahead.

Who would she turn to and for how long could she keep her secret? The questions hammered at her brain then she stopped suddenly as a new panic seized her. Where was she? She had been walking aimlessly and for how long? Her frightened eyes were taking in the shabbiness of the area, the hovels, the filthy middens – did people live in such dreadful conditions? But of course they did. Abruptly she wheeled round and walked a few yards then turned down another road. She blundered on, feverishly looking for some sign and seeing a blurred light she went towards it. With her heart thumping painfully she rubbed the misted glass with her glove and almost cried out in relief. It was a teashop. She was safe. She would go in and order a pot of tea then ask for directions to the station or better still a cab to get her there.

The wooden handle turned, a bell clanged and a girl came forward, a floor brush in her hand.

'We're just closin'.'

'Please, if I could just have a pot of tea?'

'There's nothin' much left to eat.'

'That doesn't matter.'

'In that case sit yersel' doon, onywhar yer like.' Her brush went against the wall and she dusted her hands with the skirts of her gown before going over to the dresser heaped with thick white china.

Susan sat at one of the small tables; the cloth was stained where soup had been spilt and there were tea stains but Susan was past caring. She was just too thankful to be inside. The girl was quick bringing milk and sugar and setting a place with a cup and saucer. When the large brown teapot arrived it had a chipped lid. Susan tried to pour tea into the cup but her hand was shaking so much that she had to replace it.

'My, but that's a fair state yer in. Here let me dae it.' The thin wrist lifted it as if it were a featherweight. 'Milk?'

'Yes, please.'

'Sugar?' But before Susan could answer she was spooning in a liberal quantity. 'It's shock yer sufferin' frae by the looks o' ye and sweet tea's the best thing fer that.'

Susan tried to smile but her lips were stiff. 'You're very kind.'

The sweet tea did help. Used to fine china the lip of the cup felt strange but she drank from it thirstily. The girl halted her cleaning to see if she wanted her cup refilled but Susan shook her head.

'No more, thank you but that has helped. I feel much better.' She smiled. 'If you could tell me how to get to Queen Street station I would be very much obliged. I seem to have lost myself. Is it possible to get a cab from somewhere nearby?'

The girl opened her eyes wide and stared. 'There's no cab hereabouts but the station's no' that far. Tak' the short cut – no, mebbe no, yer could be losin' yersel' again.' She bawled through to the back shop. 'Mind the shop, Bella, I'll no' be lang.'

Hauling a knitted cardigan from a chair she put it on. 'If this is summer Gawd help us in the winter.' She grinned.

Susan had her purse out and handed over some money.

'A meenit and I'll get change.'

'No, the rest is for yourself.'

'It's ower much.' She was swithering but there was a hopeful look on her thin narrow face.

'Please take it,' Susan said shakily. 'You can't know how helpful you've been.'

She took Susan's arm and led her through a warren of back alleys, careful to avoid the piles of decaying rubbish.

'Naebody will harm ye. Fowk hereabouts dinnae deserve the reputation they get.'

In a remarkably short time one of the alleyways brought them out almost at the station.

'Cannae lose yersel' noo.' But she kept Susan's arm until they were right into the station.

Susan glanced at the clock and sighed with relief. 'Thanks to you I'll catch my train.'

'Cheerio and remember nothin's ever as bad as it looks.'

'Thank you again.'

The girl waved then hurried away.

Utterly weary, Susan dragged her feet across the station and over to the platform where the train was already waiting. Returning shoppers had made the train busy and Susan found herself having to share a compartment with three well-dressed ladies who were chatting animatedly. Thankful that none was known to her she gave them a polite smile and sat down. A few efforts were made to draw her into their conversation but her reluctance to participate eventually discouraged them and she was left in peace.

Peace – as if she would ever know peace again.

Slowly and in a cloud of steam the train moved out of the station and as it began to gather speed Susan closed her eyes. Another time the rhythmic sound of metal clanging against metal would have been pleasant but now it was like a hammer in her head. Her plight was so dreadful that her brain could no longer cope. With so many stops the train never got up much speed and Susan had always liked to watch life in the small villages as they passed and she determined to do this and keep her mind occupied. She saw the rolling, purple-tinted hills in the distance, a stark contrast to the miners' rows of ugly brick houses. Opencast mining had provided the only means of livelihood until the opening of the Aranvale Papermill. The scars where the seams had been worked out were well hidden by the long, rough grass and bracken. In spite of herself a smile tugged at Susan's mouth as she watched the barefooted children egging on two boys as they raced their bogies down the slope in an attempt to keep up with the train. Susan knew what a bogie was, as a boy her papa had had one. It was made from the base and wheels of an old pram with a wooden box for the driver to sit.

She must have dozed off and it was a change in the rhythmic motion that brought her awake. In a few minutes they would be in Aranvale station and Ramsay pacing the platform, no doubt relieved to see her safely back.

The ladies were going further on and she wished them good day as the train squealed to a halt. They answered but coldly; her standoffishness had offended them.

Another time and she would have laughed at the look on Ramsay's face.

'My, but I'm that glad tae see ye, m'am,' he said as they walked to the carriage. 'Proper tizzie I've been in.'

'There was no need, Ramsay,' Susan said gently, touched by his concern. 'The fog was patchy and I managed very well.'

Before taking the turning to Hillview Susan looked across to the grey splendour of Aran Heights standing aloof and proud in its commanding position and her eyes filled. If only – oh, if only she were back there and all this a bad dream. She, like her papa, loved its wild ruggedness yet at times she knew that she had likened it to a prison. A place where she had been over-cosseted and protected and her rebellious nature had stormed against it. And where had it landed her? Those secret, stolen hours with David Cameron had ruined her whole life. Why, oh, why, had she been such a fool? Aunt Rachel had seen the dangers and warned her against furthering an acquaintance with a young man so totally unsuitable but she had chosen not to listen.

Susan swallowed nervously as the carriage turned into the drive and sat still until Ramsay opened the door and helped her down. With a murmured 'thank you' she went through the doorway that was still unfamiliar and into the vestibule with its flowering plants from Aran Heights.

Mary, the maid, was in the hall and at the sight of her mistress her mouth fell open and she stared.

'What are you gaping at, girl?' Susan snapped. 'Don't you have work to do?'

'Yes, m'am,' she muttered as she scuttled away.

'I'm getting rid of that girl,' Susan decided. 'I can't stand her, there's something about the creature I find loathsome.'

Once in her bedroom Susan let out a shuddering sob and, catching sight of herself in the full-length mirror, she had to admit that it was small wonder that the maid had gaped. Her face was chalk-white, her boots filthy and the hem of her skirt bespattered with mud.

Really she would have to get a grip on herself. She had almost two hours before Edward returned from the mill and in that time she must tidy herself, act normally through the meal then later . . .

First she must get out of these clothes and wash herself thoroughly. There was no telling what she may have picked up in the waiting-room. Just thinking about it the disgusting stench was with her. Her stomach heaved and she stood quite still until the nausea wore off then she was conscious of another ache, an ache of emptiness and she remembered that she hadn't eaten since breakfast and then only sparingly.

Polly! She could ring but that might bring Miss Wilson or Mary. Better to go along herself. The passage was quiet and when she went to what had once been a storeroom, she found Polly stooped over a gown and painstakingly unpicking the seams.

'M'am!' she said springing up.

'Polly, I'm afraid I've got myself into a filthy mess.' She tried to make a joke of it but it ended in a gulp.

'I'll get hot water and bring it right away.'

'And get Mrs Carson to prepare a tray, just a sandwich and tea. I'll be dining with the master later.'

Back in her bedroom, Susan stepped out of her clothes, kicking them aside before reaching for her robe. Slipping her arms into it she was tying the belt when the idea came to her. She stood stock still. It was so simple she couldn't think why she hadn't thought of it before. Babies were born prematurely, she could be having Edward's baby or rather she could pass it off as Edward's. All she had to do was hide her condition and that shouldn't be too difficult. She would watch her posture and Polly was letting out the seams of her gowns. And the looser style, though not to her liking, was fashionable.

Even as all this was going through her mind and a part of her was grasping at it she knew that she could never stoop so low. How could she cheat Edward so shamefully and live with herself? Her head went up. She would be honest, and delaying her confession would only add to her torture. The decision made, she felt a calmness and a new strength flow through her veins to help her face the ordeal.

Polly arrived panting from the exertion of carrying the ewer brimful of hot water. In her usual quick fashion she filled the basin, checked that there was soap and placed two folded towels on the edge of the marble slab.

'No, don't go, Polly. Get me fresh underclothes and a gown – the blue sprigged one I think.'

Polly turned her back while Susan sponged herself all over.

She took the underclothes from a drawer then drew along the hangers and took out the gown her mistress wished to wear. Very carefully she spread it over the large double bed.

'M'am, I told Mrs Carson. Mebbe it's ready and if that's all you'll be needin' – '

'Wait! Get rid of these.' She gave a backwards kick with her heel. 'Put them in the furnace,' she said with a shudder.

'M'am!' Polly was scandalised.

'Do as you're told,' Susan said sharply then regretted her tone. 'They are old and dirty and I have no further use for them.'

'There's many that would be glad of them, m'am,' Polly said stubbornly.

'You want them for yourself? Haven't I given you enough?'

'No, m'am, not for mysel',' she said, sounding hurt. ''tis a shame to waste what could be put to good use that's what I'm sayin'.'

'Very well, do what you like with them, just get them out of my sight.'

'I'll be seein' about the tray now,' she said as she scooped them up in her arms.

In the dining-room they sat at either end of the long table saying little to each other. The maid served the meal from the silver dishes and Susan was vaguely aware of Edward's eyes following her movements around the table. When she had gone his eyebrows rose.

'I see we have a change of table-maid.'

'Yes, Polly is an accomplished needlewoman and I had Miss Wilson reorganise the duties to allow her some time in the sewing-room.'

'Very good, you are learning, my dear, and with a little practice that young woman has the makings of a good table-maid.'

'You may be right, Edward, but I don't care for her. I don't like her manner.'

'Give the girl a chance, she's probably nervous.'

Nerves were the last thing Susan thought Mary suffered from. When she had finally departed Edward dropped his voice.

'Adrian Beverley – you know – '

'Caroline's father?'

'Yes.' He paused. 'He's committed suicide.'

'Surely not!' Susan said, shocked. 'But why, what on earth had come over him?'

'Rumours have been going around for some time that he was in financial difficulties and it would appear he couldn't face the disgrace of bankruptcy.'

'Poor man, I'm very, very sorry. What about his wife, poor soul, she's a bag of nerves at the best of times?'

'Gone to make her home with her widowed sister.'

'Where did you get all this information?'

'I had occasion to go into Airdrie and met Henry McCall, but don't ask me where he got his information.'

'That leaves Caroline on her own. She's an only child, you know.'

'From all accounts she's staying calm and intends seeing to the winding up of her father's affairs.' There was admiration in his voice. 'Caroline is not just a pretty face.'

'Papa always said that.'

With the meal over they moved into the sitting-room and Edward waved a hand. 'Won't be long before we have our own furniture. Have you thought how you are going to arrange matters?'

'We can make use of the guest room while our bedroom is being redecorated.'

'Is that really necessary, the redecoration I mean?'

'I would have thought so. Better now than having another upheaval.'

'We could stay with my parents until we are all square.'

Aran Heights would be more convenient, nearer the mill.'

'True, but your father is a semi-invalid and I'm not particularly keen.'

'Very well, we'll stay here.'

Edward lowered himself into the chair, stretched out his

long legs and reached for his newspaper. 'Now, if you please, Susan, let me read this in peace.'

Susan sat on the edge of the horsehair chair, her fingers tightly locked together. 'Don't open your paper just yet, Edward, there's something I must tell you.'

'You had every opportunity at the table.' Edward's expression tightened into irritation. This was the time he liked to get up to date with the financial news and Susan should know that by this time. Still, she was looking a bit tense, he thought, better hear what she had to say and get it over. Some domestic detail no doubt, women got into a state about such trifles.

'Very well, Susan, you have my undivided attention.'

She moistened her lips, tried to speak but no words came.

'It can't be that bad surely?'

'I'm pregnant, Edward,' she blurted out.

His lips twitched then slapping his knees he hooted with laughter.

'My poor, sweet innocent, we haven't been married a month yet. Darling, if it should prove to be the case I'll be absolutely delighted but you can't know for some time yet. Heavens! Didn't your mother tell you anything?'

'Edward, I am not totally ignorant and I have been to see a doctor.' The desperation in her voice got through to him.

'When? Where? A doctor, what on earth are you talking about?'

She was shaking badly but she had to go on. 'I was in Glasgow today and saw a doctor there.'

His eyes bulged and he said incredulously, 'Are you trying to tell me you went to Glasgow on your own?'

'Ramsay drove me to the station. The – the doctor confirmed that I am pregnant.'

'I never touched you before we were married.'

'No.'

'Who was it?' His voice cut like steel and Susan flinched. 'I'm waiting for an answer.'

What could she say? Papa had let drop that David Cameron

173

was no longer employed at the mill. No doubt, she thought bitterly, he was seeking his fortune in London.

'No one you know, Edward, I can assure you of that and no one I shall ever see again.'

'You'll tell me who it was,' he said threateningly, 'or do you want me to force it out of you?'

Susan felt near to fainting. 'His name would mean nothing, he's no longer in this country and I only knew him for a very short time.'

'Long enough apparently – and you acting Miss Innocent on our wedding night.' The words were tumbling out but Susan caught an edge of bewilderment and pain.

'Edward, I'm so very, very, sorry.'

'Is that all you can say?' He was out of his chair and there was something frightening and menacing in the way he was bent, like an animal about to strike and Susan shrank back in terror.

As if getting a grip on himself he moved back with his mouth curled in disgust. 'Don't worry about your physical safety, my dear wife.' He spat the words. 'I've never struck a woman in my life but God knows I've never been nearer.' He moved unsteadily and slumped back into his chair.

'You must believe me, Edward,' she said despairingly, 'I didn't know. Had I even thought it a possibility I would never have married you.'

'I can hardly bring myself to look at you. My God! Do you know what you've done? You've sunk to the lowest trick a woman can play, trapping me into marriage to give your bastard a name and save your precious reputation.' He continued with some more choice expressions and she was sickened by his coarseness.

'It's not true,' she shouted hysterically. 'I swear I didn't know, you've got to believe that and if you just think about it, Edward, you would realise I couldn't possibly – '

'Oh, granted, you couldn't be certain but you knew it to be a possibility and you were taking no chances.'

'No. Oh, why won't you believe me?'

'Tell me this – that sudden change of heart, that decision

174

of yours to propose marriage and that is what you did. Was it because you decided that you loved me after all or was there another reason? Be honest, Susan, you owe me the truth.'

She tried to be completely honest and haltingly she began to explain that it had been to put her father's mind at rest regarding the mill. But as she faltered to a close it sounded hollow even to her own ears.

'Of course he wanted me for a son-in-law, my presence is needed in the mill. You knew that and used it for your own ends.'

Susan was resigned now. 'It really doesn't matter what I say, Edward, does it? You've made up your mind not to believe me.'

'You've used me and that is something I'll never forgive. But the question is where do we go from here, tell me that?'

'That rests with you and whatever you decide I shall abide by it,' she said very quietly.

Getting up abruptly he walked to the door and when he reached it he stood still with his back to her then slowly turned and for a long moment looked at her.

'How could you, Susan? How could you do this to me?'

She shook her head. What more was there to say?

'I need to be alone, need to think,' he mumbled. The door closed and she was left alone.

A strand of hair fell across her face and she pushed it behind her ear. What punishment would Edward exact? He was a proud man reeling under a heavy blow and forgiveness did not come easy to him. But how could she expect forgiveness, hadn't she sinned in the most terrible way by proposing marriage to Edward while David Cameron's seed was growing inside her?

Fires were lit in the evenings when the weather turned unseasonably cold. The kindling was already there and all Susan had to do was ring for a maid to put a light to it, wait until it caught then add coal. Two or three times her hand went to the bell but each time she drew back. Time went on, midnight was approaching and a bone-chilling coldness settled over her. As she got up weariness and a numbness of the limbs had her catching at the furniture for support. She would go up to bed, she decided and was almost at the door when it opened and Edward stood there blocking her path.

'Get back to your chair,' he thundered. 'You'll leave this room when I tell you but first you are going to hear what I have to say.'

Even before she smelt it on his breath Susan knew that he had been drinking. She had steeled herself for another verbal lashing but now she was much more nervous. Drink unleashed the devil and she had already experienced what it did to Edward.

She hastened back to her chair and watched him stumble to his. After sitting down and crossing his legs the palms of his hands went together as in an attitude of prayer. Drink hadn't slurred his speech only made it slower, each word carefully articulated.

'I have done a great deal of thinking – '

She waited and her tiredness vanished as a new kind of terror took hold. What was he going to do to her? He was keeping her waiting, playing cat and mouse. 'Say what you have to say,' she said harshly.

'Ah, a great relief to you, my dear. You see I have decided to give your bastard my name though God knows what tainted blood it may inherit.'

'Not that word, Edward. Please, not that word,' she whispered.

'Why not? A child conceived outside marriage is a bastard. I didn't invent the word. And now if you will allow me to go on. Let's call it *it*. It is to have my name but that is all. Never shall I accept it as mine so don't make the mistake of believing that time will change that. Nothing will.' There was a grim finality in the words.

'It is more than I expected and I am grateful.'

'You should be. It is far more than most men would be prepared to do but I am not finished. No one makes a fool of Edward Brodie – '

'I didn't – '

'Be quiet,' he thundered. 'I repeat, no one makes a fool of me and that is what I would be made to look if this ever came out. Apart from that there is my position in the mill.'

'Papa would never make you suffer for my mistake.'

'Maybe not but I am not prepared to take that chance and in any case it is bound to sour relations and be awkward. No, my dear wife, my mind is made up.' The blow to his pride drove him on remorselessly, bitterness and resentment pouring from him in an unleashed torrent. 'You and I shall continue to behave towards each other as a happily married couple for the benefit of relatives and acquaintances.' His speech was becoming slurred, some of it almost unintelligible. 'That maid, the table-maid, what did you call her?'

'Mary.'

'I told her to move my clothes and other things into one of the guest bedrooms where I propose to remain until your bastard is born. After you have recovered we shall share a bedroom only until such time as you bear me a son. After that I shall have no further use for you.'

She swallowed hard and a spot of colour burned in each cheek.

He saw it and his mouth twisted in contempt. 'In other words the less I see of you the better.' With that he got up abruptly, too abruptly, lurched unsteadily, righted himself and then with a venomous look in her direction opened the door and was gone.

The guest rooms in Hillview were located in the east wing, a corridor and a half separating them from the main bedroom which they had shared until tonight.

After giving him ample time to reach his new sleeping quarters she left the sitting-room and crept upstairs like a thief in her own house. Mary had done a hasty job of transferring Edward's belongings, leaving the bedroom untidy but Susan barely noticed. All she wanted was to be alone and to have somewhere to lay her head.

She undressed as quickly as her tired limbs would permit and got into bed. Lying between the cold sheets she curled her feet up in her nightdress for warmth. She shivered,

missing the familiar warmth next to her. Beyond sleep but
with her body resting, Susan found her mind clearer than it
had been all day.

Papa need never know and for that she was deeply grateful
to Edward. A shudder went through her as she thought
of the shame and disgrace she would have brought on
the family. Mama, she guessed, would have taken to her
bed, distanced herself from her friends, unable to cope with
shame. Mercifully her parents were to be spared the pain and
humiliation. Edward, for his own reasons, was determined to
show the outside world that they were an affectionate loving
couple and she would willingly play her part.

How badly she had let Edward down and she had deserved
everything he said. He had treated her gently, reverently;
only that one time when he'd had too much to drink had he
taken her ruthlessly. And now he would seek his pleasure
with other women.

Sleep eventually claimed her and it was like a drugged
sleep, taking her some time to adjust when she awoke. The
warmth of Edward's body was missing and she stretched out
her hand to the emptiness before it all flooded back. She had
slept late but it was a matter of indifference. So much easier
to breakfast alone than try to make conversation.

What would the maids think? Separate rooms so soon,
so early in their marriage. It was humiliating to think of
the whispers and giggles that would go on in the servants'
quarters. She remembered her mother once saying, half
in annoyance, half in amusement, that the servants knew
more about the affairs of their employers than the employers
themselves.

As she brought fresh tea and toast into the breakfast-room
Mary's expression was inscrutable. But what had she told the
others? Still, what did it matter what any of them thought,
they were only servants.

Day followed day with monotonous regularity. Edward said
only the minimum and she felt if she didn't have something
to do she would go out of her mind. Occasionally she had

afternoon tea with her mother but her mother had a busy social life and not a great deal of time to spend with her daughter. Now Susan had a new routine. Hamish had changed his hours in the mill. Before, he had gone in the afternoon, now it was morning. And he had been pleased when Susan suggested she come over most afternoons to Aran Heights and help with the paperwork.

Ramsay had just deposited her at the entrance to Aran Heights and after leaving her cape with one of the maids she went along to the drawing-room to find her parents sitting together.

'Here comes the worker,' Hamish said jovially.

Susan kissed them both and marvelled at the change in her mother. No longer did she look disapproving when she and her papa disappeared to the library to discuss the affairs of the mill. Hamish treated her as a partner and seemed content when she was with him. Edward's name was seldom mentioned and sometimes she wondered if all was well between them.

'Susan, Winnie is being very tiresome.'

'That doesn't sound like her.'

'She wants a quiet wedding and I went along with that. About the same number of guests as at yours I suggested.'

'Mama, my wedding was anything but a quiet affair.'

'Nonsense. With more time for arrangements your wedding would have been a much more elaborate occasion. You only had one bridesmaid.'

'Hannah was enough.' Then Susan giggled. 'I didn't mean that the way it sounded. I only wanted one bridesmaid and Hannah was my choice. Who has Winnie decided on?'

'A cousin on her mother's side.' She gave a deep sigh. 'A mere handful of guests is all she wants – indeed all she'll have. When she makes up her mind Winnie is a very determined young woman.'

'What does Mr Clapperton have to say?'

'It's Winnie's day and if it is her wish so be it.'

'Then be pleased, Mama, it'll save you a lot of worry and work.'

179

'But I would have enjoyed arranging something special,' Mrs MacFarlane said regretfully. 'Admittedly yours was a worry but this one I could have enjoyed because it wouldn't have been entirely my responsibility.'

'I give up.' Susan smiled.

'I did a long time ago,' her father grunted as he got up gingerly. 'We'll get along to the library, lass, and leave your mother free to try more persuasion on Winnie.'

'Waste of time but I will pay a visit to find out how the work is coming along at Holmlea.'

'When I spoke to Matthew and Winnie they seemed delighted with the renovations to their new home.'

'Much needed renovations, I can tell you. Nothing has been done at Holmlea for years and the interior is a disgrace.'

'Which is why the price was so low,' Mr MacFarlane said, pausing at the doorway.

'And now they can do it up the way they want,' Susan added.

'Yes, I suppose there's that.'

CHAPTER TWELVE

Keeping her secret had been easier than she had dared hope but as was inevitable the day came when Susan felt herself being studied surreptitiously.

'I'm wondering, Susan dear, if you're keeping something from me?'

Susan had herself well prepared. 'No, Mama, but I wanted to be sure.'

'And you are?'

'Yes.' She gave a smile she hoped would pass for a happy mother-to-be. It must have been convincing because Sarah got up and hugged her daughter.

'How lovely, I'm absolutely delighted. Maybe I shouldn't say this but I can't help hoping your first-born is a boy. Your papa would be overjoyed.'

'Then I hope it is a boy,' Susan said quietly.

'What is Edward saying? He must be over the moon.'

'Prospective papas usually are,' she said lightly but she had to bite her lip to keep her mouth from trembling. This should have been such a wonderful time and it would have been if only she had been carrying Edward's child. In truth the dreadful atmosphere at Hillview was getting worse by the day and she was finding it more and more difficult to put on an act. Edward, on the other hand, would have made a good actor she thought; he could switch on the charm for the benefit of others and wipe it clear once they were on their own.

'Lilian and John will be pleased at the news though of course they are already grandparents so it isn't quite the same thrill for them as it is for us.'

'No, I suppose not.'

'You'll be seeing Edward's doctor?'

'Yes. Edward has arranged for him to visit regularly.' That part was true and showed a little regard for her well-being.

'You are keeping well? No problems with sickness?'

'A little nausea earlier on but I'm all right now.'

'Then think yourself lucky. I had quite a dreadful time with the three of you.' She paused. 'You must be careful, try to eat sensibly and take plenty of rest.'

'Mama, you're fussing already,' Susan said, laughing, 'and it's early days.'

'With cause, you've never been very good at taking advice and I'm not taking any chances with our first grandchild.' She gave a little laugh. 'I must say you and Edward haven't put off much time, have you?'

Susan could feel the colour creeping up her neck and, unable to look at her mother, fell to admiring the needlework with an unusual display of interest. 'This is quite lovely, Mama, and something I could never do.'

'More's the pity but with the coming baby you must take less interest in the affairs of the mill and concentrate on your other duties. If you don't Edward will be putting his foot down and I for one wouldn't blame him.'

'Mama, Miss Wilson is very efficient and everything at Hillview is running smoothly. In truth there is very little for me to do.'

'That will change when the little one arrives.'

'I can't imagine why. The nurse will deal with all that surely.'

'Don't be silly, I wasn't referring to those duties but rather to such things as engaging extra staff.'

'Dr Walker spoke about a midwife and he is to do the arranging.'

'Good! I might have known that Edward would have seen to everything well in advance.'

'Hardly an onerous task, Mama. All Edward did was approach Dr Walker,' Susan said a little sourly.

'You must have an approximate date?'

'He – he was quite vague, Mama. According to him first babies seldom arrive when expected.'

'A week or two either way,' her mother said matter-of-factly. 'What about the nursery? Have you decided which rooms to prepare?'

'No, I haven't given it any thought.'

'Then you should start thinking about it now.' She pursed her lips, a habit she had when she was considering something of importance. 'South-facing rooms would be best and yours being smallish means that bit more planning.'

'Surely that can wait,' Susan said impatiently. The strain of continually acting a part was taking its toll and there were times when she wondered if she could go on deceiving everybody, but then reminded herself that she had no choice. If Papa had been in robust health maybe she would have been brave enough to face up to the consequences. No, that wasn't true, she would have clutched at any straw to hide the truth.

Her weariness must have shown for Mrs MacFarlane was suddenly all concern.

'Susan, you are not to let the thought of childbirth worry you. It's natural to be apprehensive but just remember I'll be at hand to help you.'

'Thank you, Mama,' Susan said unsteadily. 'I know I'm going to need you.'

'Once Matthew and Winnie are married and settled in Holmlea you'll have me all to yourself. Believe me, my dear, you are approaching the happiest and most satisfying time of a woman's life.'

'You surprise me, Mama,' Susan blurted out, unable to stop herself. 'There were times when I was quite small that I felt myself positively unwanted.'

'What a dreadful thing to say to your mother,' Sarah said sharply, the angry colour flooding her face. 'You were never unwanted, indeed I was proud to have such a lovely daughter. Admittedly I found you difficult and wilful.'

'That was my reaction to feeling unloved and insecure,' Susan said, her voice harsh. 'You didn't show me much affection.'

Mrs MacFarlane looked taken aback and deeply offended.

'I never realised you were so sensitive, it certainly never showed.' She frowned. 'This isn't the first time you've hinted that I favoured the boys but why bring it up now?'

'I don't know why I'm doing it,' Susan said, distressed, 'it just all came out. I'm sorry, very sorry that I said all that.'

'You've been dwelling on imaginary slights and that is unhealthy. We all make mistakes,' she said unsteadily, 'and I'm sincerely sorry that you believed yourself unloved. Nothing could have been further from the truth.'

'Let's not say any more about it, Mama,' Susan said wretchedly. 'I don't know what is wrong with me.' Then she burst into tears.

'There! There!' Mrs MacFarlane said soothingly and bending her head she touched her cheek to Susan's. 'Pregnancy plays strange tricks and it's a time when some of us do and say things that are completely out of character.'

Susan gave a watery smile. 'I'm glad there's an explanation.'

'You'll feel better in a few minutes.' She touched her forehead delicately. 'I feel one of my headaches coming on and a cup of tea will help us both. You're nearer, ring the bell, dear.'

'My fault,' she said getting up to ring for the maid.

'No, it's been a niggling ache all day and I don't want it to develop.'

'You must lie down.'

'I should I know but I'm not sure when your papa is coming home and I like to be downstairs when he gets in.'

Susan got up and wandered over to the window. The familiar scene had a soothing effect. This was home, this would always be home. The maid arrived and after giving her instructions, Mrs MacFarlane joined Susan at the window.

'This is what I miss, Mama. There is hardly any view from our sitting-room window.'

'But then Hillview – '

'How they settled on that house name I'll never understand, a misnomer if ever there was one.'

'True, but being so low-lying you are spared the worst

of the weather. Here as you know we get the full force of anything that is going. The very thought of winter, wind, snow and the freezing cold – ' She gave a mock shiver.

Tea arrived and the next few minutes went to the serving of it. They sipped the weak tea, Susan quiet and her mother thoughtful. Of a sudden she seemed to make up her mind and putting down her cup she sat with her back rod straight.

'I think it would be better, Susan, if we cleared the air completely with no more misunderstandings. Perhaps then you will see my seeming lack of affection in another light.'

'Mama, I have apologised, isn't that enough?'

'In this instance – no, it isn't. Far better that we should talk it through.' She took a sip of tea before continuing. 'Has it ever occurred to you that the boys, particularly Matthew, may have resented the attention you got from Papa?'

'I don't recall getting more.'

'We see what we want to see,' her mother said tartly. 'Matthew was always made to feel inferior. You had the better brain and of that he was constantly reminded. Sharing Matthew's tutor was a grave mistake and something I was against from the start.' She moistened her lips and her voice hardened. 'Was it any wonder that he lost heart with his lessons? Some of us are slower to learn but what we do learn we retain.'

'Mama – '

'Let me finish then there will be no reason ever to bring this up again. When it comes to his family your papa does not easily admit to a mistake but I believe he only has himself to blame. Handled differently Matthew may well have taken his proper place in the mill and what's more made a success of it.'

'And my marriage of convenience would not have been necessary or should I say less pressure would have been put on me,' Susan said angrily.

Mrs MacFarlane was staring at her.

'Blame it on my condition,' Susan said flippantly, wishing she hadn't said it but she could see her mother wasn't going to let it pass.

'Aren't you and Edward happy?' Mrs MacFarlane asked. 'You always appear to be.'

'We get along all right.'

'Is that all?'

Susan moved uncomfortably. 'Maybe I was expecting too much.' It was all she could think to say.

'A bit of give and take, Susan, you'll both have to learn that.'

'Mama, be fair, you know perfectly well that I entered this marriage to ease Papa's worries about the mill. You can hardly deny putting pressure on me.'

'I admit to encouraging the union.'

'Oh, you did, Mama.' Then she smiled. 'I haven't much to grumble about.'

'My dear, you're suffering from a form of melancholia which is not uncommon in pregnancy though it is usually after the birth. Anyway, Susan, once the baby arrives it will bring you closer and I can imagine Edward a doting father.' There was a timid knock at the door.

'Yes, what is it?'

The door opened a fraction. 'M'am, the carriage for Mistress Brodie – what'll I tell him?'

Susan got up, anxious to get away. 'Tell Ramsay to come to the front entrance. I'm just leaving.'

'Aren't you waiting to see Papa?'

'No, I'll see him tomorrow afternoon. And, Mama,' she said hesitantly, 'Edward and I get along well enough, don't worry about us.'

'I assure you I'm not in the least worried.'

Susan put on her cape and her mother accompanied her to the door.

'Take care of yourself,' she said, kissing her cheek.

'I'll do that.'

After waving from the window of the carriage Susan leaned back exhausted. So much had come out in that talk, each learning a lot about the other. Looking back she saw a clearer picture and her mother could have been right about Matthew. She had been thoughtless and selfish; compared to Matthew she had always been so much quicker to learn. What had been so simple to her had taken Matthew such a long time to grasp and she had been eager to move on to something more advanced. But that was no excuse, she could have waited for her brother to catch up. She sighed. It was too late for regrets.

As the weeks slowly dragged on and summer faded into a browning and mellowing autumn the gardens at Hillview were constantly being cleared of the crimson and brown leaves blown into the damp earth by the frivolous wind. Today the sun did not shine, it was grey and depressing like her spirits. She turned from the window to seat herself at her desk and, picking up her pen, decided to answer the letters long overdue a reply. She wondered what to say.

It was hard to sleep. Susan tossed and turned and closed her eyes as if to shut out the suspicions. She could not have said when they had first been aroused though looking back she saw significance in what had then seemed innocent, unconnected incidents. There was the way that maid Mary stood unnecessarily close to Edward when serving him at the table. The secretive smile on her face – not quite a smile – a mere twitch of the lips as if something amused her. And that provocative swing to the hips, was it becoming more pronounced or was it all in her imagination? Maybe she would have settled for that had it not been – she smiled grimly. Fate must have played into her hands or how else at that precise moment would she have looked over the banister and seen a disappearing hemline. No more than faintly curious she had moved on to a bend in the stairway where they were in full view. She stood and watched.

Edward was quite a bit taller than the maid and he had to stoop down to whisper something in her ear. Whatever it was had her giggling and to stop her he had raised his hand to land a playful slap on her skirt.

Susan's anger, part humiliation, was in danger of boiling over but she forced herself to remain calm. An unladylike outburst would be unwise and only make Edward believe her jealous. Or then perhaps not; he didn't feel she had any affection for him. Was she jealous, she asked herself? No, just furious but in all honesty she knew it was more than that.

Next morning Susan had her breakfast brought to her in bed. Once she heard the carriage leave with Edward she would get up.

There was something magical about impending motherhood, Susan thought. Even in her unhappiness there was a creamy bloom to her skin and a healthy shine to her hair. She dressed with care, checking her appearance in the mirror. What she was about to do needed confidence but she didn't doubt her ability to carry it out. With her thick fair hair coiled elegantly and her head held high she was every inch the mistress of Hillview as someone was to find out.

With her hand on the banister she went down the graceful stairway and into the wide hall. Mary was leaning over the gleaming surface of the exquisitely carved table which had once graced the Old Mill House and which Aunt Rachel had insisted on Susan having. The maid's elbow was raised and her hand was busy with a polished cloth. She did not raise her eyes.

Standing there, Susan had to fight an urge to hurl the book she was carrying and strike that hateful creature. She took a deep breath.

'Mary!' she said sharply, expecting an instant response but instead the head went up slowly and the eyes were insolent.

'M'am?'

'Leave what you are doing and go along to the dining-room. At once, girl. I will deal with you directly.'

A lot of the insolence had gone to be replaced by a startled wariness and was there also fear? It had been the tone of voice more than the words that had brought on the change and Susan felt a glow of satisfaction as she swept through the archway to where the housekeeper had her own sitting-room. Miss Wilson was there, it was her time off.

Alarmed at seeing her mistress, she got up quickly and her prim features were troubled.

'M'am, is something the matter?'

'Only that I am about to dispense with Mary's services.'

'Oh!'

'She is in the dining-room awaiting me and when I ring I want you to come.'

'Yes, of course, I'll come right away.'

Mary was standing with her back to the window and her hands clasped in front of her when Susan entered. Sweeping past, Susan went to the head of the long, mahogany table and drew out her husband's chair. She turned it round to face the girl before sitting down. Now that the moment had come she didn't feel the least bit nervous, rather she was enjoying the other's discomfort.

'How long have you worked at Hillview?'

'Over – over a year, m'am,' she faltered.

'I see. Maybe you satisfied your previous mistress but I find you far from suitable.'

'I'm a good worker.'

'You may well be but your manner is insolent and I will not tolerate it for another day. Your dismissal is immediate, though I have decided to pay your wages for the full week.'

Mary looked dumbfounded and her face was grey with shock. But just as Susan was beginning to feel a small twinge of sympathy the girl began shouting.

'That's it,' she almost spat, 'wantin' rid of me and for what? Tell me the real reason but you can't, can you?' she screeched.

'I am not required to give an explanation for my actions. I am mistress of this house and I strongly object to your disgraceful manner.'

'Huh! We'll see what the master has to say about that,' she said, her eyes narrowing down on Susan. 'He won't have me thrown out, I can tell you that now.' A sly look came out on her face. 'Seein' as you're not a proper wife to him like – '

189

'How dare you! You – you slut of a girl,' Susan screeched, white to the lips.

'That went home,' she sneered. 'See, I knows what goes on and if the master fancies me for a bit of – '

Almost knocking the chair over in her haste, Susan went across to the hand-bell and gave it such a tug that it was in danger of coming apart.

Miss Wilson was with them within moments. Her eyes went from one to the other.

A few deep breaths and Susan was sufficiently recovered to greet the housekeeper.

'Thank you for coming so promptly.' She turned to look at the maid as if she were some particularly revolting garbage. 'This creature is no longer in my employ, Miss Wilson. Pay her her wages until the end of the week but I want her out of Hillview now. Is that understood?'

'Yes, m'am.' Miss Wilson's smile was one of quiet satisfaction.

All the bravado had gone and Mary now resorted to noisy tears.

'What'll happen to me?' she blubbered. 'Weren't my fault the master fancied me.' She turned imploringly to Susan. 'Give me another chance, m'am, please. I've no place to go – you can't just throw me out. I'm sorry, m'am, please . . .' she snivelled.

'Don't waste any sympathy on this young woman, m'am, her kind will always survive.' Then with a remarkable show of strength Miss Wilson took hold of the maid and frogmarched her out of the room.

After they had gone Susan sat down and closed her eyes. She had not expected such an ugly scene and it had upset her more than she had expected. Then there was Edward to face later on.

Miss Wilson approached her after Susan had eaten a light meal. 'She's gone, m'am, bag and baggage and we'll all be the better for it.'

'If her work was unsatisfactory,' Susan said coldly, 'it was your place to report the matter to me.'

'That was the problem, m'am, her work couldn't be faulted. It was the disturbing effect she had on the others that was the trouble but I felt I should be able to deal with that.'

'Yes, I see your difficulty.' Susan smiled wanly. 'Now we have the problem of engaging another table-maid.'

'May I make a suggestion, m'am?'

'Of course.'

'One of the kitchen maids is a bright and intelligent girl and I believe with a little training she would prove satisfactory.'

'Very well, give the girl a chance and I imagine it is easier to replace a kitchen maid.'

'It is, m'am, and thank you.'

The day's happenings had taken a lot out of Susan and she was glad to lie back on the couch with her feet up.

She wasn't really worried but she did wonder what Edward would say. She decided she would say nothing and leave it to him. Maybe a guilty conscience would keep him silent. Anyway she was ready for him if he did comment on the change of table-maid.

The book on her lap slipped to the floor, her head nodded and soon she was sound asleep. Miss Wilson came in, picked up the book, placed it on a table then very quietly went out, closing the door gently.

Flushed and nervous to hear of her unexpected promotion to table-maid, the carrot-haired Agnes carefully followed Polly's instructions as she started to serve the food. Susan stole a glance at Edward but he showed no surprise at seeing a new maid being trained. Only when they were finishing the meal did he make mention of it.

'Why have we a new table-maid?'

Susan was saved answering by Polly coming to see if anything else was required.

'No, Polly, we're quite finished,' Susan said, putting down her napkin and getting up. Edward rose too and with his impeccable good manners waited until she was ready to precede him out of the room.

Once in their customary chairs he resorted to his habit of

placing the palms of his hands together and looking thoughtful before speaking.

'Why the change of table-maid? The other one seemed very efficient to me. Where is' – he tut-tutted – 'Whats-her-name?'

'Oh, Come! Come! Edward, you can do better than that, the girl's name can't have slipped your memory.'

'What exactly do you mean by that remark?' he asked but his eyes swerved away.

'You have no idea?'

'Where is she?'

'Dismissed.'

'On whose authority?'

'Mine of course. I am mistress of this house and the servants are my concern.'

'You mean you dismissed Mary – just like that – without any warning?'

'That's right. Aren't you going to ask the reason for her dismissal?'

'Unsatisfactory work I should imagine.'

'Not at all. Her work was well up to the expected standard.'

'Then there was no reason to dismiss her.'

Susan's self-control broke. 'No reason!' she said scornfully. 'You have the nerve to say that! Listen to me, Edward, I am well aware that there will be women in your life and I don't care just as long as it isn't someone from under the same roof. Obviously you are not very particular when you stoop to taking one of your own maids.' She was breathing heavily. 'That was despicable and if you think you have a meek and submissive wife it is time you knew otherwise.'

'Meek and submissive,' he roared. 'That is what you should be. And who are you to talk of anyone. However low I stoop it will be far short of the wrong you did me.'

What could she answer to that?

He got up and poured himself a whisky. 'Do you want anything?'

'No, thank you.'

'Of course, unwise in your condition. I should have remembered.'

He finished off his drink then went out, slamming the door behind him.

With Mary's departure Susan's relationship with Edward drifted into darker waters and she became more unhappy by the day. Her ballooning figure made her feel clumsy and unattractive and it was in this mood that she sat down to read Hannah's letter. There were pages and pages of it but with Hannah's large and well spaced writing it added up to about an average letter.

My dearest Susan,

How are you? Well, I hope and obeying instructions to take care of yourself. Knowing Edward he will see to it that you do. The gowns arrived from Miss Beattie and I am almost swooning over them. The peach-coloured, your generous gift to me, I am keeping for Matthew's wedding. It is to be a quiet affair I hear but being family I take it we are invited. You can tell Matthew I fully intend to be present anyway. Aunt Sarah, bless her, finally wore Mama down and now I have a new day dress which is quite lovely. It is a silvery grey, a colour I would never have chosen but your clever Miss Beattie was right as usual and it really does something for me. May I whisper something? The bosom, Susan, there is a definite improvement, I'm sure of it. Mama says it looks the same to her but then I'm the one who should know.

Susan giggled and wiped her eyes. What she would give to have Hannah beside her – no one could be in her company for long and remain in the doldrums. She went back to the letter.

Samuel wrote a letter to me which was little better than the thank-you note one sends to an acquaintance who has

193

provided afternoon tea. Such a pathetic effort got no reply from me I can tell you.

I'm terribly depressed, feel life is slipping by me and nothing to show for it. Do you think I would make a good nurse? I read somewhere that young ladies from very good families – one or two anyway – are training to become nurses. The need, I believe, is very great. Mama is so upset and fearful that I may do something about it that she hardly allows me out of her sight which brings me neatly to the next bit – could you bear to have me come and stay for a few days? Mama says newlyweds prefer to spend their time together and if this is the case with you then you must be honest and tell me. On the other hand if you could persuade Edward that you needed company during the day then he may be agreeable to a visit from me. Please try, dearest Susan, I really am very low.

Your affectionate and loving cousin,
Hannah

Edward had taken to spending most evenings away from home. He didn't say where he was going and she didn't ask. The only time they conversed was over dinner or for a short time in the sitting-room. Susan had Hannah's letter with her as they sat down to dinner.

'Edward, I have just had a letter from Hannah and she would like to spend a few days with us if you are agreeable.'

'Quite agreeable,' he said between bites. Then added surprisingly, 'She will be company for you.'

'Just what Hannah said.' She smiled.

He looked at her sharply, his brow drawn in a frown.

'Company during the day, Edward,' she said gently. 'She knows nothing of the circumstances.'

'Yes, well, as I said, invite her by all means.' He lapsed into silence but he was obviously deep in thought. 'Hannah's parents will be coming with her?'

'I would expect so. Very likely Uncle George and Aunt Millie will stay overnight at Aran Heights.'

194

'In that case we had better offer hospitality by having your parents and your aunt and uncle at Hillview for dinner.'

Susan was pleasantly surprised. 'That would be very nice.'

He smiled faintly. 'May I mention, my dear, that your performance in company of late has been far short of convincing.'

'I'm so sorry,' she said sarcastically, 'but I promise to make a greater effort for I am no more anxious than you to show anyone the true state of our relationship.'

The dinner party at Hillview was a pleasant occasion with everyone contributing to the conversation. Even Uncle George, so often tongue-tied, had opened up. With Mr MacFarlane he was more relaxed but then, Susan thought, her papa had mellowed since his illness and his manner was much less brusque and impatient.

'Edward,' Aunt Millie smiled to her host, 'you have a lovely home and I feel almost envious of you both with your life ahead of you.'

'Millie, that is most depressing – '

'Well, we have to face it, we are getting older – '

'I'm only too well aware of that and I don't like being reminded of it, particularly since I am some years older than you.'

'You've nothing to worry about, Aunt Sarah, you always look nice.'

'Thank you, Hannah.'

She gave a deep sigh. 'I wish I were pretty – '

'Hannah – '

'No, Susan, it's true. Appearance is very important.'

'No, it's not – ' Susan began but Edward interrupted.

'Hannah is right, looks are important and it is foolish to suggest otherwise – '

'See – '

'No, Hannah, let me finish. Looks attract but personality is just as important and you, young lady, have an abundance of that.'

Hannah blushed and looked pleased and Susan shot Edward a look of surprised approval.

*   *   *

Hannah's natural high spirits brought much-needed relief to Hillview and in the evenings Edward remained at home and teased her mercilessly but she took it in good part and gave as good as she got.

'By the way, Samuel told me he wrote to you but you didn't favour him with a reply.'

'What a nerve! What a cheek! Edward, I should have brought the letter and let you read it. Goodness knows there was nothing personal in it.'

'But you did keep it,' Susan grinned.

Hannah ignored her.

'Surely you didn't expect him to pour his heart out,' Edward teased, 'poor Samuel wouldn't know how.'

'A little encouragement from you, Hannah, may have helped.' Susan smiled.

'Edward, do tell me, please, I want to know, was Samuel really upset at not getting a reply?'

'Devastated.'

'Don't tease, just tell me,' Hannah said quietly.

Edward smiled kindly. 'Yes, Hannah, I honestly believe he was disappointed but he was at pains to hide it. Samuel may have been afraid to tell you his feelings lest he frighten you off or, worse, have you laugh at him.'

'I would never do that, laugh at him I mean.'

'You do like him, don't you?'

'Yes, Susan, that's why I was so disappointed. I thought it was just a thank-you letter for being kind to him at the wedding.'

'Then put him out of his misery and write a note from here.'

'Yes, I could do that.' She turned to Edward. 'I could hug you, you really are a pet at times.'

'No running away to be a nurse now?' Susan said softly but Edward had heard.

'What's all this about nursing?'

'Nothing,' Hannah said hurriedly, 'it was just something said in fun.' She glared at Susan.

All too soon the holiday was over and after Hannah's

departure Susan made every effort to keep the atmosphere from deteriorating to its former chilly coolness and for a while she succeeded.

On a bitterly cold day in January with the frost still thick on the ground, Matthew and Winnie were married quietly in the church where Susan and Edward had taken their vows. Only close relatives and friends, shivering in their finery, had been invited for the occasion.

In a classically simple white gown with a short veil the bride looked tall and regal and serenely happy as the minister began the ceremony. And as they were pronounced husband and wife there was a radiance about her that made her truly beautiful.

Those who had not seen Winnie since her engagement to Matthew were having difficulty in equating this handsome young woman with the gauche, plain daughter of Euan Clapperton.

During the ceremony Susan stole a sideways glance at her husband, wondering what his thoughts were. Such a short time ago they too had made their vows before God. Edward must have been conscious of her eyes on him for he gave her a faint smile before turning his attention to the minister.

The words of the service were only a background to Susan's thoughts. Would her brother's marriage turn out to be happy? First-hand knowledge of the misery and despair the other could inflict had her praying silently that these two would find happiness together. Certainly Winnie would play her part and more, and Matthew would try to be a good and faithful husband for a time at least. But in restless moments what then? Would he remember with an aching longing what might have been? Caroline so delicately beautiful with such a sparkling personality and somehow so right for Matthew, the two names linked together for so long. Her papa had approved of Caroline, recognising the strength behind all that light-hearted nonsense but Matthew's head had ruled his heart.

CHAPTER THIRTEEN

As a harsh winter eased its icy grip the snowdrops bravely heralded another spring. Soon the whole countryside would awaken to the joyous sight of young lambs frisking in the fields but Susan was uncaring. Physically and mentally she felt weighed down and longed for the relief of shedding this burden and having her body her own again. There were times, more frequent now, when she hated the life growing inside her and hated herself for thinking the thoughts she did. Far less important to her now were the remarks the baby's early arrival would bring. People would believe Edward and she had anticipated marriage – well what if they did? It made no difference.

After that first embarrassing visit she had seen the folly and the uselessness of being vague with Dr Walker, a stocky, red-faced, middle-aged man with a brisk professional manner.

That the baby's 'premature' arrival would cause ripples through their circle she was in no doubt. There would be whispers from some and raised eyebrows, heavy with disapproval, from others. She managed a grim smile as she wondered how they would cope with the stark truth – that she was not carrying her husband's child.

That night, like so many other nights, Susan was alone in the sitting-room where a cheerful log fire burned. She raised her head from her book when the unmistakable noise of the heavy front door opening reached her. She heard voices too subdued to recognise and glancing at the clock wondered who could be calling. It had gone ten, too early for Edward who would let himself in noiselessly or nearly so; he'd had a lot of practice of late.

On the point of investigating, Susan was on her feet when after a light tap on the door it opened and she looked into Matthew's chalk-white face.

'Edward! Where is he?' he asked sharply, looking about the room as if he should find him there.

Startled as well as apprehensive she shook her head. 'Edward is out, Matthew, I don't know when he'll be home.'

'Susan –' He stopped, unable to go on and she knew with a dreadful certainty what she was about to hear.

'Papa! It's Papa!' she whispered, willing him to deny it but knowing he wasn't going to.

'Susan, you've got to be brave – '

'No! No! No!' she screamed and as the noise hit the room she was conscious of Matthew beginning to move, saw his blurred figure take on a grotesque shape and as the room began to spin alarmingly her hand went out and clutched at air – then she was falling – falling – falling. The sharp edge of something, the corner of the table, digging into her had her gasping, then an agonising, hot, fierce, brutalising pain shot through her followed by a piercing scream and after that only blackness and blessed oblivion.

She drifted in and out of consciousness and through it all pain, searing agonising pain that had her gasping as it held her in its terrifying grip. A white figure, two white figures, an army of white figures floated before her eyes, a face hovered near to hers and she tried to push it away but her arms were too heavy. Something cool wiped her forehead and whispered consultations went on around the bed, then came the blessed relief of sleep. Sleep from which she never wanted to awaken.

But those monsters in their white coats were pulling her back, trying to force her awake and she was deriving a curious comfort from refusing to co-operate. She had a choice but they didn't know that. Two doors were opening for her. To enter one was to invite more pain and unhappiness and she was so tired, so dreadfully tired and too weak to fight. But the other was drawing her ever nearer and from it she could hear soft, hauntingly beautiful music. Could these be the gates of heaven opening for her? Was she dying? She felt no fear just a longing to be safe but she must hurry – if she could just reach – but it was too late. With a gentle click the gates closed and there was the sound of a door closing.

Her eyes flickered open.

'She's coming round.'

'Thank God! Oh, thank God!' That was Papa's voice but it wasn't Papa standing looking down at her. It was Edward. She moved her head from side to side, she didn't want Edward, she wanted Papa. Her mouth opened, she tried to speak but she was too weak, too weak even to keep her eyes open.

'She'll be fine now, the crisis is past.' The doctor's voice was gruff but satisfied. 'What she needs is rest, plenty of it and I'd advise you both to get the same.'

'Dr Walker is right, Edward, you should go and lie down. I'll sit with Susan for a little while then I'll go home.'

That was Mama but where was Papa? Why wasn't he here? Maybe he'd gone to the mill. She could hear Edward's reluctance to go but at last he did agree. Only when she heard the click of the door did she open her eyes.

'Mama,' she said weakly.

'Oh, my darling.' The tears were coursing down her face and her mouth was quivering. 'You've been so very ill and we've all been so terribly worried.' Susan felt the wet cheek touch her own, then fear took hold of her and her hand went to the flatness that was her stomach.

'My baby!' Her eyes were wild as she tried to struggle up. 'What have they done?'

Mrs MacFarlane and the nurse exchanged looks then the nurse got up and walked away to the other end of the room. Susan's eyes followed her every movement. She saw her bend down to lift a shawl-wrapped bundle from the cradle and carry it over to the bed. Very gently she placed the baby in its mother's arms then with a smile to Mrs MacFarlane she left the room.

'Susan, dear, you have a beautiful son, he is quite, quite perfect,' she said softly.

201

Susan's eyes melted in wonderment as she looked into the tiny, crumpled face. Gently she touched the little hand with its perfectly formed fingers and felt an indescribable rush of love. Nothing had prepared her for the fierce protectiveness she was experiencing for this tiny scrap of humanity. Her son, her own child and in those moments she vowed that no harm would ever come to this child of her flesh.

'Mama?'

'What is it, darling?'

'Papa will be so happy, he wanted a grandson and now he's got one. My son is beautiful, isn't he?' she said proudly. 'I can't wait to show him to Papa.'

Sarah gave a sob. 'Susan, oh my dear, you must remember. Matthew came to tell you. It was the shock of that and you falling that brought on the baby. Darling, we've lost Papa.'

Susan looked at her mother with rising concern. What was that she was saying? Lost! How could Papa be lost? She puckered her brow trying to concentrate but she didn't seem able to keep her mind on anything and nothing was making sense.

'You're not well, Mama, you should go and lie down. And why are you wearing black? You know Papa doesn't like you in dark colours,' she said, before dropping her gaze to the still sleeping infant. 'If only he would hurry,' she said wistfully.

Her mother mumbled something, got up, opened the door and called for the nurse.

'Take the baby back, please, nurse.'

'I'll take him now, Mrs Brodie.' She lifted the baby with practised ease and settled him in the cradle. When she returned to Susan she had a bottle and a spoon. 'A little of this and just let it slide down your throat,' she said, pouring a spoonful of the mixture.

Susan opened her mouth like an obedient child, made a face at the taste and gave a slight shudder. Soon a pleasant drowsiness washed over her and in a few minutes she drifted off to sleep.

Edward was dozing in the chair at the bedside when Susan

awoke. She was studying him dispassionately when he opened his eyes and a broad smile lit his face.

'How are you feeling, Susan?' He got up and bent over the bed to kiss her brow. He touched her hand then sat down.

'I'm fine, much better,' she said unsteadily.

She saw with surprise that he was fighting some emotion and when he spoke there was a catch in his voice.

'You've been so very ill,' he said huskily, 'and you had us all desperately worried.'

'Were you, Edward? Were you really worried?'

There were dark shadows beneath his eyes and she saw the pain in them but she didn't wish the words unsaid.

'More worried than you would believe possible.'

'There's no need to worry now.' Her voice was weary.

'Is there anything I can do for you? Anything at all you need?'

'Nothing, Edward, nothing at all. All my needs have been taken care of.'

'Then I won't tire you by talking.' He smiled. 'The mill hasn't seen me for a while but I'd better put in an appearance now.' His lips brushed her cheek, his breath fanned her face then he was gone. Tears filled her eyes and ran down her cheeks. Neither of them had mentioned the baby.

Her next visitor was Matthew. He hugged and kissed her.

'Thank God you're more like yourself. No one will know what I went through, blaming myself – '

She put out her hand and he pressed it. 'I've quite recovered.'

'You're certainly coming on. Winnie's all dewy-eyed about that babe you've produced,' he said gently, 'and as for me I feel ten feet tall being an uncle.'

'Papa wanted a grandson, Matthew.'

'Yes, I know.'

'Why doesn't he come?' The tears rolled down her cheeks.

'Susan, you are only making matters worse for yourself,' he said, looking distressed. 'Blocking it off in your mind won't bring him back.'

'Papa wouldn't leave me,' she said brokenly.

'Stop it, Susan,' he said sternly. 'Father died peacefully in his sleep. It was an easy way to go. Try to think of it that way.'

She couldn't bear it. Not to see her papa again, her beloved papa. She gulped, then Matthew was holding her and she was sobbing her heart out.

'Get it out, don't fight it, Susan. Far better to give way to your grief now.'

Exhausted but more at peace, Susan lay back on the pillows. Tears were like the rain, they helped to wash away the agony. And it was strange but in those moments when she had given in to her grief she had felt her papa very near.

'Poor Mama, she'll be so lost and lonely.'

'She's coping, Susan. Mother's a very capable woman when the need arises. Perhaps worrying about you gave her less time to think of her loss.'

'Is someone with her?'

'Winnie has been spending a lot of time at Aran Heights and Aunt Millie is there. Poor Hannah is full of the cold otherwise she would have been over but she sends her love to you and the babe.'

'Matthew, what about . . .' She faltered and her eyes closed.

'Friday at two o'clock. The mill is closing for the half day to allow as many of the workers to attend as wish.'

'They'll all turn out for Papa.'

'Yes. I wish it could have been different, Susan. I feel so guilty yet I know I would never have been a success in the mill.'

'Don't torment yourself, Papa came to realise that. None of us can alter the way we are made. You are a farmer and you are going to be a good one.'

'Yes, I mean to be a good farmer,' he said confidently. 'The trouble is, things haven't worked out as Father hoped.'

'What do you mean?'

'We talked a lot, you know, these last weeks. At first he was reluctant to discuss Edward and please don't think I am being disloyal, far from it. Edward works hard, he doesn't spare himself.'

Susan propped herself up on the pillows and tucked the sodden handkerchief underneath. 'You'd better tell me, Matthew.'

'Nothing very serious, it's only that he seems to rub the workers the wrong way and the sad fact is they haven't taken to him. Father tried to be tactful, advise him.'

'But he wouldn't listen, that's Edward all right,' she said with a touch of bitterness. 'Papa hinted something of the sort to me when he was ill that last time.' She sighed. 'Edward uses the distillery as an example of how a business should be run and as he never tires of reminding me my father-in-law's workforce is better disciplined and works the harder for it or they know they are out of employment.'

He nodded. 'The rule of fear works for some, I suppose, but Father believed in a contented workforce being more reliable and conscientious and I'd go along with that.'

'Tell me what to do, Matthew. I want to keep my promise to Papa but I'm placed in an intolerable position.'

'I can understand that. Edward should listen to you, Susan. He knows you had Father's confidence and that you are well up on the management side.' He smiled. 'Added to which you are a MacFarlane. Give the workers time to get over the shock of seeing a woman in a position of authority and I do believe you would come to be accepted.'

'Am I hearing right?'

'Difficult to accept after what I've said in the past and maybe Winnie has something to do with that. She's a woman and she's capable enough.' He paused and looked at her thoughtfully. 'Once you're stronger why not get into the mill for an hour or two, get them used to seeing you about?'

'Edward would never stand for it. He thinks it is bad enough that I work at home.'

'Well, he is your husband after all.' He shrugged. 'It's up to you but forget all that just now and concentrate on getting well. And now tell me, what name have you decided to give the wee lad? When I asked Edward he said he was leaving it to you.'

'I gave it some thought before you arrived so you are the first to hear. Paul because I like the name, MacFarlane for Papa rather than Hamish.'

'I'll keep it under my hat until Edward knows.'

'It wouldn't bother him.'

'Perhaps not. Too relieved that you came through what you did. The man was nearly out of his mind when we came so close to losing you so he is to be excused if he isn't showing too much excitement at becoming a father.'

She didn't answer, there was no answer. She smiled sadly and lay back feeling exhausted.

'Oh, dear, I've stayed too long and tired you out and here is the nurse ready to throw me out.' He got up, giving the nurse his lopsided grin.

'Sorry, nurse, I know you said just a few minutes –'

She looked at him reproachfully.

'Don't scold my brother.' Susan smiled. 'His visit has done me the world of good. And once I've had a rest I'm sure I'm well enough to get up for a while in the evening.'

'We'll see. Rest now and perhaps an hour downstairs and a walk around the room. Dr Walker isn't one for keeping his patients in bed longer than necessary.'

Friday, the day of the funeral, began cold and bright but by afternoon there was some warmth in the sun. When one o'clock struck the machinery in the Aranvale Papermill came to a grinding halt and the workers made haste to their homes to change into Sabbath suits and stiffened collars. In shambling fours they walked in silence ahead of the wreath-covered hearse drawn by black-plumed horses. A very large turnout of sombre-dressed business acquaintances joined relatives, friends and workers to follow the cortège to the cemetery.

All mourned the passing of Hamish MacFarlane but for the workers apprehension overshadowed their grief. The old master had been strict but fair and had earned their loyalty. With the son-in-law, Edward Brodie, in charge jobs that had once been secure seemed less so now. Already he was showing his hand by attempting to increase the workload of each worker, causing worry and resentment along the way.

After the funeral it was arranged that close members of the family should make their way to Hillview. The highly esteemed solicitors who handled the widow's affairs had expected the reading of the will to take place at Aran Heights but Mrs MacFarlane, on the advice of Dr Walker, had this changed to Hillview. Susan, he felt, was well enough to be up and dressed and sitting in her own drawing-room but not sufficiently recovered to venture out of doors.

Mrs MacFarlane, heavily weeded, the black accentuating her pallor, had been with Susan for much of the day supervising the arrangement of chairs and had a table brought through to the drawing-room for the convenience of the solicitor. Susan marvelled at her mother and wondered how she could have suppressed her own capabilities, but supposed women of her mother's generation would consider it an affront to their husband to do other than remain in the background.

By late afternoon they were assembled in the pleasantly furnished room with the sound of desultory conversation being carried on between folk ill at ease in the unnatural atmosphere.

Matthew and Winnie sat with Aunt Rachel between them. The old lady seemed to have aged in the last weeks and the death of her brother had affected her deeply. Edward sat on his own and Susan next to her mother.

Mr Joseph Weatherspoon's arrival put an end to the murmurings and Edward got up immediately to show the solicitor to his chair behind the table. He was a short, pompous elderly man who caused hidden irritation the way he kept rearranging the papers and taking time to polish his spectacles before replacing them on his blue-veined, bulbous nose. He cleared his throat and proceeded with the reading of the will.

Hamish MacFarlane had left his wife well provided for during her lifetime. Mrs MacFarlane turned slightly to exchange a wan smile with Susan. The droning voice went on . . .

'Aran Heights is to remain the property of my wife, Sarah, for as long as she has need of it. Thereafter it passes to my daughter Susan.'

Having known of this beforehand, Susan stole a glance at her husband. In that sombre room where emotions were kept in check she thought she detected quiet satisfaction. But then love of Aran Heights was something they shared. Edward had always expressed admiration for both the house and its commanding position.

'My son Matthew who has already received his inheritance in full is to have those of my personal possessions he cares to make his own.' There was a short pause and a rustle of paper then a noisy clearance of the throat. 'After my death the ownership of the Aranvale Papermill is to pass to my daughter, Susan. Her authority is absolute and only her decisions legally binding. No changes of any nature may be carried out in the mill without her written consent.'

Matthew's eyes sought and held his sister's and he gave an almost imperceptible nod before they both looked over to Edward. That he was taken aback and outraged was evident by the hard line of his mouth.

Hamish MacFarlane had been generous to various charities and to those who had served him faithfully, including Dr Sullivan who was to benefit by a small legacy. The only moment to lighten the proceedings had come when the solicitor made mention of Hamish's sister Rachel.

'To my dear sister, Rachel, I leave sufficient moneys in the sincere hope that she will use same to purchase for herself a carriage to replace the existing one which is, and has been for a considerable time, a danger to life and limb.'

Everyone smiled. It had been a joke for many years that Aunt Rachel, generous to a fault, had refused point blank all suggestions that she replace the shabby and dilapidated carriage which she declared would last her very well for the rest of her days. She laughed with the rest but there were tears in her eyes and Matthew put an arm around her.

* * *

With everyone gone, Susan and Edward moved from the drawing-room to the smaller sitting-room.

'Susan, since you're not retiring I think we should talk.'

'What about?'

'Your father's will surprised me.'

'In what way?'

'It would have been more convenient and sensible if he'd left the mill in our joint ownership. Still, I'll make sure you're not troubled and such papers and documents that require your signature I'll have brought to you here.'

Her blue eyes regarded him steadily. 'Edward, I think my father made his wishes very clear. Indeed he discussed the mill with me on several occasions and left me in no doubt that he wished me to take control.'

'That is absurd, the man was sick and unable to make rational judgments.'

'That happens to be untrue and I'll tell you here and now that I intend to take an active part in the running of the mill.'

'Has it escaped your memory,' he said sarcastically, 'that you have an additional responsibility?'

'No, I haven't forgotten nor am I likely to,' she said icily. 'This is the first time you've even mentioned the baby, can't you bring yourself to?' she said bitterly.

'No, I can't. And you can hardly blame me for that. Instead you should be humbly grateful that he is to have the protection of my name.'

'Oh, I am I assure you, but people are going to think it strange if you never mention the baby. Are you sufficiently interested to want to hear the names I have decided for my son?'

'Of course.'

'Paul MacFarlane – Brodie,' she said slowly and distinctly.

'Any particular reason for the choice?'

'Paul because I like the name. MacFarlane – after all that is what he is and Brodie by your gracious consent.' She felt the sweat on her brow and her hands were moist but she couldn't stop herself adding, 'One day, should the truth come out, Paul can drop the Brodie.'

'And be known for the bastard he is?'

'There are times when I wonder if it wouldn't be better.'

'You don't think that at all.'

'How cruel and uncaring you can be, Edward.'

'You are so wrong, my dear. The truth is I care for you deeply and it is because of that that I can never come to terms with what you did to me.'

'Yes, Edward, I know. If only I could turn the clock back and this marriage of ours had never taken place.'

'I don't wish that at all but I can never accept your son. In the circumstances my terms were generous as most people would agree. And you could go some way to make amends by giving me control of the mill or at the very least joint control.'

'Never! That would be breaking my promise to my father and that I won't do.'

'Who is to look after your child?'

'Who looked after you and Thomas when you were small? Certainly not your mother, she left that to trained staff just as I mean to do.'

Slowly he began pacing the floor then came to stand in front of her.

'I would work very hard to see that the mill flourishes.'

'I know you work hard, Edward and nothing would please me more than that we should work together.'

'No, that's out of the question.'

'Why?'

'Because my position would be intolerable if I need your permission, a woman's permission, for everything I do.'

'Not everything. You have a great deal of responsibility, far more than you enjoyed at the distillery and I wouldn't dream of changing that.' She paused. 'That said, I intend taking up my rightful position at the earliest possible time.'

'Then don't come running to me when things go wrong.'

'Don't worry, I'm not likely to do that and now if you'll excuse me I'll say goodnight, it's been a long and trying day.'

'Of course,' he said, suddenly all solicitude. Swiftly he was over to open the door but before doing so he gave a half smile. 'Soon you'll be well enough for my company.'

She looked uncomprehending.

'Not until Dr Walker declares you fit. I wouldn't trouble you before you were completely well. You do remember our agreement?'

'Yes, I remember.'

'Susan, I want a son.'

'Yes, I do know that, Edward, but I would like a breathing space.' Why couldn't he have waited before talking like this? she thought resentfully. The horror of her experience was still fresh and she couldn't think of another pregnancy without a shudder. She made a move but before she could escape Edward had taken her arm and guided her back to her chair before sitting down himself.

'A few more minutes won't make much difference then you can go up.'

'What is it, Edward? Why can't it wait?'

'It is important to me to have a son and heir and as quickly as possible.'

Warning bells were ringing and she looked at him sharply. 'Paul is the first-born and it is he who will inherit the mill.'

He shook his head. 'That is where you are wrong. Paul may have my name but that doesn't alter anything. He is still a bastard.'

The colour rushed to her face. 'You delight in using that word knowing how it distresses me.'

'The truth can be cruel.' Then he smiled and leaned forward. 'Later on you'll feel differently when our son is born, yours and mine, Susan.'

She got up and almost ran from the room.

Undressing quickly, Susan got below the covers and lay rigid, staring into the darkness. How could Edward possibly cheat Paul? It was her mill, she was the legal owner. What had she to fear? Yet the unease persisted. It was a man's world and the law would bend backwards to accommodate its own. Should Edward be able to show her as incompetent, unable to

NORA KAY

manage her affairs, or if the workers refused to have a woman in charge . . . Surely it would never come to that, but if it did he would have a fight on his hands. She would fight him tooth and nail. She wouldn't fail her father. According to Matthew Edward had not endeared himself to the workers and provided she was strict and as fair as her father had been she would get the same loyalty. It was a challenge and she was ready to meet it. In two weeks whether or not Dr Walker declared her fit she would make her first entrance into the mill. She liked Matthew's suggestion of an hour or two to begin with. That settled in her mind, she turned to the matter of her marital obligations. To be pleasurable that side of marriage needed love and respect and both were in short supply in her marriage. He was desperate for a son. Thinking about it now she decided to forget her fears. The sooner the better, she wanted it over.

Paul MacFarlane Brodie gave only a tiny whimper during the christening service and only when the minister took him in his arms and splashed holy water on his head did he give a howl of outrage. Throughout it all Edward was very correct and very wooden but no one appeared to notice. Paul was the centre of attention and all eyes were on him. Hannah, much to her delight, had been given the honour of carrying the baby and declared to one and all that Paul was absolutely gorgeous and she wished she could run away with him.

In the days that followed, Edward was careful to put on a convincing show as the visitors began to arrive to see the baby and leave their gifts. Both grandmothers called frequently as if they couldn't allow a day to go by without seeing this new addition to the family.

'He is absolutely adorable, Susan,' her mother-in-law enthused as she and Mrs MacFarlane joined Susan in the drawing-room.

'Such a good baby, we left him gurgling away happily,' Susan's mother added.

'No question about whom he resembles,' Lilian Brodie gushed. 'Paul's a Brodie. John was very dark when he was

212

younger with the same almost black eyes. He is very much John's grandson. You did see the resemblance too, didn't you, Sarah?'

'Well – yes – a little but there is quite a bit of Susan too. The shape – '

'Of course there is a little of Susan too,' Mrs Lilian Brodie conceded generously.

The maternal grandmother managed a smile but Susan could see that she was decidedly piqued.

CHAPTER FOURTEEN

The cold April sun shone brightly and the walk to the village then back by the farm road had put the colour in her cheeks. Not ready to go indoors Susan lingered in the gardens and then, seeing Nanny Ferguson leaving the house and wheeling the high pram, she hurried to meet them.

'Good morning,' Susan said, but her attention was on the sleeping babe. After breakfast she'd gone to the nursery and gazed at the fuzz of dark hair which covered her baby's tiny, perfect head and felt her heart swell with love and pride.

'Good morning, m'am.'

The infant stirred, his eyes flickered then closed and he settled again.

'Good as gold,' Nanny Ferguson said in her throaty voice that was at odds with the soft hazel eyes and homely face. Miss Morag Ferguson could have been any age with her round figure, ample bosom and hair beginning to show salt and pepper but Susan knew her to be only in her thirty-eighth year.

'Don't venture too far,' Susan warned with an anxious glance at the sky which had darkened.

'I won't, m'am, though there's no harm in a soft April shower and Master Paul won't get wet. There's a rain cover under the quilt if it should be needed.'

Susan was annoyed with herself, she didn't want to fuss, something she deplored in others. 'Yes, of course you're well prepared,' Susan said as she turned away.

Daffodils withered and disappeared as spring gave way to summer but Susan barely noticed. The truth was she was bored and restless. She wasn't needed, the house almost ran itself. Dr Walker, though pronouncing her fit, insisted

215

she take plenty of rest. The daily visits were unnecessary and she had annoyed him by saying so.

For something to do she went over her wardrobe with Polly. Gowns that Susan would have carelessly cast aside were quickly examined and hummed and hawed over.

'Hardly worn it is, m'am and such lovely material.'

'It's too slack.'

'That's 'cos I let out the seams. I can take them in again.'

'If I allow myself to listen to you, Polly, I'll never have anything new. All right, this once then. Take them with you to the sewing-room and if I'm satisfied I may wear them once or twice.'

Edward had a drink by his side and was reading the business news.

'I told Dr Walker that there was no need for these daily visits.'

'Wasn't that rather rude? He's been most attentive.'

'I certainly wasn't rude and he can spend more time with patients who do need him.'

'Well, I'm glad to hear that you have recovered.'

'Well enough to go into the mill for an hour or so. I want to accompany you tomorrow and have you introduce me.'

'You must be out of your mind! The answer is no, a very decided no. However, if you feel you must contribute more than your signature then I dare say I can arrange to have a little work brought here.'

'Don't be so patronising,' she snapped. 'To hear you one would imagine you owned the mill.' She took a shaky breath. 'Whether we travel together is up to you but I intend taking my place in the mill and if, as I suspect, you are already established in my father's office, then kindly vacate it and return to your own. And make no mistake, if you don't I'll take steps to have you removed.'

'As well as edging on the hysterical this is absurd,' he spluttered, the pages of his paper scattered on the floor. 'Everyone accepts me as being in charge.'

'Then the sooner they realise that you are merely standing

in for me the better.' She paused to moisten her dry lips. 'You have always been so anxious for our marriage to appear a success and our difficulties kept private but that can't go on if you are to take up this attitude.'

'More important for you I would have thought,' he sneered.

'Not any more, Edward,' Susan said quietly. 'Now that I am financially independent I can face up to the consequences of my mistake.'

'You couldn't stand the disgrace.'

'That was true when my father was alive but I could face it now.'

She hadn't intended saying that but now that she had she knew it was true.

'Very well,' he said, stumbling to his feet with his face twisted in anger. 'You can have your damned office and with you in charge we'll be facing ruin in no time.' Not bothering to pick up his newspaper he got up and halfway to the door turned. 'I'm going out, a change from your company will be more than welcome.'

'What about tomorrow?' she shouted after him. 'Do we travel together or not?'

'Go to hell.'

Susan gaped at the closed door. No one had ever sworn in her presence. Papa, she knew, had occasionally said damn but as her mother explained, that word was permissible from a man under a considerable strain.

Susan was shaking with anger. How dare he speak to her like that! She would show him, show everyone, that under her guidance the mill would go from strength to strength. It needed determination but she wasn't short of that. By putting her back into the work she could only gain the respect of the workers, for above all they wanted security of work and a living wage and who better to give them that than herself.

Her mind made up to defy Edward she went upstairs and began to look out the most suitable clothes for her first time in the mill. Being still in mourning reduced the choice. The black gowns she put aside as unsuitable and finally selected a skirt in dark grey with enough fullness to allow her freedom of movement and with it a black silk blouse.

Her anger, quick to rise, seldom lasted long and with it gone she felt a twinge of guilt. Maybe a child of Edward's would lessen the bickering which was tearing them apart and making them both miserable. She would rather like another child herself. In that mood she had even toyed with the idea of having her husband's belongings brought back to her bedroom then dismissed it. If she knew Edward he would be consoling himself with drink and the sympathetic ear of some woman. Tonight it was unlikely he would have need of her.

Morning came and Susan was keyed up. Edward overslept and she had finished breakfast before he appeared. With the maid fussing about they greeted each other civilly. She was standing dressed in cloak and bonnet and fastening her gloves but he made no remark. After a hasty breakfast he scraped back his chair and left the breakfast-room without a look in her direction. It would be undignified to follow but she could feel her lips twitching in amusement. They were both acting like children.

To pass the time before Ramsay's return Susan went along to the nursery. Paul was awake and rather timidly she bent down to take her baby in her arms. She thought he was going to protest and looked over to Nanny Ferguson in alarm.

'The wee mite won't object to a cuddle, m'am. More than likely he'll raise a rumpus when you put him down.'

Feeling the endearing warmth of the tiny body Susan cuddled him closer.

'My own precious darling,' she murmured and touched the petal-smooth cheek to her own. 'Nanny, how soon do babies recognise – I mean how soon before he knows me?' She felt foolish asking the question but Miss Ferguson only smiled kindly.

'From the very beginning, m'am, a baby knows its own mother.'

'Really?' She smiled in wonder. 'I must go,' she said handing Nanny her precious bundle.

'A proper charmer Master Paul is going to turn out.'

'I shouldn't wonder,' Susan said proudly as she left.

Nanny Ferguson watched her go then spoke to her young charge. 'Your mama loves you dearly, my pet, but as for your papa – ' She shook her head. 'Unnatural I call it, proper unnatural. Not once to my knowledge has the master come near the nursery.'

Baby Paul MacFarlane Brodie gurgled his complete indifference.

'Where to, m'am?' Ramsay asked as he helped his mistress into the carriage.

'Holmlea Farm, Ramsay, please.'

The roads were thick with dust. Everyone seemed short-tempered and she wondered if the long, dry spell was responsible.

'How long do you think this dry spell will continue?' she asked Ramsay as they approached the farm track and she asked him to stop.

'I feel a change, m'am.'

'I hope you're right. Don't wait, Ramsay, Mr MacFarlane will bring me back.'

'Very good, m'am.' He waited until she reached the gate into Holmlea Farm then he set the horses to a trot.

Susan closed the gate behind her and walked slowly along the hard, uneven path to the house. To right and left of her was a wide panoramic view of rich farmland but in the oppressive heat the countryside had a tired look. Already the shaws were drooping in the potato fields and the only splash of colour was in the hills, bright yellow with broom and touched in patches by the pale purple of heather not yet showing its full colour.

She hadn't noticed Matthew until he shouted. She waved and he waved back then, after saying something to the farmhands, he hurried over to meet his sister.

'This is a nice surprise,' he said, giving her a brotherly kiss, 'and how are you?'

'Absolutely fine, Matthew.' She smiled. 'Except for the

heat, but I have it from Ramsay that there is a change in the air.'

'Let's hope he's right.' He wiped his brow. 'It's got to break sometime.'

Holmlea was a substantial two-storey, stone-built house with no claim to splendour but since Susan's last visit a tub of flowers graced each side of the doorway. Winnie had the door open, a welcoming smile on her face.

'Susan, how lovely, come along in.'

'Just for a minute then.' She looked apologetic. 'Actually I came to see if Matthew would take me to the mill, that is if it isn't inconvenient,' she said glancing at his heavy boots and working togs.

Winnie gave a peal of laughter. 'Don't be misled by appearances. To look at him one would think he was to tackle the farmhand's job instead of just giving orders.'

'And let me tell you, my good woman, I am no stranger to manual labour,' he protested.

Susan laughed with them and felt real envy. This was how marriage should be.

'Before we say any more how is my nephew?'

'He's gorgeous, Matthew,' Susan said softly.

'And now what is this all about, Susan?'

'It can't be any surprise to you that Edward is against me setting foot in the mill and I can hardly go in by myself. I mean I'd feel a fool not knowing where to go.'

'Did you ask Edward?'

'He refused.'

'Matthew, go and change and Susan can give me all the news about little Paul.'

At the end of the recital Winnie sighed. 'I just hope you appreciate how lucky you are,' she said enviously.

'Your turn will come.'

'I hope so. It won't be for want of trying,' Winnie said without a trace of embarrassment, then saw Susan's shocked look. 'Sorry! Sorry! Sorry! We farming folk are much too outspoken but why it should embarrass you, a married woman, I don't know.'

Matthew came in soberly dressed. 'I'm ready.'

'Stay a bit longer next time,' Winnie called as Matthew had the carriage brought round.

'Oh, I shall.' She sat down beside her brother. 'I'm nervous.'

'Don't be. We'll find Mr McNeil. Father had a great respect for him and there's not much he doesn't know about the mill.'

Matthew could see that Susan was tense and kept up a flow of conversation. 'Many's the time he's covered up for me and I had reason to be grateful.'

'Edward thinks he's an old fool.'

'He's anything but that.'

Crossing the yard Matthew stopped. 'A word of brotherly advice.'

'I'm listening.'

'Edward is going out of his way to be awkward but don't be too hard on him. I have yet to meet the man who would enjoy taking orders from a woman and remember your husband has more than his share of pride.'

'But I thought you were in favour – '

'I am but you have to be careful how you go about this. The mill needs you and so does the workforce though they don't know it. Edward isn't a success, he's resented but even so they may prefer him to working for a woman.'

'Then I have to prove myself.'

'That's the spirit.'

'Matthew, I hate the way things are.' She paused and swallowed painfully, 'All I want is for us to work together but it's hopeless.'

'Things must be pretty rough for you at home.'

'Let's say they could be a lot better.'

'Don't rush things and when I think the time is right I'll have a quiet word with Edward – man to man – after all he has to accept the situation sometime. He was there at the reading of the will and Father made it clear enough that you were to be in charge.'

'You're happy, aren't you, Matthew?'

221

'Yes, Susan, I am. Winnie is right for me.'

'I envy you both.'

'Things will work out for you two and of one thing you can be sure. Edward loves you, Susan; if it isn't obvious to you it is to everyone else.'

'We'd better go in.'

The elderly man sweeping up the debris watched them cross the yard and go in to the mill. Matthew MacFarlane he recognised as the old master's son but only when they got closer did he see that the fine-looking woman was young Mistress Brodie. There had been plenty of rumours going about, some of them plain daft. Whoever heard of a slip of a lassie taking control of the likes of the Aranvale Papermill!

A clerk weighed down with ledgers murmured, 'Mornin', Mr Matthew, sir,' then flushed crimson. 'Beggin' your pardon, Mr MacFarlane, sir.'

Matthew smiled but made no remark. They walked along the corridor to where the offices were. Taking Susan's arm Matthew stopped opposite a door with a large brass plate, highly polished and bearing the late master's name. Seeing it brought a lump to Susan's throat and she could see Matthew was affected too. Matthew opened the door and Susan went in first. She walked to the centre of the room, a spacious room, and looked at the large mahogany desk placed across the length of window with a leather chair behind it. Cabinets lined the office but even so there was an overspill on the floor. There was a framed parchment on the wall and she went over to read it.

> Rags make paper
> Paper makes money
> Money makes banks
> Banks make loans
> Loans make beggars
> Beggars make rags.

Matthew came up behind her. 'Good, isn't it? It dates from the eighteenth century and Grandfather had it put on parchment. Later on it was framed. Father was very proud of it.'

Susan smiled. 'You know it reminds me of when we were children. Don't you remember Aunt Rachel having us stand on a box so that we could see the wagonloads of rags going into the mill?'

'You remember that too?'

'Of course, it was the highlight of our day. She told us about the clothes being sorted and all the buttons and fastenings being removed before they could be put in the boilers.'

'And that, my dear Susan, was known locally as the Buttony.'

'The what?' She giggled.

'It's true. The Buttony produced some high quality buttons which managed to find their way to the cottages. Father knew that it went on and he turned a blind eye but he often said that the villagers might be shabbily dressed but most of them sported a fine row of buttons.'

'I miss him terribly, Matthew.'

'I know,' he said gently, then pointed to the desk. 'Try it for size.'

'What?'

'Sit behind the desk and get the feel of your new position. I'll see if I can find Mr McNeil.'

Sitting in the chair that had once been her father's brought him very close but not in a tearful way. She had shed her tears, now she was going to do the job she had been entrusted with.

Mr McNeil was well beyond middle age with a face devoid of any healthy colour. He was a small man who held himself stiffly erect as if in defiance of his advancing years.

Susan came a little self-consciously from behind the desk and joined her brother. After the introductions Matthew said, 'My sister is to be in charge of the mill, Mr McNeil.'

'Father spoke very highly of you,' Susan said quietly.

'T'was a sad day for the mill when he went. The maister was a man among men.'

'We would be better sitting,' Matthew said, bringing three chairs together. He straddled his own and leaned forward.

'Mr McNeil, Mrs Brodie would be glad of your assistance until she gets settled.'

'A privilege, m'am.'

'As you probably know, Mr McNeil, I've been trained in financial matters but I'm completely ignorant about the rest and my husband is tied up with – with other matters.'

His blue-veined hand went to stroke his chin and his eyes were thoughtful.

'You see problems?'

'Oh, I do but 'tis better to face up to them than pretend they don't exist. The maister liked plain speaking and I'd be thinkin' a daughter of his would be like-minded?'

'Please go on.'

'There are some who thrive on causin' unrest and the ithers are like sheep – easily led.'

'I'm aware of the difficulties. Because I am a woman I am not accepted.'

'They'll be wary. To them you'll represent an ambitious young leddy with a few new-fangled ideas. But you've this to mind too, they've no choice but to accept you but it could be a grudgin' acceptance.'

'How would they show it?'

'A machine breakin' doon for no apparent reason, orders held up, that sort of thing.'

'That's not going to help them either and surely they'll give me a chance before resorting to that,' she said impatiently.

'Mebbe aye and mebbe no.'

'Working together is for our mutual benefit.'

'Give them time to get used to you.'

'Then let's hope they don't take too long about it,' she said crisply.

'Oh, I see a day when they won't just accept you. Mark my words, Mistress Brodie, they'll not only accept but respect you.'

'I can only hope that you're right and I'd like to meet those you feel I should meet.'

'Arrange a meeting, Mr McNeil. No need to give an explanation, just make sure they attend.'

He winked. 'The auld maister knew the value of involving the charge hands,' he said slyly. 'It gied them an inflated sense of their own importance and output improved because of it.'

Matthew hooted with laughter and Mr McNeil got up stiffly.

'I'll be gettin' back then but afore I go may I say how fine it is tae see that seat about to be occupied by a MacFarlane.'

'Even a female MacFarlane?' she teased.

'When she's a MacFarlane I mak' an exception.'

'Quite a character, our Mr McNeil.' Susan smiled when they were alone.

'And fiercely protective you'll find him. Even with me he was. No one knew better than Mr McNeil just how hopeless I was but heaven help anyone else who dared suggest it.'

CHAPTER FIFTEEN

'**E**dward, are you to be present?'
They had just finished the main course and Edward placed his knife and fork side by side on the plate before answering.

'No.'

'Then I'll make your apologies.'

'Do that.'

The rice pudding, browned on the top the way Edward like it, was served and when the maid had gone he shook his head as if in exasperation.

'If you would only listen to reason, Susan. I am thinking of your welfare.'

'My welfare?'

'Yes. If you insist on being in charge then it means visiting all departments and some are positively hazardous.'

She smiled. 'I do know that, Edward, and I'm assuming you mean the Beater House. My father explained to me about the boiling of the rags, the pulp being spaded into the beaters and that the floor was always awash. He likened it to a giant wash-house.'

'Well, then – '

'It's not all like that, the machine-house by contrast is clean and dry but my place is in the office. My father spent most of his time there leaving the chargehands to look after their own areas of work. And now won't you give me your support?'

'No.'

'Very well, I'll give the reason as pressure of work,' she said sweetly.

In truth Susan was relieved, knowing that his presence would only add to her nervousness.

* * *

When eleven struck Susan took her place at the head of the highly polished oval table. She looked cool and in control but her hands in her lap and out of sight were tightly clenched. The faces round the table seemed lengthened with disapproval but she told herself that could be imagination. Maybe they always looked grim and forbidding.

Somehow she had to get the right mix, show a reasonableness and at the same time assert her authority from the start.

In his slow and precise manner Mr McNeil had introduced each one by name and occupation but little of it registered. Her mind was on what she was going to say.

Mr McNeil took his place on her left but before doing so frowned deeply at the accountant, the youngest there. Faced with such beauty and poise young Mr Harper was experiencing great difficulty in keeping his mind on business. If the more mature were similarly affected they hid it behind their long faces as they sat stiffly upright in the matching brass-studded high-backed chairs.

That she made a very attractive picture in that solemn room Susan was completely unaware. Her aim had been to look neat and businesslike but the contrast between the black of her mourning and her own fair beauty was quite startling.

She took a deep breath.

'Gentlemen,' she began and wondered if that was how she should have started. 'Now that I have taken over my late father's position in the mill I wanted this opportunity to meet you.' She was glad her voice was firm and clear and paused for a moment but there was no alteration in their expressions. 'The continued prosperity of the mill depends, among other things, on a good relationship existing between management and workers. My father did not underestimate its importance and while training me for this position, stressed its value. You have that same duty to those under you.' A few heads nodded, the accountant beamed his approval.

'Changes will only be made where these are shown to be an aid to efficiency and smooth working and will in no way constitute a threat to the workers. In all matters I intend

228

to follow the example set by my father and I hope that the same loyalty you gave to him you will now extend to me.' She smiled. 'That is all, thank you.'

No one spoke as they shuffled out. Some bowed stiffly, others merely nodded and the accountant looked at her with undisguised admiration. Mr McNeil, at her request, remained behind.

She bit her lip. 'Is it always like this, Mr McNeil? Don't any of them make a comment?'

Mr McNeil looked shocked. 'If ye'll forgive me sayin' so, m'am, ye've a lot tae learn but you were fine, just fine,' he said hastily. 'What you said was enough to keep them from worrying, but Mistress Brodie, when ye want their opinion ye hae tae ask for it. That aside it's nae often the likes o' them is invited tae the boardroom, but ye'll mind it was Mr Matthew's orders.'

She smiled. 'It's a good thing I have you by my side to keep me from blundering.'

'We'd a' tae crawl afore we could walk, m'am,' he said with a twinkle in his faded blue eyes.

'Before you go, Mr McNeil, I want you to arrange for some-one – no, on second thoughts make that someone yourself – to show me the mill and each process of paper-making. In theory I know it, in practice I want to see it.'

Murdoch pursed his lips in disapproval. 'Some of it, m'am, if it's insistin' ye are, but a lot o' it is no' fit for a leddy tae enter.'

'Why should that be?'

'The stench, m'am, frae auld dirty rags and the boilin' o' them would hae ye reelin'. My ain stomach's been turned at times.'

'Mr McNeil,' Susan said severely, 'if my workers can spend whole days in such unpleasantness surely I can put up with it for a few minutes.'

'I'm nae sae sure,' he said stubbornly.

'Nevertheless, I intend going through with it. Indeed some improvements in their conditions may be possible if it is as bad as you suggest.'

After Mr McNeil had left Susan stared at the door that he had gently closed behind him and smiled with satisfaction, then she went through to her own office. There was a spring in her step as she walked to the cabinet, used her key to open it and carried the ledgers over to her desk.

She felt the thrill of ownership and a new confidence in herself. Doubts and uncertainties were now cast aside; she had inherited her father's shrewd business sense and the only risks she would consider would be those carefully calculated. A gambler took chances but she wasn't that way inclined. She would use her judgment and not be inhibited by those too unimaginative to see the long-term advantages.

Susan would never forget that first visit to the rag house. Mr McNeil had warned her but even so she was unprepared for the stench that almost stopped her breathing. Piles and piles of rags lay about the floor and on small stools women sat snipping away with scissors, the discarded buttons and fastenings falling at their feet ready to be swept up and emptied into containers. The women, most of them elderly, looked up at their visitors, their faces grey with tiredness but eyes bright with curiosity.

Hiding her shock and with physical sickness a distinct possibility, Susan left the premises quickly and Mr McNeil followed, looking at her with concern.

'Shouldnae hae let ye go in,' he muttered.

'You had no choice. Just give me a minute or two in the open and I'll be all right.' They went out to the yard and when she felt sufficiently recovered she shook her head. 'Mr McNeil, how can they stand it?'

'Fowk get used tae onythin' in time. Yon wimen mak' no complaints and if they did there's ithers ready and willin' tae tak' their place.'

'Surely a few improvements could be made without incurring too much expense?'

'Time enough when they seek it. Ye've enough on yer plate withoot lookin' for mair.'

'You could be right at that.' She paused and looked a little shamefaced. 'Regarding the other areas of the mill we needn't rush and do them all at once.'

'No, m'am.' Mr McNeil hid a smile.

The days became weeks and the weeks months, but Susan was hardly aware of the passing of time. Her days were fully occupied, her brain active as she put heart and soul into the work. No longer did Edward object to sharing transport in the mornings and at the least encouragement she discussed the day's events with him. Perhaps he was accepting the situation or at least making the best of it. Certainly she welcomed the thaw in their relations and now that they were sharing a bedroom she tried to be a loving wife. Not that he made it easy with his swift changes of mood, she thought, but would she ever understand her husband? He could be so gentle and tender and she could feel herself responding, then without warning he would change to a rough, demanding, frightening stranger and she would recoil from him.

Working in her office longer than usual, Susan looked up when Edward walked in unexpectedly and flung himself in a chair.

'You've done it now and don't say I didn't warn you.'

Annoyed at the interruption she frowned. 'Don't be tiresome, Edward. If something has happened then tell me what it is.'

'Number two machine, Dry End number two has broken down again and if we can't keep to our delivery dates we'll lose the order altogether.' He looked smug. 'If you'd paid attention in the first place and allowed me to order a replacement machine for that one and – '

She interrupted. 'Don't you find it strange, Edward, I know I do, that the machinery should break down so frequently?'

He shrugged. 'It's old but are you suggesting carelessness?'

'Or perhaps more than that,' she said carefully.

'Deliberate?' He looked thoughtful. 'Possible, I suppose, but it would be difficult to prove. Could be their way of bringing the problem to your attention. In any case,' he said impatiently, 'we can afford new machinery so why not replace it now?'

'I quite agree the machinery is old and no longer dependable and the matter has been receiving my attention.'

'Well, then, what do you intend to do?'

'Have you studied this article?' She handed him a trade magazine with a pamphlet keeping the place.

'No, I haven't. I've neither the time nor the inclination.'

'Then I suggest you stay where you are and read it. After that we can discuss the subject of new machinery.'

He gave her a dark look but settled down to read and she continued with her own work. Once she looked over at him briefly and seeing his raised eyebrows smiled to herself.

'Mmmmmm!' he said at last. 'Very impressive.'

'German-made but my father had a healthy respect for their workmanship and when their representatives were over here a year or two back they declared themselves very impressed with a design improvement our head machineman had thought out. Since then we've kept up the contact and should we decide to order we could be guaranteed a respectable discount and early delivery.'

'That may well be so, Susan, but this is a revolutionary design and even with a generous discount we still couldn't afford that kind of money. Far better to settle for a replacement, it has served us well in the past – '

She leaned forward eagerly. 'But don't you see, Edward, if we do that and our competitors go for this German invention we are going to lose out.'

'I see the possibility and getting in first would give us the edge – '

'Exactly. In time we could double our production,' she said excitedly. 'We have to act now and not miss this opportunity.'

'How do you propose to pay? Get the bank to finance it?'

She shook her head. 'The cost of borrowing is too high. No, I've worked it out and my figures have been checked by the accountant. We can manage – just.'

'Leaving nothing? Cleaned out?' he said aghast.

232

'Using my own money would let us have a small working capital.'

'Count me out, I like a bit of security at my back.'

'Quite right too,' she said briskly, 'and anyway it isn't needed.' She looked at him steadily. 'What I want, what I need is your co-operation; you can help if only you will.'

'If it is for our mutual benefit I am not likely to refuse,' he said stiffly.

'We both want what is best for the mill.'

He smiled. 'What sort of help is it you require?'

'Let the workers know that new machinery is ordered but that in the meantime we cannot afford stoppages. In fact, go as far as to tell them that their own jobs are only secure if production is kept up.'

'Quite the business woman, aren't you?' But he wasn't sneering.

'Yes, Edward, I am and I enjoy this life.' Her face softened. 'This is perhaps not the right place to announce it but we are alone so why not? I'm pregnant.'

'You are? You're absolutely sure?'

'Yes, I've seen Dr Walker.'

He got up and grasped her hand. 'When?'

'Late September.'

'You can't even begin to know what this means to me,' he said unsteadily.

'I think I do.'

'You must stop working, give all this up,' he said anxiously. 'We can't take any chances with our first-born.'

She stiffened and withdrew her hand. 'Our second,' she said coldly, 'or had you forgotten Paul?'

'He doesn't count, he isn't mine,' he said dismissively. 'This one will be a Brodie, my own flesh and blood.'

Susan gave a deep, resigned sigh. Nothing was ever going to change his attitude to Paul and quarrelling about it only set them at each other's throat.

'You must take care of yourself.'

'I shall do nothing foolish but having a baby is not an illness as every doctor is at pains to explain. It is perfectly all right

233

for me to work so stop worrying. When the time comes and I'll know when that is, then I'll cease coming to the mill and instead work from home.' She paused and looked at him steadily. 'Once the baby is born and a few weeks to regain my strength then I'm back to working in my office in the mill.'

'I appear to have no choice in the matter but at least promise me that you won't overtax your strength.'

'I can promise you that and you can reduce my workload by seeing to the ordering of this German machine.'

'Leave it to me. Heavens! I feel like celebrating.'

She laughed. 'Just keep your mind on your work. I'm not exactly throwing you out but I have a lot to do and I work better on my own.'

'Hint taken, my dear,' he said without resentment. Then, picking up the trade magazine, he sketched a salute and departed.

Susan allowed herself to sit back for a moment and her mouth curved in a gentle smile. From now on things are going to be better, she thought. Edward is thrilled at the thought of the baby and one day soon he'll forgive me and accept Paul and we can settle down to a happy life. Without warning the sun went behind a cloud, darkening the window and some of her optimism vanished. Wishful thinking was all she was engaged in. Forgiveness for her perhaps but what chance had Paul of ever being accepted?

Shortly after Paul had celebrated his first birthday with a nursery tea-party Winnie gave birth to a son, whom she called Duncan. Such excitement that followed had never before been witnessed at Moorend. Matthew's own delight was enormous but Euan Clapperton could not contain his joy, his face was suffused with it. The farm manager right down to the most humble of the farmhands were sent to the huge kitchen at Moorend for a wee dram to drink the health of his grandson.

Susan was having a trouble-free pregnancy and only gave up

going into the mill when her condition could no longer be disguised. Throughout the months Edward had been quietly attentive to her needs and when she was at home he took time to discuss the day's happenings, knowing how much it pleased her. The order for the new machinery had been confirmed, its transport arranged and sooner than expected was in position in the Aranvale Papermill and working perfectly. In the weeks and months that followed efficiency was much improved with the workers taking a pride in the latest machinery. Delivery dates were cut, resulting in an upsurge in new orders and this in turn meant engaging more workers.

The benefits filtered through to the village with the shops doing more business and the public houses doing even better. If Susan did not receive the credit she was due, at least she was accepted as being no longer a threat.

On a mild September morning Susan's daughter was born and all she could feel was an overwhelming disappointment. She had been so sure it would be a boy. But if Edward wanted a son, he was delighted when he looked at the tiny rosebud mouth and the fan of thick lashes that lifted from eyes that stared into his own. He drew in his breath, almost ashamed of the rush of tenderness which filled his heart.

'I'm sorry, Edward,' she whispered.

'Whatever for?'

'You wanted a son so much,' she said, tears of weakness spilling over.

Bending over her he took up her hand and kissed it. 'Don't upset yourself, darling. She's lovely, absolutely beautiful, our little daughter. Thank you, Susan.'

She felt a sudden rush of love and clutched at his hand. 'I love you, Edward, and next time I promise you a son.'

'That is the first time you have ever said that to me, Susan.' He was about to say more but the doctor came in.

'Mr Brodie, your wife needs a rest after all that hard work so I must ask you to leave.'

He seemed reluctant to go and stopped beside the baby's cot.

'She's a little beauty, isn't she?' he said, gazing adoringly at the tiny face peeping out from the snowy white covers.

'Quite perfect,' Dr Walker agreed in a voice that suggested he was taking full credit.

From that first peep at his daughter Edward was besotted and visited the nursery each day. As with Paul both grandmothers were frequent visitors.

'Such a lovely name, Susan,' her mother-in-law said. 'Who decided on Victoria?'

'Edward did and we both decided Lilian for her second name.'

'I'm very honoured.'

Victoria Lilian Brodie, according to Mrs MacFarlane, was just like Susan at that age except that Victoria's hair was turning to a reddish blonde.

'Yes, Sarah,' Lilian Brodie agreed, 'this one is a MacFarlane, no doubt about that. She's going to be a beauty like her mother and her grandmother.'

Sarah demurred but blushed with pleasure at the compliment.

'Paul, now,' Mrs Lilian Brodie continued, her hand on the banister as they came slowly downstairs from the nursery, 'is getting more like John each time I see him. John doesn't see it but he's very proud just the same.'

'Paul's adorable.'

'He is and you're so lucky,' she said turning to Susan. 'It's such a pity Thomas doesn't have a son, that's three girls and a miscarriage and Elizabeth seems disinclined to have more.'

'And who could blame her,' Susan said, feeling real sympathy for the unfortunate Elizabeth. 'After going through all that it's hardly surprising.'

'Oh, one quickly forgets all that,' her mother-in-law said with a wave of a plump hand, then added with a knowing smile, 'I don't imagine she'll have too much say in the matter.'

Back at the mill work had been accumulating in her absence and Susan was kept busy getting up to date. Edward got through a power of work and his manner when dealing with employees had improved of late. Victoria's arrival seemed to have mellowed him and relations were much better with the foremen and managers.

Each day without fail Edward paid a visit to the nursery and lifting up his daughter he had her squealing and gurgling with delight as he played with her but the dark-eyed toddler who looked on silently was totally ignored. Once Paul had ventured a hand on Edward's leg but the cold look he received had him running back to Nanny Ferguson, his lips trembling as he buried his head in her lap. Miss Ferguson cuddled him and her lips tightened in anger as she led her darling charge away. There was something far wrong when a father treated his little son like that and drooled over his daughter. She vowed there and then to have a word with the mistress and risk the consequences.

'Yes, of course, Miss Ferguson, I've time to see you,' Susan said, inviting her to be seated.

'It's about Master Paul,' she began nervously.

A cold hand touched Susan. 'There's nothing wrong? Paul isn't unwell, is he?'

'No! No! He's in good health.'

'Then what is it? I don't imagine Paul causes you too much trouble?' she said with a smile, wondering what this was all about.

'None at all, m'am.' Miss Ferguson bit her lip. 'It's just that Master Paul, young though he is, he's sensitive . . .'

'Yes?' Susan prodded.

'If you will excuse plain speaking, m'am, the way the master ignores his son and makes such a fuss of Miss Victoria, well, m'am, that can be real harmful, especially to a sensitive child.'

'I see,' Susan said slowly. 'It was good of you to bring this to my attention and I'll have a word with my husband. I can assure you it is unintentional. You don't seem to understand, Miss Ferguson, that some fathers make a fuss of their daughters but feel it is bad to lavish too much attention on a son.'

'Then it's wrong, m'am, that's all I can say,' Miss Ferguson said spiritedly. 'Maybe when they are older that may apply though I am not so sure it does but when they are small it is cruel.' She paused and looked at her mistress, knowing she had gone too far but unable to stop herself. 'Children should be treated alike and that way they feel equally loved.'

How very true, Susan thought, her mind going back to her own childhood. Miss Ferguson knew what she was talking about, but even so she had to be loyal to Edward and show Nanny that she was overstepping the mark.

She drew herself up, her back straight and looked like her mother at her most disapproving.

'That is quite enough, Miss Ferguson,' she said sharply. She stood up to show the interview was at an end and Miss Ferguson got up, her face flushed and alarmed.

'I'm very sorry, m'am, no disrespect intended I assure you.'

'Very well, I accept that you have the interest of your charge at heart and will overlook your outspokenness this time.'

'Thank you, m'am.' She gave a bob and all but fled from the room.

After she had gone, Susan sat on, thoughtful and deeply worried. There was cause for anxiety, of that she was certain. It had taken a lot of courage on Miss Ferguson's part to speak out. Surely if Edward was made to realise the seriousness of his callous treatment of Paul he wouldn't continue to ignore him. Tonight she would tell him of Miss Ferguson's fears, plead with him if necessary but surely it wouldn't come to that.

'I enjoyed that, it was delicious,' Susan said, touching her lips with the napkin and looking down the length of the table to her husband.

'Mmmm. Very nice but for myself I prefer the meat less well done.'

After finishing the meal they went through to the sitting-room where a recent addition of fresh logs had the fire spluttering and crackling.

'Shall I put up the guard?' Edward asked.

'No, it hides the fire and I think it's settling.' She waited until he had poured himself a drink and taken his usual chair. 'Nanny, Miss Ferguson, came to see me.'

'About what?'

'About Paul.'

Deliberately he put down his glass and reached for the newspaper.

'She's very worried about your – your indifference to Paul and its damaging effect in later years. Before Victoria was born you never went near the nursery.'

'Are you objecting to my visits there?'

'Of course not, quite the opposite. It's just that you make such a fuss of Victoria and Paul is bewildered – he's just a little boy and he cannot understand – ' She stopped.

'Have you quite finished?'

'Edward, please – please don't do this to Paul.'

'Your memory can be conveniently short when it suits you.'

'But –' she said desperately.

'No. Do I have to repeat it again?'

'No, you don't, I remember it very well including the rest.'

'The rest? What rest?'

'Once I give you a son you will have no further use for me.'

'That was said in anger.' He managed a smile. 'That side of our marriage is perfectly satisfactory.'

'Then I hope from our union that I am already with a child and pray to God that it will be a boy. Then, Edward, we can live our separate lives and I no longer will have to feign pleasure from your advances.'

It was cruel and not altogether true but it had gone home. His face was a dull red. 'Indeed you won't for I shall look elsewhere for my pleasures.'

Her lips curled. 'Before we were married you had women and you still have. I imagine that the only difference will be that you'll take a mistress instead of spreading your favours.'

'How dare you speak to me like that!' He looked on the point of springing at her but she knew he wouldn't and she didn't flinch.

'The truth can be cruel as we both know.'

He took up his paper but whether to read or hide his anger she could not tell. Her own book was open but not to read. It was something to occupy her hands while she stared at its pages. She knew only too well that the fragile improvement in their relationship was smashed beyond repair. Too much had been said, too much bitterness existed between them. But that was unimportant compared to Paul's happiness. The innocent must not suffer. Yet she was not without blame; the mill had been claiming more and more of her time and energy but it should be possible to change that now. Business was good and the order book healthy – she'd achieved more than she had dared hope. It was time to delegate some of her work on to others and two of the senior clerks, one in particular, had impressed her. Yes, she could and would rearrange her day so that more of it could be spent with her children. She would make more visits to Holmlea. Little Paul adored his Uncle Matthew's farm and shrieked with joy when Matthew carried him shoulder high to see the animals.

Edward was still reading when Susan looked across but now as she turned the pages of the book the words made sense. Her immediate problems were partly solved, at least for the time being. For what remained of the evening the only sounds were the ticking of the clock, the occasional movement of logs settling to a new position and the turning of the page.

CHAPTER SIXTEEN

That winter there was no snow until after Hogmanay and then a darkening sky let loose a fluttering of snow to cover the hills like a feather pillow. In the middle of January a storm lashed the west coast, sending boats scuttling for shelter and the full force of its fury was felt as far inland as Aranvale. Some said its like hadn't been experienced since January 1885.

Impossible though it seemed, by morning the storm had spent itself and in the uneasy calm that followed folk ventured out to see the extent of the damage and assess the cost.

Edward was in his heavy outdoor clothes when Susan met him in the hall.

'I've just been out to check,' he said, blowing on his hands, 'but apart from a few broken slates lying about and a bit of devastation in the garden we appear to have escaped. Comes from being so low-lying.'

'Yes, it must have helped and we must be thankful. I've never heard anything like it. Never!' she said, giving a shudder.

'You were terrified.' Their glances met.

'Yes, I was,' she admitted, then remembering how she had clung to him during the worst of the storm she turned away and spoke too quickly. 'The children – I've seen Nanny Ferguson and they both slept through it. Unbelievable isn't it?'

'Children sleep through anything, I suppose. Take my tip, Susan, and stay indoors today anyway; a rest won't do you any harm.'

It was a change to feel protected and rather nice she had to admit. Though she could quite easily have accompanied him, she decided against it.

'I'll take your advice.'

'That's a change.' But he was smiling. 'I'll deal with anything urgent.'

'Thank you and remember if you are busy get Mr Lamond to assist; he is proving very dependable.' She laughed at his look of disbelief. 'I'm learning to delegate.'

'And not before time.' He hesitated.

'What is it, Edward?'

'To put your mind at rest I'll call in at Aran Heights and then see Matthew before going on to the mill.'

'I'd be grateful but don't forget Croft House – your parents.'

'No, I won't but I'm not going to get much done at the mill, am I?'

'Never mind that, it can wait. To be honest I am anxious about Mama being on her own. A storm like that gets her in a bit of a panic.'

'Like most women.'

She smiled at him with genuine tenderness and before he left she turned her cheek for his kiss, the first in a very long time.

Edward was a strange mixture. Would she ever understand her husband? For weeks hardly an unnecessary word had been exchanged yet here he was putting himself out for her. Matthew would be busy enough with the animals to settle and maybe unable to get to Aran Heights until later. Edward would see that her mother was all right and of course Mrs Dunbar was there.

She spent longer with the children but Nanny Ferguson had her routine and she was upsetting it. What was there to do? How empty her life would be without the mill.

Miss Wilson approached her. 'Good morning, m'am. I'm afraid we're short-staffed, two of the maids haven't arrived yet.'

'After such a night it's hardly surprising. Have you heard if there is much damage in the village?'

'Ramsay says a fair bit but it's mainly slates and the like.'

'Bad enough if it lets in the rain and there'll be a lot of

clearing up to do.' She paused. 'Miss Wilson, keep work to a minimum today and tell Mrs Carson a simple, easily prepared meal will do very well.'

'I'll do that and thank you, m'am.'

Susan watched her departure and thought back to Miss Wilson's appointment as housekeeper. Then she had lacked confidence but then so had she. They had both grown together and Miss Wilson had proved her worth. She was good with the staff, not over-friendly and not over-strict. There was a pleasant atmosphere and at least on the domestic front she wasn't troubled by conflict. Not since the departure of that slut Mary.

By evening she was looking forward to Edward's return and when he appeared she had to hold herself back from bombarding him with questions.

'Well, tell me,' she said impatiently.

'The roof of the cutting-house is damaged.'

'Badly?'

'A gaping hole but it was all hands on deck, everybody got stuck in to see it rainproof and it should hold until the job can be properly done.'

'Excuse me, m'am, the meal is ready to be served.'

'Thank you.'

Susan kept the rest of her questions until they were seated and the first course served.

'We must get someone on to it as quickly as possible.'

'Don't worry about it,' he said, picking up his cutlery, 'the mill will get priority. And now for the rest of the news.' He swallowed a mouthful of food and had the next prepared on his fork. 'Someone must have been very concerned about your mother. Euan Clapperton was a very early visitor, I just missed him.'

Susan smiled. 'That comes as no surprise, Mr Clapperton is very attentive to Mama. You found her quite well then?'

'Oh, she made the most of it, you know your mother. She said she was petrified but Mrs Dunbar left her own room to sit with her. Needless to say your mother had the comfort of her bed and Mrs Dunbar was huddled in a chair wrapped in a blanket.'

Susan giggled. She could picture the scene. 'Good, she's all right then?'

'Quite perky and oh, before I forget, your mother is paying you a visit tomorrow.'

'Coming here you mean? When?'

'Late afternoon and she expects you to be here and not in the mill.'

'Of course I'll be here when I know she's coming. My mother can be the limit. A social visit or is it something more?'

'Haven't the foggiest.'

'Did you manage to see Matthew and Winnie?'

'I did and there is quite a trail of damage. Matthew was doing some clearing up and using some very colourful language.'

'Mama wouldn't need to hear him. Is the damage really bad?'

'Winnie says it is nothing like as bad as your brother is trying to make out. She is very matter-of-fact and as she so rightly says the buildings can be repaired and she is just thankful that the livestock escaped injury though they could hear the animals whimpering with fright.'

Mrs Sarah MacFarlane arrived at Hillview in a cloud of lavender perfume, a little overdone Susan thought. Greeting each other she got a strong whiff. After seeing her mother comfortably settled in the sitting-room Susan rang the bell, the signal for tea.

'This is a lovely surprise, Mama.'

'Hardly a surprise, I told Edward to tell you I was coming.'

'Oh, he did.' Susan smiled. 'I don't recall seeing that gown before and that shade of dull rose is very becoming to you.'

'Thank you, my dear, and no, you won't have seen it. After so long in black I felt the need of something new and Miss Beattie suggested this as being pretty and not too bright.'

244

She's on edge, Susan thought, watching the nervous movements.

'Mama, what is it? Is it something you have to tell me?'

'Is it so patently obvious?' she said turning pink then, recovering, pointed to the tray which had just arrived moments earlier. 'That tea will be getting cold and you know how I dislike tea that isn't fresh. Are you pouring or am I?'

'Sorry, I'll pour.'

Nothing more was said until Mrs MacFarlane was nibbling at a biscuit and sipping at the tea. At last she put down the cup and leaned back.

'You must be honest with me, Susan. Should I decide to remarry would it distress you?'

'Mr Clapperton – '

'Yes,' she said, colouring like a young girl. 'Euan has proposed and I have promised him his answer just as soon as I have your approval and Matthew's.'

'Mama,' Susan said gently, 'you don't need our approval – ' Then seeing her mother's face hastened in with, 'I mean of course you have my approval. You are entitled to your happiness and it is not as though you are going off with a stranger.'

'Well, I'm glad that is over. This has been quite an ordeal for me. You and your papa were so close and I didn't want you to – to – it's no disrespect to your father's memory.' Her voice faltered and Susan got up to give her a warm hug.

'Papa would want you to be happy so don't feel guilty.'

'There are some who won't be so generous.'

'Does it matter?'

'No, it doesn't,' she said firmly. 'I won't let it.'

'That's the spirit and I assure you Matthew won't object.'

'No.' She laughed. 'In fact he and Winnie were getting quite hilarious about the complicated relationship. Cheeky too! Says he can stand me as a mother but is less certain how I'll measure up as a mother-in-law. Until he mentioned it I hadn't considered the complication.'

'Didn't occur to me either but now that I think about it it is amusing. When is the big day?'

245

'It won't be, it'll be very quiet and quite soon.' Her delicate eyebrows shot up. 'What is the point of delaying at our time of life? We are both lonely and last night's storm – well, that's when he asked me.' She blushed. 'Tina told me it was all she could do to keep her brother from going out at the height of the storm to see if I was all right.'

'Oh, Miss Clapperton, I had forgotten about her. Isn't this going to put her nose out of joint, you becoming the mistress of Moorend?'

'Susan,' her mother reprimanded, 'that was a most unlady-like expression.' She sniffed. 'No doubt being a business woman you think it acceptable but I can assure you it is not.'

'I apologise,' Susan murmured, trying to keep her face straight, 'but you haven't answered my question.'

'Tina is not in the least put out, she made that very clear to me. There is a vacant cottage in the village and Euan means to buy it for her. It is walking distance from Moorend and she is quite looking forward to settling down in a house of her own.'

'Then our approval was anticipated?' Susan teased.

'Euan foresaw no problem,' she said tartly, 'and now to the piece that concerns you. Once I move to Moorend Aran Heights becomes yours, you hadn't forgotten had you?'

Susan's face paled then flushed and her eyes were bright. 'I hadn't thought – hadn't realised – but it's true, isn't it?' she stammered. 'Aran Heights will be mine,' she said wonderingly. 'Mama, how can you bear to leave it?'

'Very easily.' She gave a short laugh. 'That big barn of a house! And don't look so shocked. All those years I put on an act, a convincing one and your father never suspected. Aran Heights never meant to me what it did to your papa and you. My dear, you are very welcome to it.'

Susan's eyes misted. She was going back to Aran Heights but different this time. It was to be hers. Her children would grow up in it and perhaps one day another son or daughter

246

would be born there. Aware suddenly that her mother was watching her Susan gave an embarrassed laugh. 'I'm sorry, I'm just so thrilled.'

'And I'm happy for you. You've never liked Hillview, I've known that.'

'Because my heart was in Aran Heights. You think I am being ridiculous about a house, don't you?'

'No, you are a bit of a romantic. How will Edward take the news?'

'He'll be delighted.'

'We should discuss the furniture.' She made a face. 'As you can imagine everything will have to go at Moorend. Tina will take what she wants, Winnie too and the rest can be disposed of.'

'You'll be able to furnish Moorend from Aran Heights.'

'Some of it,' she said carelessly. 'I rather fancy buying new.'

'And I think Mr Clapperton will give you anything you set your heart on.'

'And why not? The money is there and Euan has prepared himself for my expensive tastes.' She needled her brow in thought. 'There was something else I had to tell you, now what was it?' Her face brightened. 'How could I have forgotten that?'

'Forgotten what?'

'Hannah and Samuel have announced their engagement and your Aunt Millie said in her letter that Hannah would be writing to you herself.'

'That's lovely news. I'm really delighted and I think they are perfectly matched. She will bring Samuel out of his shell and he'll have a restraining influence on her. You're pleased too, aren't you?'

'Very pleased. Samuel has a good family background and though he is a strange young man – '

'He isn't, Mama, not when you get to know him. He's shy, that's all. Is it to be a long engagement?'

Mrs MacFarlane drained the rest of her tea but declined another cup.

'I don't think so but there is no date fixed as yet.'
She got up.

'You're not going so soon?'

'I must, but a few minutes with my grandchildren first.'

Susan was humming under her breath when Edward breezed
in.

'Someone is happy by the sound of it.'

'I am, I've got marvellous news.'

'So have I. You'll never guess but our Samuel has proposed to Hannah, or come to think about it it may have
been the other way round; anyway they've got themselves
engaged.'

'I know.'

'Oh!' he said deflated.

'Mama told me.'

'So what is your news?'

'My mother and Mr Clapperton are to be married.'

'That comes as no surprise, I thought there was something
in the wind.'

'You do realise what it means?'

'I suppose you'll be gaining a stepfather and God knows
what it makes Matthew.'

'It means, Edward, that Mama will be going to live at
Moorend.'

'And Aran Heights becomes ours or should I say yours?'

'Ours, Edward, and I'm so happy I could cry. You won't
mind leaving Hillview will you?'

'Not in the least. Hillview has served its purpose but it is
a doll's house compared to Aran Heights.'

'Oh, come, that's a bit strong.'

'A good time, Susan, the house market is buoyant and it
should be possible to get a good price for Hillview.'

Six weeks later there was a small gathering at the church.
Susan sat with Edward in one of the front pews along with
close relatives to witness the joining of Sarah MacFarlane
and Euan Clapperton in marriage. It had been a unanimous

decision that the children should have a tea-party at home with Nanny Ferguson.

Before the actual marriage it had been easy to give her blessing but now as they stood before the minister Susan could only feel sadness and resentment. How could she? How could her mother marry this burly man who had suddenly become an intruder? The light glinted off the stained-glass windows and tears pricked at the back of her eyes, forcing her to blink fiercely. She could feel Edward's eyes on her and she turned to smile but it was a poor effort.

'What's the matter?' he whispered.

'N-nothing, I was just thinking about Papa.'

After the ceremony the new Mrs Clapperton looked serenely happy and Euan Clapperton, nervous throughout the service, smiled as if he had come through an ordeal and was now ready to claim his prize.

Carriages took the guests the three miles to the recently opened Burnbank Hotel where a splendid meal awaited them. There was only one absentee from the family. Aunt Rachel had given no excuse for declining the invitation, instead writing a note to Susan wishing her niece and family every happiness at Aran Heights.

Knowing how devoted Aunt Rachel was to her brother, Susan could readily understand her feelings, her own were similar, but even so she wished her aunt could have forced herself to put in an appearance even for a short time. Though her mother would never admit it she must have felt hurt at the slight.

When Hillview reached the market it attracted a large number of prospective buyers and Miss Wilson was kept busy showing the various interested parties around the house then, something Susan had insisted on, leaving them the freedom to walk about the gardens at their leisure. She apologised for the additional work but Miss Wilson dismissed it.

'M'am, I am only too happy to assist. It is such a relief to know that I am to work at Aran Heights. I've been very worried.'

'Then I do apologise and indeed I would have been greatly distressed had you not been prepared to come.' She smiled. 'You thought Mrs Dunbar would be staying – '

'Yes, I did.'

Susan shook her head emphatically. 'My mother couldn't do without Mrs Dunbar.'

Polly passed by with an armful of linen and when she was out of earshot Susan said, 'Polly was at Aran Heights and appears quite excited at the prospect of returning.

'Yes, she is, she has told us.' Miss Wilson spoke with the weary air of someone who had heard it all too often.

'Susan? Where are you, Susan?' Edward called out as he hung his coat on the hallstand.

'I'm here,' she said, appearing at his side.

'In here,' he said, leading her through to the sitting-room and closing the door.

'Whatever it is it must be good by the look on your face.'

'I've made a substantial profit on the sale of Hillview.'

She noted the 'I' but smiled. 'Glad to hear it.'

'The joy of an unexpected windfall, we timed it beautifully.'

'What do you propose doing with it?'

'Banking it of course. Why? Have you any suggestions?'

'Well, it is found money, Edward. I'd be inclined to have a little flutter, buy shares, study the stock market, have a little excitement.'

'And risk losing it? Certainly not, I like security.'

'So do I and it's true you could lose. But on the other hand you could also gain substantially.'

'It's going in the bank until I find something without a risk and a guaranteed return.'

'Unfortunately there's no such investment.' She laughed.

Later Edward was to wish he had taken Susan's advice but then no one could have guessed . . .

The west of Scotland was bathed in sunshine when Mr Euan Clapperton, smart in a grey suit, and his wife, dressed in a dark blue travelling habit and matching bonnet, took

250

themselves off to the Lake District for two weeks to escape the workmen.

Moorend had never seen such an upheaval; dust was everywhere. There were alterations, redecorating, the laying of carpets and the movement of furniture. Servants deplored the rate of progress and itched for them to finish so that they could climb up the ladders to hang the curtains. Mrs Dunbar, with so much responsibility placed upon her, grew ever more worried and excited. She began giving orders and contradicting them in the same breath. Panic developed when after ten days instead of the arranged fourteen the master and new mistress of Moorend arrived at the farmhouse.

Mrs Dunbar apologised profusely for what was in no way her fault and the new mistress of Moorend graciously accepted her apologies. Apparently torrential rain for much of their stay in the Lake District had eventually dampened their enthusiasm for sightseeing and shortened their honeymoon.

An amused Matthew and Winnie came to the rescue and the honeymooners spent the next three days at Holmlea.

Much less traumatic was the move from Hillview to Aran Heights. All that Susan decided to take was the furniture gifted by her parents and of course the other wedding presents. The new owners had shown a cautious interest in the remaining furniture and furnishings and Susan, anxious that they got it cheaply, reminded Edward that they had no use for it. After a show of reluctance Edward let it go at what he thought a ridiculously low figure.

The children's voices were high with excitement as they charged about the house they still thought of as Grandmama's.

'Mama, am I getting Uncle Matt's bedroom?' Paul asked, pink with pleasure.

'Yes, dear, and I really think now that you are a big boy that you should start saying Uncle Matthew.'

'Uncle Matthew,' Paul repeated, 'all right.'

'Yes.' Susan smiled, delighted at his enthusiasm. And Victoria will get the one I had when I was a little girl.

251

Long used as a storeroom the schoolroom was to revert back to its original use. Her plans she would discuss with Edward but with or without his approval she would go ahead. Then she stood still and pondered the change in herself, some of it not to her liking. It was one thing to be a business woman but was it at the expense of her femininity? She was so used to making decisions in the mill and now she was doing the same at home. Then she shrugged and gave a satisfied smile. No, she hadn't lost her femininity, she told herself, she still had the assurance that sprang from seeing desire in the eyes of men at those functions and dinner parties she attended with Edward. She was woman enough to get a glow of pleasure not only from that but from Edward's obvious pride in her appearance.

People changed, circumstances altered but Aran Heights alone defied time and the elements. Looking down from the top of the stone steps her eyes roved the scene. Summer brought a pastoral and gentle beauty filled with tranquillity. Pinks and mauves spilled forth from the magnificent rhododendron bushes and beds and beds of roses flowered for the second or third time.

In this house I grew up and now my children will enjoy it and for the rest of my life it is to be my home. Susan hugged the thought as she went indoors and up to the library, the room that drew her as no other did. As a rebellious child she remembered the atmosphere portentous with brewing storms, her papa's stern warnings when she had gone too far. Then he had seemed huge and terrifying as she suffered the harsh rasp of his voice. Suitably cowed she had promised tearfully to behave herself and give her mama less trouble and before dismissing her he had patted her on the head as if to take some of the sting out of his words.

The library looked strangely naked and on an impulse she sat down in her father's chair and surveyed the room. Her own desk, the instrument of her changing fortunes, was back in its position and for a fleeting moment she pictured someone else there. Where was he now? That young man she had once loved and whose son would one day inherit the mill and Aran

252

Heights. Had he prospered? She would never know. She came out of her daydream and gave a small shiver. In Paul, the growing boy, she was seeing the resemblance to David Cameron becoming more pronounced and it was disturbing.

How impressed David had been with the shelves and shelves of books; she remembered the longing in his face. Her father had been an avid reader and she had shared his love of books. Paul was going to be the same, she was sure of that.

In the hall the grandfather clock chimed the hour and she rose to go, closing the door quietly behind her.

CHAPTER SEVENTEEN

T here was a breath of spring in the air when Susan gave birth to her second son but it was a false spring, one that occasionally comes in February or early March, raising the spirits but cheating the land so that the buds begin to sprout then blacken and be killed off when the severe frosts return.

Paul was almost seven, a tall nice-looking boy though too serious for his years. His sister Victoria was a bouncy, precocious child with a mop of reddish fair curls and given to temper tantrums when she didn't get her own way.

For much of the time with this pregnancy Susan had felt unwell but with Dr Walker assuring her that there was nothing to worry about she had tried to keep as much as possible to routine, spending a few hours most days at her office in the mill.

As if to make up for it the birth itself was easy, so easy that Susan couldn't believe it was over. But the baby was small and frail with barely enough strength to suck milk and when his birth weight dropped alarmingly it was feared he would not live.

Edward had been anguished.

'Why?' he demanded of the doctor. 'Why is he like this when my daughter was – ' He broke off and looked at the doctor then the nurse but she turned away.

'Both your children,' the doctor corrected him, 'were healthy babies. No one can say why it happens this way but in many families there is one child weaker than the others.'

In bed a few feet away from them Susan listened and could only feel guilt as she heard the rise and fall of their voices. Edward had been over the moon when told he had a son but that had quickly turned to disbelief verging on anger when he gazed upon the pitifully weak infant with his fragile hold on life.

Susan put out her hand and he came over. 'Edward, our son is going to be fine, all he needs is careful nursing and he'll get that.' Her blue eyes were soft and appealing and he nodded, forcing a smile.

'Yes, he'll get that.' Then added softly, 'If it's enough.'

'Don't think like that, Edward, I'm not, I'm going to will my baby to live and you must too.'

'That's the spirit, Mrs Brodie,' Dr Walker said approvingly. 'I've seen some underweight babies thrive against all the odds.' He went off and beckoned to the nurse to follow, leaving Susan and Edward alone.

'We should get the baby baptised as soon as possible,' she said quietly, nervously plucking at the bedcover.

'Yes.'

'The name we chose – ' She hesitated. 'John after your father?'

His face twisted in pain. 'No, I don't want him called John. Had he been – ' He left the rest unsaid.

'Then what name, Edward?'

He looked at her bleakly. 'You said you liked James.'

'I do.'

'Then call him that,' he said, getting up. 'You'd better get some rest.'

'I'm all right,' she said tonelessly, wanting him to stay but knowing he wouldn't.

James did live though he wailed plaintively, causing consternation to those around. Susan had arranged for the nurse to stay on in order that the baby should have special care. Both grandmothers called but they were subdued, neither rushing to claim a family resemblance with this one.

Gradually though, James began to take a little interest in his surroundings and in those early weeks Susan spent a lot of time with her baby, nursing and cuddling him as she had never done with Paul and Victoria. Eagerly she watched for some improvement and when it came she took a personal pride in each small achievement.

'He is coming on, Nurse?'

'His progress, m'am, is what one expects in any underweight baby. Each stage is slow and you must accept that.'

'Oh, I do, but surely now that he is feeding well and gaining in weight he'll come on?' she said anxiously.

'Perhaps,' she said, but without conviction. The nurse, brisk and efficient, did not believe in raising false hopes, rather she was of the firm opinion that parents were better equipped to deal with a situation if they understood it.

Susan was aware of this and gave a sad little smile.

'I'm not looking for miracles, Nurse, but that doesn't mean I'm not hoping. Compared to my other children Master James is backward but as long as he is happy and contented.'

'That is the best attitude to take,' the nurse said approvingly, as with a slight nod she disappeared with the baby in her arms.

James was painfully slow in every way but Susan wouldn't go beyond admitting that James was backward and was angered when Edward hinted that their son was more than backward, that he was severely mentally retarded. One day she had come on him in the summer house sitting on a low chair, his elbows on his knees and his head in his hands. Her heart went out to him in his silent agony but their relationship was such that no words of hers would give comfort.

Edward continued his visits to the nursery but James was not responsive and when he began whimpering Edward would turn to Victoria and scoop her up in his arms until she was squealing with delight. Paul, used to being ignored, would go over to the cot and comfort James in his childish way. He was fiercely protective of his little brother and James seemed to settle when Paul was near.

One morning on the way to her own bedroom Susan heard the sound of quarrelling coming from the nursery and went along to investigate. She had opened the door and could hear them though they were unaware of her presence.

'Papa doesn't love you, he only loves me and James,' Victoria said in her childish treble, her curls bobbing as she tossed her head.

'I don't care,' Paul said with his mouth set in a stubborn line, but his eyes belied the words. Susan saw the hurt and misery and closed her eyes, feeling his pain hers.

Oh, my darling, you do care and it is breaking your heart. Her own guilt returned to torment her but her hatred was levelled at her husband. Only a monster would treat an innocent child as he was doing. Walking into the room she was fearful that she would strike her daughter and kept her hands rigidly at her side.

'How dare you, Victoria! How dare you say such a wicked thing!' Susan spoke with a harshness never before heard in the nursery. She was shaking with rage. 'You will apologise to your brother at once. At once! Do you hear?' she said, her voice rising to a shout.

Victoria stared back at her mother, her feet set apart, and looked mutinous. Had Susan but known it it was a stance she too had taken and Victoria and the young Susan looked very alike in those moments.

'I'm waiting,' Susan said with a dangerous quietness.

Just then the door opened and Nanny arrived, breathless from hurrying.

'M'am, I'm so sorry but I had to see Mrs Carson about the children's menu.'

'That's perfectly all right, Nanny, you cannot be expected to be with them every minute.' Susan tried to modulate her voice but her eyes were smouldering.

'Is there something wrong, m'am?' Nanny asked, taking in the scene. Paul stood silently, his eyes downcast and Victoria was backing away looking a little afraid.

'Yes. Miss Victoria has been rude to her brother and refuses to apologise. See that she is put to bed half an hour earlier than usual and without supper.'

'Mama! No!' Victoria wailed. 'I'm sorry, I'm very, very sorry.'

'Your apology comes too late, young lady,' Susan said

coldly, then with a smile she turned to Paul. 'Come along with me, dear.'

The air was warm with a gentle breeze and the sky was so penetratingly blue that its shimmering clarity had one blinking. Together Susan and her son walked along the path with its neatly trimmed hedges and Paul kicked at a stone and said awkwardly, 'It's true, Mama, Papa doesn't like me. What Victoria said is true.'

'Of course it isn't true, Paul,' she began, then stopped herself from going on. It was no use, his face made it all too clear that he was well aware that Edward held no love for him. To change the subject she said brightly, 'Tomorrow is Saturday and you have no lessons. Would you like to go over to Aunt Winnie's and see the new baby? You could play with Duncan.'

'Oh, yes, please, Mama, and will Uncle Matthew be there?'

'I expect so.' She smiled.

'I wish Uncle Matthew was my papa,' he said wistfully.

'Paul,' she said gently, 'it's wrong to say that or even to think it.'

'I can't help if I think it,' he said reasonably.

'Don't keep kicking the stones, dear, or you'll ruin your boots,' Susan said, fighting her tears.

'Have you got to go to the mill, Mama?'

'Yes, Paul, I must, there is a lot of work awaiting my attention.'

'All ladies don't work, why do you, Mama?'

'I enjoy it, Paul.'

'Will I work in the mill when I'm big?'

'I hope so.'

'Duncan is going to be a farmer like Uncle Matthew.'

'That's nice. Now run along, dear, or Nanny will be annoyed at me for keeping you so long.'

She watched him run over to the side door then turn and wave. She waved back then went in search of Ramsay. He was in the courtyard.

'Bring the carriage round in ten minutes, Ramsay.'

NORA KAY

Once in the mill and behind her desk Susan began to tackle the backlog of work. Both before and after the birth of James she had given less of her attention to the mill and she was uncomfortably aware that Edward was taking on more and more responsibility and making decisions she was only advised about once the changes had been adopted.

All that was going to cease. She was back in command.

In a light grey costume, with touches of white at neck and cuffs, Susan looked neat and businesslike and her manner matched her appearance. Her fair head was bent over the columns of figures which at a quick glance appeared to be in order and she put them aside. Next to receive her attention was the accounts ledger and here her frown deepened as she studied the entries and compared them with the previous month's. After jotting down some names she rang the bell which sounded in the main office where the clerks sat on high stools at their desks. The insistent ring, jarring the silence, brought the most junior clerk to Susan's office.

'Have Mr Lamond come here immediately,' she ordered, glancing up briefly.

'Yes, m'am.' He hurried away. When the lady boss spoke like that it was trouble for someone and that could be Mr Lamond. He grinned. Having been severely reprimanded that very morning for untidy figures the young clerk saw no reason to warn his superior that Mrs Brodie was on the warpath.

'Come in.'

'You wished to see me, m'am?'

'Yes, I think you have some explaining to do.'

His grey eyes blinked nervously and he licked his lips.

'I'm afraid I don't understand, m'am,' he stammered.

'Neither do I, Mr Lamond, which is the reason I sent for you,' she said icily. She turned the ledger to face him. 'Kindly explain why these accounts haven't been settled? Has it been an oversight?'

'Not at all, m'am. I mean, it wasn't an oversight, it's the new policy.'

'Really!' she said sarcastically. 'Do go on.'

'Well, m'am, these customers know they will be paid and won't push for early settlement. By waiting a few more weeks the money can be working for us – begging your pardon – for the mill I mean,' he said hastily.

'And you think that makes good sense?'

'Oh, yes, m'am.'

'Who authorised this?'

'Mr Brodie,' he answered as if it were a foolish question. 'I see.'

He smiled with relief and shifted his feet. Susan was holding in her anger with difficulty. Mr Lamond had only been obeying instructions, not hers to be sure, but then he would assume Edward to have full authority in her absence.

'There have been a few misunderstandings, Mr Lamond, which need to be cleared up now that I am back in charge. Perhaps there is wisdom in delaying payments but it has never been the policy of the Aranvale Papermill and it is not mine.' She tapped the ledger. 'See that these accounts are settled today and a letter of apology for the delay enclosed with each. Have this done immediately and brought for my signature. Is that understood?'

'Yes, m'am,' he said meekly.

'And in future kindly remember that your instructions come from me and no one else. Have I made myself clear?'

'Yes, m'am,' he repeated, bowing himself out.

Susan put a hand to her brow and stared down at the desk. She would make no mention of this to Edward, there was no need. Mr Lamond would be extremely careful in future. Should he fail to do so she would have him dismissed and this possibility would undoubtedly have occurred to him.

By evening her mind was on Paul and her rage was at boiling point. It was all she could do to restrain herself until after dinner. As usual Edward's first move was to the drinks cabinet.

'May I get you something, dear?'

'No, thank you and I do wish you would stop offering, you know perfectly well I do not drink.'

261

'On your high horse are you?' He smirked as he poured himself a whisky.

She ignored the remark, took a deep breath and her eyes bored into him. 'Your precious daughter, that precocious child, has been goading Paul with the remark that you only love her and James.'

'An observant child.'

'She's becoming impossible.'

'You don't like your daughter, you never have.'

Susan was taken aback. 'That is ridiculous and totally untrue. I love my children but I do not like the child Victoria is becoming and it is your fault. You have her absolutely ruined.'

'Exaggerating as usual.'

Her hands were shaking. 'Edward, can't you see that what you are doing to Paul is monstrously cruel and unless you – you change your attitude to the child I am going to tell him the truth. Once he realises that you are not his natural father then he will find your attitude towards him easier to understand.'

'And when he is old enough to understand how that came about, what then? What will he think of his mother?' he jeered.

'I'll have to take that risk but perhaps he will be more charitable and forgiving than you,' she said bitterly.

Leaning against the mantelpiece and sipping his drink he looked at her thoughtfully and shook his head.

'Don't think I wouldn't carry it out, Edward. Don't think that for a moment. Paul is my son and means the world to me whilst you are my husband in name only.'

The glass was arrested before it reached his mouth and he was looking at her oddly, seemingly at a loss for words. She saw it and felt satisfied with her performance.

Among the passengers getting off at Queen Street station was Matthew MacFarlane. Until recently Euan Clapperton had attended the market but now he had confidence in his son-in-law and Matthew was only too happy to take his place. He enjoyed farming talk and frequently joined a group who continued their discussions over a refreshment in a nearby hotel. Today Matthew declined their invitation as he had promised Winnie to call in at Morton's in St Vincent Street. His father-in-law's birthday was on Sunday and Winnie wanted special tobacco that only Morton's stocked.

Leaving the shop he found himself face to face with Caroline Beverley, only now, he had to remind himself, she was Caroline Saunders. For an instant they stood staring at one another, each startled by the change read in the other's eyes. Caroline saw a tweed-suited man still with his boyish good looks but now there was an air of confidence lacking before. For his part Matthew saw a strikingly lovely woman in a cherry red costume with a nipped-in waist accentuating her dainty figure. The colour was superb with her blue-black hair and dark eyes but the soft appealing look that had been so much a part of Caroline had gone.

'Matthew! Well, hello,' she said, holding out a gloved hand. 'It's been a long time.'

'Yes, it has. You're looking very well, Caroline.'

Matthew secretly marvelled at his good luck; he had been wondering how he could get in touch and here she was.

'I was about to ask you what you are doing here but of course it's market day and may I say you look every inch the successful farmer.'

Did he detect a hint of sarcasm or was it just his imagination? 'Yes, Caroline, I've been at the mart and now I'm on my way to get a bite to eat before heading home.'

'May I invite myself?' She smiled into his face. 'I haven't eaten.'

'I was about to invite you. The Royal all right?'

'Yes.'

It was a short walk to the hotel and once inside the entrance hall they took the left passage leading to the red and gold dining-room. Small tables were set for luncheon and they were shown to a vacant one in the corner then supplied with menus and left to make their choice.

Caroline barely glanced at hers. 'I'm not very hungry. Do you think I could just have a lightly poached egg on toast?'

263

'I imagine so.' He beckoned for the waitress, ordered for Caroline and something more substantial for himself. The dining-room was filling up and the occupants of one table were taking a great interest in the couple at the corner table.

Caroline leaned forward, an elbow on the table and a hand supporting her chin. 'This is like old times, isn't it?' She smiled.

Matthew gave an uncomfortable smile. 'Caroline, I was very, very sorry to hear about your father. I wanted to write – '

'But in the circumstances you didn't know what to say,' she said harshly. She paused and said bleakly, 'I found him you know, he would know I would. He chose a time when my mother was staying with my aunt.'

The waitress came to adjust the cutlery and Caroline leaned back.

Matthew waited until they were alone. 'That must have been dreadful for you.'

'Oh, it was, Matthew, it was I can assure you.' She had been speaking softly but her voice dropped to a little above a whisper. 'He shot himself, Matthew. Hard to believe, isn't it, that my strong, God-fearing father should take his own life.' There was the hint of tears in her voice. 'I needed someone so badly but there was no one. No one to help. I had it all to do and face up to the fact that my father left nothing but debts. Matthew, I needed you, needed you so badly but you weren't there.' She gave a half sob. 'You treated me very shabbily.'

'Caroline, we weren't engaged, I made no promises,' he said defensively but only too aware that he had behaved badly.

'Everyone expected us to marry. I expected it, Matthew, after all we'd been to each other.'

'Caroline, you're married.'

'Oh, yes, Matthew, I'm Mrs Charles Saunders. Like you I married for the wrong reasons. You married that clumsy girl Winnie to get your hands on Moorend and I married a man more than twenty years older for security. Charles was a widower with no children and a large bank balance.' Her eyes glinted. 'One day I'll be all right but meantime he keeps a tight grip on the purse-strings.'

'You're wrong about Winnie,' Matthew said, the angry colour showing on his face. 'I happen to love my wife and our two little sons.'

'Very cosy,' she said as their meal arrived. In silence they each ate a few mouthfuls then Caroline put down her fork and knife and pushed back the plate.

'In the beginning,' Matthew said, striving to be honest, 'Moorend was the attraction but not any more. You may believe it or not but it happens to be the truth. Winnie is a lovely person and I am very lucky.'

'Well, I'm not. Charles is old, dull and I hate it when he touches me.' She shuddered.

Matthew discovered he wasn't hungry and was only eating to save the waitress asking if there was something wrong with the food. Before Caroline left him he had to find out.

'Caroline, are you seeing Edward Brodie?' he asked abruptly.

'What if I am, what business is it of yours?'

'I don't want Susan hurt.'

'Coming from you that's rich. My feelings weren't important when you dropped me.'

'Edward Brodie is a married man.'

'So he is,' she said sarcastically, 'but from what I gather that too was a marriage of convenience.'

'You used to like Susan.'

'I do like Susan and unlike you she managed to write me a letter and somehow she found the right words.'

'Would there be anything else?' the waitress asked politely.

Matthew looked at Caroline and she shook her head.

'No, thank you, just bring the bill in a few minutes.'

Caroline reached over and took hold of his hand. 'I'm sorry if I've sounded bitter, Matthew, but life hasn't been all that kind to me.' She kept hold of his hand and said playfully, 'Edward is a pet but I'd give him up like a shot if we could meet sometimes. It shouldn't be too difficult and it would make my life just bearable.'

'No, Caroline,' Matthew said firmly. 'I have a good marriage and I don't mean to do anything to spoil that or hurt my wife.'

She snatched back her hand and stood up. 'Then I'll say goodbye, Matthew. I've just remembered some shopping I want to do.'

He sat and watched her trim figure walk away and what did he feel? Relief, sadness and oh, yes, the shameful reminder of how little consideration he had given to his one-time love.

It was a beautiful but cold autumn day when Susan and Paul set out for Moorend. Unlike her brother Victoria was afraid of the animals and made no fuss at being left behind.

Paul was warmly dressed and laughing as he waded through the mounds of gold and brown leaves before leaving them to turn into the village Main Street. The cottages were of old standing but had been added to by room and kitchen houses built on either side of the road to meet the needs of the influx of Irish workers for the mines and quarries.

Next they came to the school. The classrooms were on the ground floor and upstairs was occupied by the dominee and his family with access by an outside stair.

Soon they were into Clapperton land with the cows lifting their heads from grazing to watch their approach, then Holmlea farmhouse was in sight and Paul took to his heels. The dogs began to bark excitedly and Winnie appeared to subdue them. She came to meet them and the sisters-in-law kissed.

'Winnie, I'm not being a nuisance bringing Paul, am I?'

'Of course not as you very well know.' She bent down to Paul. 'Hello, Paul, fancy your mama suggesting that you could be a nuisance.'

Paul grinned. 'Hello, Aunt Winnie, where's Duncan?'

'Not far away. Look, there he is,' she said pointing to a small figure pushing a wooden barrow. Paul ran across to his cousin and Susan and Winnie went indoors.

'And now tell me how is baby Peter?'

'Sound asleep, he's a night bird and chirpiest when all good

266

people are in bed.' They tiptoed through to an adjoining room and over to the cradle.

Susan very gently moved the cover to get a better look at the sleeping babe. 'He's gorgeous, Winnie,' Susan said, taking another lingering look. 'Peter resembles your side I think.'

'Not so likely to be a heart-throb then, is he?' Winnie said bitterly and Susan looked at her quickly. Now that she was studying her properly she could see that something was wrong. Since her engagement Winnie had been particular about her appearance but her hair today was lank and she wore an unbecoming gown.

'What is it, Winnie? Something's troubling you?'

'Nothing is and do sit down,' she said when they were in the sitting-room. 'I'll go and see about tea being brought through.'

She made to go but Susan caught her arm. 'Later, Winnie.'

Winnie sat down, her hands in her lap. 'How is James?'

'He's well enough I suppose.' Susan sighed.

'He'll come on, just try not to compare him with Paul and Victoria.'

'I know.'

'You've accepted the situation, Susan, but Edward hasn't, has he?'

'Having a backward son isn't easy to accept.'

'No, it can't be.' They lapsed into silence.

'Winnie, don't try putting me off. I know there is something wrong and if it was the other way you would force it out of me.'

'You may as well know, it'll be common gossip before long. Matthew is seeing Caroline Beverley or rather Saunders.'

'That I do not believe, not for a moment.'

'Then you should, you of all people. You warned me before our marriage that this could happen.'

'That was a very long time ago and we were both young and silly,' Susan protested. 'Matthew is a very different person now and a very contented husband and father.'

'Susan, I got it from a very reliable source.' Her face twisted with pain.

'Have you tackled Matthew?'

'No, and I don't intend to.'

'Why not for heaven's sake? He probably has a very good explanation.'

'They dined together, even holding hands at one stage I believe.' She laughed mirthlessly. 'Now I know why Matthew is always so keen to attend the market and save Papa.'

'Caroline is married.'

'That doesn't appear to be a hindrance. She married someone old enough to be her father and is no doubt bored with him and looking for a bit of excitement. Probably Matthew is bored with me and they are consoling each other.'

'It doesn't make sense to me.'

'Then it should. Matthew married me for the farm, I knew that, you knew that and I accepted it. With having the children I thought,' her voice broke, 'thought it would be enough.'

'But it isn't?' Susan said gently. 'You need Matthew?'

'More than I believed possible, yet I've always known it was Caroline he loved and would have married if things had been different.'

Everything Winnie said was true or had been but even so she couldn't believe Matthew would do this. There had to be another explanation for seeing Caroline.

'Try not to worry, Winnie, I'm sure things will work out.'

'Perhaps, we'll see.' She brightened. 'I must tell you about Duncan but for goodness sake don't tell your mother.'

'What's the little monkey been up to?'

'Aunt Tina drops in and takes Duncan for a walk, usually into the village.'

'Is she still doing her "good works"?'

'Yes, she is and it was the turn of the McGregors to get some advice and a basket of goodies. While they chatted Duncan went outside to play with the children.'

'Did you mind?'

'Not in the least, good for him. Anyway after a while Aunt Tina went outside to see what all the hilarity was about.' Winnie laughed. 'There he was, the young master, barefooted and tramping the blankets with the others.'

'Tramping the blankets?' Susan said, mystified.

'You wouldn't know of course. Well, to enlighten you it's a yearly event or perhaps twice yearly when the blankets are washed. A tub is filled with soapy water, the blankets put in and the family, adults first, jump up and down to get them clean. The children then get a turn and it makes sense you know. Washing by hand isn't nearly so effective or perhaps I should say doesn't get so much of the dirt out.'

'And that's what young Duncan was doing?' Susan laughed.

'Having the time of his life according to Aunt Tina and she had quite a job tearing him away.'

'Did you tell Matthew?'

'Yes. He thought a lot of people in Aranvale would have clean feet for a change.'

'Cheeky.'

'And now that tea. Just let me ring for Edith.' Winnie pulled at the bell and a rosy-cheeked girl knocked and opened the door.

'Tea, please, Edith and some scones.'

'How are the love-birds?'

'Happy as the day is long. Mind you, Susan, I thought Papa might have rebelled at some of the changes at Moorend but not a bit of it. He doesn't seem to mind just as long as your mother is happy.'

'I'll drink this then I must go. There's a mountain of work to be done.'

'I hear you are well thought of in the mill.'

'Thank you, Winnie, thank you for telling me that. I do know that I've been called that bossy young woman and that description I could do without.'

'Don't let it bother you. In your position you have to assert your authority. Forgive me asking but how does Edward feel about taking orders from his wife?'

'I do very little ordering and though the position isn't to his liking Edward has come to accept it.' She shrugged. 'He has to, after all.'

The tea arrived and Winnie poured. The scones were delicious and still warm and Susan couldn't resist another.

'Before I go, may I say something and please don't be offended.'

'I'll try not.'

'Don't let your appearance go. You've been looking marvellous but just now your hair is a mess and do get rid of that gown.'

'You are a bossy boots and a real little madam, but all right I'll take your advice. It was just that I couldn't be bothered when –'

Susan hastened in with, 'That makes it doubly important. Now I really am going. Tell Paul to be good and maybe Matthew will bring him home.'

'Yes, he'll do that.'

When the carriage from Holmlea trundled up the drive Susan was at the door awaiting it. Paul was tired but happy and needed no prompting to run indoors to Nanny.

'What's this? Aren't I being invited in?'

'Could we take a walk, Matthew? I need to ask you something?'

Was that unease she saw? She couldn't be sure.

'Fine by me,' he said as they fell into step.

She didn't waste time. 'Is it true that you are seeing Caroline?'

'Whatever made you ask that?'

'Is it true?' Susan persisted.

'I've seen her, yes,' he said guardedly.

'You dined together.'

'Suppose you tell me what this is all about. And who has been gossiping?' He sounded distinctly annoyed.

'I have no idea but I do know that it has reached Winnie. How could you, Matthew? How could you hurt Winnie like that? She worships you and the children.' Her eyes flashed dangerously. 'You are my brother, more than that, my twin, and I love you dearly but if there is any truth in this, about you and Caroline, then I am not only disappointed but I'm disgusted.'

'Have you quite finished?' he said icily.

'Matthew, I don't want to believe it.'

'Then don't.'

'Are you saying that you haven't been seeing Caroline?'

'No, not exactly, we had a meal together that was all.'

'But why, Matthew? You must have known that if you were seen together tongues would wag. Remember, you two were practically engaged.'

'We were not.'

'Then there is nothing between you?

'Nothing. I'm not in love with her and to be honest, Susan, I don't think I knew what love was until I married Winnie. Caroline is beautiful and her gaiety is infectious but exhausting and now it's all a bit forced.'

'Then you do love Winnie?'

'Yes, I do,' he said quietly, 'She is the best thing that ever happened to me.'

'Then you stupid, stupid boy tell Winnie that. She still thinks you married her for the farm and but for that Caroline would have been your wife.'

'Maybe at the beginning that was true but she must know. Surely she still doesn't think,' he said incredulously, 'she can't – '

'She does, I can assure you of that and it's up to you to put things right between you. Incidentally I'm curious, why did you have a meal with Caroline and what did you talk about?'

His eyes fell. 'I can't tell you that, I'm sorry.'

Susan raised her eyebrows in surprise. Why the secrecy? But she didn't pursue it. 'Make sure you tell Winnie if you can't tell me. It isn't good to have secrets from her.'

He smiled. 'Just as soon as I get home she shall be told all.'

Matthew put off no time in getting back to Holmlea; he was shaken by what he had just heard but he managed to wait until Duncan was in bed and asleep. He wanted no interruptions.

'Winnie, come and sit down.' He indicated the space beside him on the couch.

'I'm busy, I have things to do.'

271

'Leave them, this is important.'

'Very well,' she said, sitting down but in the chair opposite.

'I've been talking to Susan and she tells me – '

'Susan had no right, what was said was in confidence.'

'Thank God she did tell me.' He paused. 'You have been a bit strange recently but I thought you were just off colour. Winnie MacFarlane,' he said slowly, 'I love you, I love the life we have together and I adore our two little sons. Is that enough for you?'

Her lips were trembling. 'No, Matthew, it isn't enough. I have to know about Caroline. I can't, I won't share you.'

'Come over here, woman.'

After some hesitation she got up and sat beside her husband but sideways so that she could look at him.

'Tell me why you were with Caroline. The truth, Matthew, you owe me that.'

'Yes, I owe you that. All right here it is. I happen to know that Caroline and Edward are seeing each other.'

Winnie stared. 'Oh, Matthew, and all you were doing was trying to put an end to it.'

'That's right and I wasn't successful I'm afraid. Caroline isn't the girl she used to be, she's an embittered young woman.'

'Hardly surprising,' Winnie said, feeling generous now that her own happiness wasn't at risk. 'Her father's suicide and then marriage to a man so much older.' And losing you, my darling, she added silently.

Matthew's arm went round her, drawing her close and she snuggled in.

'I love you so much, Matthew, life without you would be meaningless.'

Very gently he eased himself away and got up to close the curtains and in the dim light from the one oil lamp they made love.

Winnie's arrival at Aran Heights surprised Susan.

'Matthew said I would catch you, that you only work a half day on a Wednesday.'

'As a rule,' Susan smiled. 'And I'm delighted to see you.'

'I believe I would have ventured into the mill if you hadn't been at home.' She laughed, her happiness brimming over.

'You look wonderful,' Susan said approvingly. 'Now tell me what has brought on this change.'

'As if you didn't know,' she said softly.

'Matthew has made his peace with you?'

'More than that, he has explained everything. Caroline means nothing to him and it's true, Susan. Matthew loves me,' she said wonderingly, 'he really does.'

'Of course he does and you had better believe it. And now forgive me for being a nosey parker but why was he seeing Caroline? He wouldn't tell me.'

'Nothing important, really it wasn't, they just had a chat,' Winnie said evasively and glanced away so that she didn't meet Susan's eyes.

'You can tell me, I'm no gossip.'

'I know that but I'm afraid I can't tell you.' She was beginning to look agitated.

'This gets curiouser and curiouser.' Susan laughed. 'Anyway, just as long as you are satisfied with his explanation.'

'Oh, I am,' she said and Susan had the uncomfortable feeling that she was getting an oddly sympathetic glance.

Tea arrived and after being refreshed they went upstairs to the nursery. James was lying on cushions on the floor surrounded by soft toys which held no interest for him. He was staring at the ceiling and didn't move his head as they came over. Susan felt the familiar tightness in her throat as she looked at her child, her poor, damaged child as she thought of him.

'Come on, lazybones,' Winnie said, scooping him up and kissing his cheek. His eyes were a very pale blue, almost colourless and his fine hair was gingery fair.

'Here, he's a solid weight, Susan,' Winnie said as she put him back on the cushions.

'I know. Nanny is trying to get him to walk a little but so far without success.'

273

'Paul and Victoria are in the schoolroom,' Susan said as they walked towards the main stairway.

'That's what I meant to ask. Are you satisfied with the governess?'

'She is quite excellent, Winnie. Appearances can be very deceptive. She looks so severe, mannish almost but she's very good with children. Victoria needs a firm hand and she gets that from Miss Loudon. I expected ructions from that young lady but strangely enough she gives Miss Loudon no trouble.'

'What about Paul?'

'He's very good and very quick. Before another year passes I must see about engaging a tutor. I had the advantage of sharing Matthew's and I consider myself very fortunate. Should Victoria show a willingness to learn she'll get every encouragement. She'll continue with the governess for a few years then we'll see.'

'And James, can anything be done?'

'Very little but there is a light at the end of the tunnel. Miss Loudon is beginning to spend some time with him, she's had some experience with handicapped children and slow learners and once the other two are through her hands she'll take on James.'

'That's a big relief. Duncan isn't all that keen on schooling.'

'Like Matthew.'

'Yes, like Matthew but it doesn't really matter. Duncan wants to be a farmer like his papa and his grandpapa. And now I must go, I hadn't intended staying this long.'

'I've enjoyed it, we must try and do this more often.'

'Yes, we must and, Susan, thank you for – for everything.'

It was Susan's day for checking the ledgers and she didn't welcome the interruption.

'Yes, Edward, what is it?' she said, trying to hide her impatience.

'Letter from Frankfurt,' he said, putting it down in front of her.

'From Herr Wilhelm Rolfe?'

'No, his son, Helmut.'

'What does he want?'

'An order I expect. The fellow is to be in Scotland and would like to pay us a visit if we are agreeable.'

'Quite agreeable but put him right concerning an order, there'll be nothing in the forseeable future,' she said, glancing over the letter and then shaking her head. 'No, Edward, he's not after an order it's no more than a courtesy visit.' She smiled up at him. 'Be a dear and reply to it and offer whatever hospitality you feel necessary.'

'Yes, all right and it is to be hoped he speaks English as well as he writes it.'

'I'm sure he will. His father and mine exchanged the occasional letter – in English of course,' she added.

It was March, but a bitterly cold day with a blustery north-west wind beating gusts against the windows of Aran Heights as the carriage took Edward to the station to meet Herr Helmut Rolfe. Susan had brought work home so that she could be at Aran Heights to meet their German visitor. Edward had suggested that after a light refreshment he would take Herr Rolfe to the mill and show him around. Then about one o'clock they would return to Aran Heights for luncheon. Hopefully their guest would have departed by early afternoon and Edward saw no reason to alter his appointment.

To receive her guest Susan wore a deep blue gown with a stand-up collar and a double row of real pearls at her throat. She thought that the total lack of fussiness made it suitable for a luncheon where, she imagined, the conversation would be mainly about business. What Susan failed to realise was that the gown's sheer simplicity showed her slender figure to advantage.

Her ears caught the sound of the carriage stopping in the drive then a little later she heard masculine voices but only when the door opened did Susan get up from her seat at the fire and go forward. Edward made the introductions and at the touch of the German's hand Susan raised startled eyes and saw her own awareness mirrored in his. She turned away sharply as a tingle of excitement went coursing through her body.

What, she wondered, is the magical formula that instantly draws two people together? Herr Rolfe was far from being unattractive but her own husband was more handsome. The German was shorter with broad shoulders and a slim athletic body and like most of his countrymen he was fair. His dark blond hair was longer than convention dictated. It was very thick and a lock of it fell on to his wide forehead. The face was squarish, denoting strength, the nose straight and the eyes a light blue.

Not quite recovered and feeling her colour high, Susan was glad of Edward's ease with guests. He talked while she rang for the maid. Coffee was served and as is the British custom the conversation centred around the vagaries of the weather.

'You didn't pick the best day for your visit, Herr Rolfe.' Susan smiled.

'The cold does not trouble me, Mrs Brodie,' he said in a voice only lightly accented, 'but the wind!' He gave a mock shudder. 'If it is like this now what, I ask myself, is it like in the depth of winter?'

'Very much worse.' Susan laughed. 'But we are quite snug here. My father had Aran Heights built to withstand the elements.'

'And it certainly does that,' Edward added. 'During one of the severest storms we've had in this part of the country there was hardly a building that didn't suffer damage yet Aran Heights, in the most vulnerable position, got off with losing a few slates.'

Herr Rolfe turned to Susan. 'My father was deeply upset to hear about Mr MacFarlane's death and I do know he misses the occasional letter they exchanged.'

'Thank you.' She paused. 'Does Herr Rolfe keep well?'

'Father is slowing down and becoming forgetful but otherwise, allowing for his age, he is remarkably well.'

'Your English is so good, isn't it, Edward?'

'Excellent and I feel ashamed that apart from a smattering of French I speak only my own language.'

'Forgive me, Mr Brodie, but we call that the arrogance of the English, expecting everyone to speak their language.'

'That lets us out, Herr Rolfe,' Susan said mischievously. 'We are Scottish and some of the English have great difficulty understanding us.'

They all laughed.

'Look at that, a blink of sun!' Susan said as a shaft of bright sunshine came through the parted curtains. 'By afternoon the wind may have dropped.'

As the maid cleared away the coffee cups Edward got to his feet. 'I think we should get on our way, Herr Rolfe. Among other things you'll want to see your own machinery working.'

'Indeed I would and I trust you have no complaints.'

'On the contrary,' Susan answered, 'we are very well satisfied.'

Anxious to be gone, Edward moved to the door and the German followed him. 'We should be back by one, Susan.'

Alone, Susan took herself to task. She was being utterly ridiculous, acting like a lovesick seventeen-year-old instead of a married woman and the mother of three children. Well, she would get down to some work and that would put this nonsense out of her head, only it didn't. She found that she couldn't concentrate and, sighing, put aside the papers and sat in unaccustomed idleness dreaming impossible dreams.

They were punctual, a few minutes before one o'clock but everything was prepared. Game soup was to be followed by slightly underdone roast beef with garden vegetables and roast and boiled potatoes, and the sweet was an almond pastry. Edward had selected the appropriate wines.

Earlier Susan had remarked to Edward that perhaps they should have made it a light lunch but Edward hadn't agreed. 'Germans have hearty appetites, my dear Susan.'

They were using the main dining-room and dining three people at such a long table posed problems. Susan solved it by making use of the top end of the table. Edward sat in

277

his customary place and she and Herr Rolfe sat opposite one another. The conversation during the meal had been general but Susan had a burning curiosity to know more about this German.

'Are you married, Herr Rolfe?'

'Yes, I am married and we have a small daughter. Marlene will be seven next month. And you, you have a family?'

'Two sons and a daughter.'

She saw his face cloud. 'How I envy you both. I was a one child – is that how you say it?'

'An only child,' Susan said gently.

'I was an only child and I did not wish that on Marlene. I felt too much was expected of me but then,' he shrugged, 'it was natural that my father would want his only son to take over the business.'

'You would have preferred to do something else?'

'Perhaps, Mrs Brodie, but I cannot be sure. Painting, unless one has exceptional talent, should be no more than a hobby and honesty forces me to confess that I fall into that category.'

Edward was frowning and his eyes kept going to the clock.

'Edward, I'm sure Herr Rolfe will excuse you.' Then to the German. 'My husband has an appointment.'

'Then I must not keep – '

'No, there is no hurry for you, Herr Rolfe. My wife will look after you and our coachman will be ready to take you to the station when you wish to leave.'

Herr Rolfe was on his feet. They shook hands. 'I am indebted to you for your kindness and maybe one day you will bring your charming wife to Germany. We have a very beautiful country and the journey is less tedious than it used to be.'

'One day I hope to do just that and now you must excuse me.'

With Edward gone Susan suggested they return to the drawing-room.

'That was a delicious meal,' Herr Rolfe said as he sat in the chair near to hers.

'I'm glad you enjoyed it,' she said breathlessly. His nearness was affecting her and she rushed in with the first thing that came into her mind. 'My elder brother was killed in an accident and my other brother had no interest in the mill. Matthew always wanted to farm and now he has got his wish. You would see the farm on your way here.' She was babbling.

'Yes, your husband pointed it out. He also said that one day both farms would be his.' He grinned. 'Your brother married a farmer's daughter and very sensible too.'

'They are very happy,' Susan said defensively and wondered what Edward had been saying.

'I do know quite a lot about your family, Mrs Brodie. Your father gave a glowing account of his daughter's capabilities and frankly I was in awe of meeting this exceptional woman.' His voice dropped. 'One thing he could have added was beauty: you are very beautiful, Mrs Brodie.'

'And you know how to flatter. I'm sure your wife – '

He didn't let her finish. 'My wife never recovered from the birth of our daughter. I believe your term for the condition is melancholia.'

'Oh, I am sorry, that must be very distressing for you.'

'Yes. Very distressing. Poor Helga was a lovely, lively girl but now she has no interest in anything. No interest in her daughter and no interest in her husband.'

'How do you cope?'

'Eva has been our salvation. She is my wife's sister and unmarried and I persuaded her to come and live with us.' His face softened as he spoke of his sister-in-law and Susan felt a sudden stab of unreasonable jealousy.

'Is she beautiful, your sister-in-law?'

'Eva beautiful? No, far from it but she is good and we all love her. That is not to say she is plain, she has – ' He seemed to be struggling for a word.

'An interesting face,' Susan finished for him and he let out a guffaw of laughter.

'An interesting face! I like that and it is true, I shall tell Eva and I know she will be much amused.'

279

If his marriage was dead a man like Helmut would need a woman, Susan thought and wondered if Eva supplied what was missing in his marriage.

'Are you and your husband happy or is that a question I should not ask?'

'No, you shouldn't. But why do you ask it?'

'Perhaps I notice more than I should; forgive me, we'll say no more about it.'

'We have our difficulties but that is all I am going to say,' Susan said firmly.

'Mrs Brodie,' he said abruptly, 'I am to be in Glasgow for a little time. Is it possible that we could meet?'

She shook her head weakly.

'Why not?' he said softly. 'You must know that something has happened between us.'

Yes, she thought, I do know. Raising her eyes, she felt the full power of his magnetism. Without taking his eyes from her Helmut Rolfe got up and drew her gently to her feet. She didn't try to pull away when his arms went around her and when his mouth found hers it was a kiss that transported her to another world. Sighing, she moved out of his embrace and went over to the window. After a while he joined her and they stood looking out at the gardens and beyond to the hills.

'It amazes me that you are surrounded by such peaceful countryside yet a few miles away is Glasgow, a city of such contrasts.'

'Yes, my father always said we had the best of both worlds, but you can't know Glasgow well?' She turned to him and as if by common consent they went over and sat on the couch.

'I have seen some of its impressive architecture and magnificent buildings but I have also seen its squalor and the hovels where some must live. We, too, have that in Frankfurt. It is an unfair world, Mrs Brodie, but happily you won't have seen that side of Glasgow.'

She smiled and shook her head but in those moments she was remembering a time when, sick with worry, she had stumbled into its mean streets and only chance had taken her into a dreary teashop and safety.

He touched her hand. 'You were miles away and I was asking you about shopping, surely you could make some excuse?'

'It's true I do shop in Glasgow occasionally.'

'Well, then – ah, I see, perhaps you are not permitted to travel alone?'

Susan frowned. 'Herr Rolfe, I do not require my husband's permission. I am a matron not a young girl.'

'A woman of spirit is what you are, Mrs Brodie, and that I admire.' He gave a slow smile. 'This formality is it not ridiculous? Please, I would like you to call me Helmut and may I address you as Susan?'

'Yes.' She smiled, amazed that in a few short hours they should be so at ease with one another.

'You promise to come to Glasgow but when?' he persisted.

A recklessness came over her. 'Tuesday would be best.'

'Tuesday and at what time?'

She thought for a few minutes. 'In the late morning. The train gets in to Queen Street at eleven fifteen.'

'And must you return the same night?' he asked, so softly that she almost didn't hear.

Her own gaze dropped in confusion and as if sensing a withdrawal he spoke quickly. 'Please do not misunderstand, the accommodation would be as you wish. You have nothing to fear.'

She nodded, knowing that she could trust him but wondering if she could trust herself.

'And now,' he said regretfully, 'it is time I left for the station.'

'Yes, it is,' Susan said, and with a glance at the clock pulled at the bell.

'You rang, m'am?'

'Yes. Tell Ramsay to bring the carriage round. Herr Rolfe is ready to leave.'

Sitting back in the carriage taking him to the station Helmut Rolfe's thoughts were only of Susan Brodie. He had to keep reminding himself that she was another man's wife but it didn't stop the strong desire he felt for her. It had been a very long time since a woman had aroused in him such a hungry passion. His wife never had. Pretty, spoiled Helga had hated the intimate side of marriage and had never pretended otherwise. Her mother had had a lot to do with that, he always thought. They had been very close and Helga would never have questioned anything her mother said.

He frowned in perplexity. What was wrong with the Brodie marriage? Susan had been genuinely surprised that he had noticed something amiss. It was no light tiff but something deep-rooted and he guessed correctly that Susan would never speak of it. Even so, it continued to intrigue him. Edward Brodie was a fortunate man indeed for his wife had everything, beauty, poise, charm and a keen mind. Then his thoughts went to Tuesday. Would she come? Would she keep her promise? Yes, he was almost sure she would. Susan Brodie would not readily break her word.

Soup was not served that night. Susan had requested a two-course meal with biscuits and cheese to follow. Edward, concerned at what he thought was the beginning of a paunch, made no complaint.

'Rolfe got away then?'

'Yes.'

'Seemed favourably impressed with everything, do you agree?'

'Yes and I think he enjoyed his day.'

With the German dismissed from his mind Edward was unusually talkative about a business deal which had left him in a pleasant mood. Once they'd moved to the sitting-room and before he reached the business section of the paper, Susan had decided to broach the subject.

'Edward, I'm planning to do some shopping in Glasgow and Tuesday seems most convenient,' she said in a casual, offhand manner.

'Mmmmm.'

'I may decide to stay overnight rather than rush the shopping in an afternoon.'

He looked up. 'In that case you can pop into Browns and see if the book I ordered has arrived.'

'Yes, no trouble.'

'You remember where it is?'

'That lane off St Vincent Street.'

'Yes, that's it.' His attention went back to the paper and after a few minutes Susan excused herself and climbed the stairs to the library. To protect the books the room was always heated and comfortable to sit in and Susan was spending more and more of her time there rather than the sitting-room. With her elbows on the desk and her chin resting on her hands she marvelled at how easy it had been. Edward hadn't questioned her at all. Of course he would assume that she would be staying overnight with Agnes and Duncan Stewart. On the occasions when they made a foursome for the theatre or went to a concert Susan and Edward remained overnight at the Stewart home in Maryhill. Other than that they rarely saw the Stewarts so she had little to fear. And if she felt the faintest touch of guilt she had only to remember how often Edward left her alone.

It was Tuesday and Susan felt a growing excitement and was amazed how everything had worked for her. Even the weather, by one of those sudden twists so common to the west, had become warm and springlike. Dressed and ready, Susan took one last look in the mirror and smiled at her reflection. Her costume was fashionable with the jacket nipped in at the waist and the shade of soft rose pink set off her fair complexion. To complete the outfit she wore a saucy hat with a long feather. Some time ago Charlotte Beattie had closed her salon but even before that, Susan, like so many of the ladies of her acquaintance, was shopping in Buchanan Street and Sauchiehall Street. Glasgow, it was agreed, was very nearly as good as London for stylish clothes.

Ramsay drove Susan to the station and saw her safely on the train. Then as they moved off suddenly and unexpectedly,

Susan was full of doubts. Until then she had carried the memory of Helmut's face but now she couldn't remember what he looked like. Was he, too, experiencing doubts? Would it be politeness that brought him to the station? Well, that needn't be a problem, they didn't have to go through with it, did they? Herr Rolfe would understand and no doubt be relieved when she told him that she had changed her mind. Then she could do a little shopping, collect Edward's book and return home. That settled in her mind, she sat back and tried to enjoy the rest of the journey.

The train puffed into Queen Street station a few minutes before its scheduled time of arrival and Susan joined the others walking along the platform. Of Helmut Rolfe there was no sign. Relief, disappointment and a damaging blow to her pride were battling for place. Then just as suddenly her whole world changed. Helmut was coming towards her, almost running, his face wreathed in smiles and her own face lit up. The hug he gave her was quick, satisfying and completely natural. Just two people so happy to meet again. Relieving her of the bag, he tucked her arm in his and together they walked out into the spring sunshine. They stopped on the pavement and Helmut looked at her with eyes full of admiration.

'You look enchanting, my dear Susan, and do you know I was in torment fearing you would not come.' He laughed and she smiled at the boyish gesture as he pulled his fingers through his hair. 'You cannot begin to imagine the joy it was to see you walking along that platform.'

Should she tell him of her earlier doubts? she wondered but decided against it. They were together and that was all that mattered. Oh, there was risk and danger, she was aware of that but somehow it only added to a sense of adventure.

'Helmut, I want to do something before I forget. My husband ordered a book and I said I'd collect it.' She was sorry to bring up Edward's name so early but Helmut didn't seem troubled.

'But of course, we will get a cab.'

'No, really, it isn't far and I would enjoy the walk.'

They strolled happily along West George Street saying little, just content to be together. When they reached Browns bookshop with its small bow-fronted window Helmut remained outside until Susan appeared with the wrapped package.

He took it from her. 'And now?' He smiled.

'I'm quite thirsty.' She didn't tell him that she'd been too excited to eat breakfast. 'And I do know there is a teashop a few doors away.'

Miss MacGregor's Teashop was famous for its home baking. The wonderful smell of hot loaves and pastries made Susan realise how hungry she was. They were shown to a table with a fresh white tablecloth and in the centre was a pot containing a few sprigs of white heather.

The waitress arrived and Helmut ordered a pot of tea and a selection of pastries.

'That is white heather, Helmut, and supposed to be lucky.'

'Then I must have a bit,' he said, taking a sprig of heather and fixing it in his buttonhole.

Putting down the plate of pastries and a pot of tea Susan saw the waitress glance at the heather and raise an eyebrow.

'You must charge the gentleman for that.' Susan smiled. 'My fault, I told him it's supposed to be lucky.'

'And so it is.' She smiled. 'But the gentleman is welcome to the white heather and there is no charge.'

After serving the other tables the waitress, who looked to be in her forties, hovered nearby. The couple interested her. Not young lovers but lovers all the same, she thought with a pang of envy. A married lady, she wore a ring, but the gentleman she was with was not her husband. She could always tell the married couples. They seldom made eye-to-eye contact and for much of the time they sat in a comfortable silence. The lady was very, very pretty and a toff, that was easy to tell. The gentleman was handsome enough and though his English was good she was quite sure that he was a foreigner. The generous tip he left was very welcome and a boost to her meagre wages.

Susan felt completely happy and carefree as they walked and talked and had lunch at a restaurant. Helmut signalled for a cab and they had a short tour of the city then at Susan's suggestion they dismissed the cab at the Suspension Bridge and arm-in-arm walked across it. How safe it looked at this time of day with people coming and going but Susan knew from her father how different it was when darkness fell. A sudden need to warn Helmut made her clutch at his arm.

'Helmut, you must promise me never to come here at night.'

He smiled. 'Thank you for your concern, my dearest Susan, but I have more sense. All cities have their unsafe areas and bridges are a magnet for undesirables.'

'My father told my brothers and me that at night drunken beggars sleep here and half-starved, barefooted children roam around begging for pennies.'

'Poor little wretches. We live in an unfair world, Susan.'

'Yes, I know, but there is little we can do about it.'

'Now I cannot agree with you there; we should all make some effort to improve conditions.'

'How?'

'Cheaper houses and basic education for all.'

'My father would have agreed with that. I do too though I am ashamed to say I haven't given it a great deal of thought.'

He was silent for some moments then when he spoke again it was hesitantly. 'You do know I have been staying at the Majestic?'

'Yes, you said so in your letter.'

'So I did.' He paused and Susan, knowing what was coming, avoided his eyes.

'As I said before you have nothing to fear. It would, of course, be unwise for us to stay there and I have booked accommodation at the Park Inn. The food there is very good or so I am told and I have booked a table for dinner.'

'That sounds lovely.'

They had eaten an excellent meal with Susan taking more

wine than she was used to but even so it didn't dull her mind. Instead it left her with a feeling of euphoria. She was here with Helmut, enjoying the company of a charming and intelligent man. Their table was in one of the alcoves and she supposed that had been at Helmut's request.

When she put down her coffee cup he caught her hand and kissed it with passion. 'You are very beautiful, my dear Susan,' he said softly, 'and I speak the truth when I say I have never wanted a woman as much as I want you.'

Susan saw the longing in his face and feeling her own body responding she dropped her eyes in confusion. Not certain of what it meant, Helmut sat back in his chair and she saw him bring out a key and place it between them on the white tablecloth.

'I am a gentleman of my word, Susan, and if you wish to spend the night alone that is your key.'

For a long time Susan looked at it. She didn't deny to herself that she wanted Helmut and what harm were they doing? she asked herself. One precious night, that was all it would be. They would never meet again, no one need ever know. Helmut would return to Germany to his unsatisfactory marriage and she to the coldness of hers.

She shook her head and Helmut put the key back in his pocket. Then they got up and climbed the stairs. Helmut unlocked the door and she went into the comfortably furnished room with its large four-poster bed. Coming behind her, Helmut turned her to face him then put his arms around her. His mouth came down on hers and she was aware of the strength of his body and could feel his heartbeats blend with hers. When he began to undo the buttons of her blouse she made no attempt to stop him. She felt no shame, only shivering with desire when his hands touched her bare skin.

Across the breakfast table Helmut gazed at her adoringly but there was sadness in his expression.

'I shall always remember you, Susan, and those precious hours we shared gave me more happiness than I have ever experienced. In English I do not have the words to tell you but you understand?'

'I understand, Helmut,' Susan said almost in tears. 'For me it was very special too but now,' she said, fighting for normality, 'time is short and we have shopping to do. I can't go home empty-handed. I must buy gloves for myself, ribbons for Victoria, a book for Paul and a toy for James.'

'Don't forget you promised to help me with mine.'

'I hadn't.'

Inside the large store Susan looked at Helmut enquiringly. 'You'll have to give me some idea.'

'Marlene is no problem. She likes adding to her collection of dolls.'

'Good, the children's department is on the ground floor.'

The assistant was very helpful, showing dolls of all sizes. 'You choose, Susan.'

'I like this one, it has such a lovely face,' she said, touching the china doll.

'That one then,' Helmut told the assistant.

'I shall tell Marlene the doll's name is Susan,' Helmut whispered when the assistant was out of earshot.

'I'm honoured.' Susan laughed as she left Helmut to pay and went off to select something for Paul and James.

'So far so good, now what do I get my wife?'

'Does she sit about a lot?'

'Most of the time.'

'Then I suggest a fine-knit shawl.'

'Excellent,' he said when that was purchased. 'And now my sister-in-law.'

'Something to wear?'

'I think not.'

They had moved to the china department. 'What about a little Wedgwood dish?'

'Yes, that would do very nicely.'

'Helmut, I'm going to leave you here while I do some shopping on my own, then we can meet at the entrance.'

'That is fine, I shall arrange for these to be sent to the hotel.'

Susan bought two pairs of gloves, a selection of hair ribbons for Victoria and at a sudden thought bought some for Helmut's daughter.

He was there at the entrance watching the faces as the customers came out and when Susan appeared he was over quickly, taking the packages from her.

'Those are ribbons for your little girl,' Susan said, handing him the small packet. 'If she's anything like Victoria she'll be for ever losing them.'

'Yes, she does and that was very thoughtful of you. And this is for you.'

'Oh, no, Helmut, you shouldn't, I didn't want – '

'It is only perfume, Susan, something you may well have bought for yourself.'

She looked at the beautifully wrapped box and felt close to tears. 'I have nothing for you.'

'My darling, you gave me the greatest gift of all, you gave me yourself.'

So engrossed were they with each other that they were unaware of eyes watching them until they heard the voice.

'Susan, it is you, for a moment I wasn't sure.'

Seeing who it was, Susan found it difficult to hide her dismay.

'Hello, Beccy,' she said, knowing she looked guilty. Beccy and Adrian Brownlea were friends of Edward's and occasionally joined their circle of friends. Though Adrian was pleasant enough, Beccy had a sharp tongue and a nose for gossip.

'Herr Rolfe is a business friend from Germany,' Susan said after making the introductions.

'Really!' she said, fixing Helmut with her green eyes. 'And how do you like our country, Herr Rolfe?'

'Very much and I am indebted to Mr and Mrs Brodie for their hospitality and to Mrs Brodie for helping me with the difficult task of choosing gifts to take home.'

Susan breathed more easily, grateful to Helmut for his quick thinking.

'Is this trouble for you, Susan?' Helmut said worriedly as Beccy disappeared into the store.

'No, not at all, I'm sure your explanation satisfied her.'

Susan wished that she were as confident as she sounded but when three weeks went by she relaxed, though she should have known better.

As usual Edward waited until they were in the sitting-room.

'Adrian mentioned that Beccy met you in Glasgow in the company of that German, Rolfe.' His eyes narrowed. 'How did that come about?'

Susan's stomach was churning with nerves. How much did Edward know or guess?

'Strangely silent, aren't you? Incidentally I took the trouble to find out from the Stewarts if you had remained the night with them. Apparently you hadn't.'

Susan's nervousness vanished and anger took its place.

'How dare you check up on me.'

'You are my wife.'

'That doesn't stop you having other women.' Her blue eyes were flashing dangerously. 'This is the first time I have been unfaithful to you and yes, I'll be happy to tell you all about it.'

'Have you no shame?' he shouted, his face purple.

'No shame at all, Edward.' She smiled. 'Helmut Rolfe made me feel young and desirable and those hours with him in Glasgow were the happiest I have had in a very long time.'

'Love at first sight,' he said sneeringly but behind the sneer there was uncertainty and she could see that he was shaken.

'No, not as strong as that but I was very, very attracted to Herr Rolfe.'

'What about his wife, had you given any thought to her?'

'It would not affect her. Helmut has returned to Frankfurt to his unsatisfactory marriage and I am back to the sham that is ours but don't worry, Edward, life will carry on as before.'

CHAPTER EIGHTEEN

No other institution is regarded with the same respect as the bank. From the humble depositor of a few coppers to the giants of industry all use its services with complete confidence and its solid reliability is never in question. For a variety of reasons a small business or one of its larger sisters may go to the wall but for a bank to fail is beyond comprehension. Yet in that year of 1898 it happened to the Lomond Bank.

Virtually disregarded were the first faint rumblings that preceded its collapse. Though the City was nervous no one seriously doubted but that the position would steady. There was no cause for alarm.

When its collapse did come the whole country was shaken and repercussions were felt far beyond its own doors. Other banks were quick to realise that if they were to survive, withdrawals must be kept to a minimum. Ugly scenes followed as customers, rushing to get their hands on their savings, were refused.

In the Aranvale Papermill the machines were silent, the workers gone home but a gas lamp still burned in one of the offices. All day there had been rumours and counter-rumours. Too disturbed to settle to anything, Edward had gone by train to Glasgow to see the position for himself. Barely had he arrived than the news broke. The horrified groups hanging around saw the heavy wooden doors of the Lomond Bank close, heard the massive bolts snap into position. There was a surge forward to read the notice posted on the outside. With their worst fears confirmed, the more hysterical among them made to break down the doors. Hurriedly more police were drafted to the scene before it got completely out of hand.

Edward was pale and shaken when he returned.

'My God! You wouldn't believe what I saw, Susan, it's mass hysteria.' Backwards and forwards he walked the floor and Susan's worried eyes followed him.

'Edward, we mustn't let ourselves panic and overreact. Undoubtedly the bank has serious problems but the fact that they have seen fit to shut out the public may only be to assess the true position.' It was bravely said but she didn't believe it herself.

'The true position!' Edward repeated bitterly. 'What might that be?'

'A panic to withdraw, Edward, they have to avoid that, no bank could stand . . .' She trailed off.

'It's the end, Susan, it's ruin for us and others like us.'

Susan was pale but spoke firmly. 'I refuse to think along those lines. The full facts are not available yet and until such time as they are –'

'You'll go on hoping?'

'Yes.'

Flinging open the cabinet which had at one time lodged a variety of bottles, he stared at the office paraphernalia which now occupied the space. The door banged shut.

'Why the hell don't you keep this place stocked? Your old man did. Right now what I need is a good stiff drink.'

'What we both need, Edward, is to go home and try to get some rest. Tomorrow the news may be better and even if it isn't we'll be better able to face it after a night's sleep.'

He smiled at that. 'Cool as always, aren't you? Maybe I envy you the ability to distance yourself from reality.'

'If you believe that you'd believe anything,' she said tartly. After locking the cabinets she picked up her belongings. 'Are you coming?'

'I suppose so.'

Tomorrow confirmed their worst fears but Susan was anxious that it should be business as usual. A workforce plagued by uncertainties and worried about the security of jobs would not give of its best and it was vitally important that the wheels of industry keep turning.

'Edward, I'm calling a meeting of the chargehands right away,' she said, having made up her mind that moment.

'What do you intend telling them? That there is no money and they can whistle for their wages.'

'It hasn't quite come to that,' she said quietly. Edward didn't look like removing himself and she wanted to be alone. 'On your way out, Edward, would you mind asking Mr McNeil to come and see me?'

'What for?'

'To arrange the meeting. Incidentally, do you want to be present?'

'I do not.'

'Very well,' she said to his departing back.

'This is a richt bad business, Mistress Brodie.' Mr McNeil's expression was serious and his eyes troubled.

'Yes, Mr McNeil, this is something no one could have foreseen.' She paused. 'I feel I should see the chargehands, speak to them personally. The others I can talk to at a later date.' Her eyes went to the clock. 'Will you arrange it for – say – eleven thirty in the boardroom?'

His eyebrows rose when she said boardroom.

'I know! I know! Mr McNeil, but it suits me better and these are special circumstances.'

'I'll grant ye that.'

In an unguarded moment Susan closed her eyes and Mr McNeil saw the strain and tiredness in her face.

'You're a fighter, Mistress Brodie, you'll come through.'

'If only my father were here,' she whispered, 'he would have known what to do. I thought I was equal to the responsibility but I'm not so sure now.'

'Tch! Tch! What kind of talk is that comin' from a MacFarlane? I've found the maister gie low at times but he pulled through and you'll do the same, never fear.'

'I hope you're right, it would break my heart if I failed.'

'There's no such word.'

Susan looked with affection at the old man who had been both employee and friend to her father. 'What would I do without you, Mr McNeil?'

'Ye'd manage I dare say but could I gie ye a word o' advice?'

'Say whatever you have to say.'

'Maist fowk like tae feel needed. My advice is, dinnae haud back. Let the workers know the true position, that survival is possible if a'body pulls th' gither,' he said gruffly. 'Test their loyalty and I dinnae think ye'll find it wantin'.'

'Thank you, Mr McNeil, I was thinking along those lines myself.'

The chargehands filed into the boardroom looking ill at ease in such hallowed surroundings but when Susan addressed them the posh upholstery was forgotten and she had their undivided attention.

She took a deep breath before beginning. 'Gentlemen, you are all aware of the gravity of the position. I don't need to emphasise it.'

There were murmurs and nods.

'It is my firm belief that honesty is the best policy and I want you all to know the position.' She had been standing with her hands splayed on the table but now she sat down as her legs threatened to buckle. She had made some notes on a pad but she didn't refer to them.

'Due to the collapse of the bank we have suffered a crippling blow and we are quite unable to meet all our debts. However we do have one advantage.' She paused and looked at the faces turned her way. 'My father preferred to pay his accounts promptly, believing that should we ever be in financial difficulties we would be treated more sympathetically than those others who chose to wait until the last minute to settle.'

A thin-faced, anxious-looking man raised a hand tentatively and Susan acknowledged the movement with an encouraging nod.

'A word, m'am, if ye'd be so kind,' he said, glancing nervously around the table as if searching for support.

'Comments are welcomed.' She smiled.

With a calloused hand he brushed the moisture from his moustache and lumbered to his feet.

'Is it likely ye'll be payin' aff some o' the workers?' he asked worriedly, then sat down quickly, drawing his brows together. All those present had wanted to ask the same question and were grateful that one of their number was bold enough to voice their concern.

'I very much hope not,' Susan said quietly, 'the very last thing I want to do is that.' Leaning forward she spoke earnestly. 'To avoid such a measure I need your help and those under you. Uncertainty is bad for business, bad for everybody. It is absolutely essential that you reassure the workers about their jobs. Let them know that for the foreseeable future their position in the mill is secure.' She paused to sip from the glass of water thoughtfully placed there. 'Unfortunately and I very much regret this, but it may become necessary to cut their wages. Not just theirs,' she hastened in with, 'each and every one of us will be called on to make sacrifices.'

Another chargehand begged to be allowed his say. This man was older with a scalp speckled like a thrush's egg.

'M'am, I dinnae think I'm speakin' oot o' turn when I say that a cut in wages, unwelcome though that is, is preferable to nae job at a'.' His eyes sought the approval of those round the table and he got it in the murmurings that followed. 'There wis a time when, like mony mair, I had ma doots aboot a woman, beggin' yer pardon, m'am, takin' o'er frae the maister.' He swallowed noisily and cleared his throat. 'I hope I'm man enough tae admit I've bin proved wrang. Ye've earned oor respect, m'am, and ye'll get frae us the same loyalty we'd hae gi'en tae the maister, rest his soul.' It had been a long speech and his colour had risen before he finished.

Susan was having difficulty with a lump in her throat.

'Thank you, each and every one of you. I am deeply moved and I hope I'll always be worthy of that respect.' She tried to smile but her lips were trembling too much. 'My confidence has been given a boost now that I know we are facing this together,' she said unsteadily.

Recognising how near Mistress MacFarlane was to breaking down, Mr McNeil took it upon himself to bring the meeting to a close and Susan escaped to her office. Once inside she turned the key, went to her desk and sat behind it, staring at the wall opposite. Once she felt more composed, she sent for the accountant. They would go over the books again.

Neither she nor Edward had an appetite for the food placed before them, merely picking at it. For much of the time they had been silent, each engrossed with thoughts that could not be shared.

Later on they sat in the sitting-room and Edward poured himself a drink.

'God! I wish I'd taken your advice, Susan, and invested the money from Hillview. Even a gamble would have been a spot of excitement,' he said, staring moodily into the amber liquid. 'As it is I might just as well have poured it down the drain.'

'Surely you'll get a small percentage, they'll be able to pay something.'

'So small it'll be negligible.' His face darkened as he put down his glass then his fist crashed down on the table, disturbing his drink and splashing some over the rim. 'Susan, I hear myself saying all this yet deep down I'm not believing it has happened.'

'I know, Edward, I'm the same. The enormity of it hits me one moment and in the next I am hoping to awaken from a nightmare.'

'We'll have to cut down expenses. Get rid of some of the servants and make the others do a bit more for their wages.'

Her blue eyes resting on him were cold and hostile.

'Maybe that will come but it will certainly not be our first economy, but I can tell you what that will be.'

'Then do.'

'The first to feel the pinch and I apologise for the unfortunate choice of expression, will be your mistress.'

'What the devil – ' he spluttered.

It was a shot in the dark but since Winnie's evasiveness she was becoming more and more convinced that she was right. 'Caroline is too expensive, Edward, she is a luxury you can no longer afford.' Her lips curled. 'Unless of course, the lady is sufficiently taken with you to supply her services free.'

Edward's face had turned a mottled red. 'You bitch,' he breathed. 'Brother Matthew's doing I suppose,' and followed nastily with, 'Resents someone else having a bit of fun when he has to be content with that cold fish of a wife.'

With difficulty Susan kept her temper. 'Wrong on both counts. Matthew and Winnie happen to enjoy a particularly happy marriage and I did not hear about you and Caroline from Matthew or indeed from anyone.' She paused to let her words sink in. 'It was a chance remark which aroused my suspicions and you, yourself, have just confirmed its truth. I recall you once saying how attractive you found Caroline.'

'I do believe the lady is jealous!'

'Wishful thinking on your part, Edward. I am not in the least jealous. Caroline is a decided improvement on that slut of a maid.' She gave an exaggerated mock sigh. 'Sadly though, the Carolines of this world do not come cheap.'

Edward threw back his head and laughed heartily.

'Susan, you never cease to surprise me. Who would have guessed that the innocent maiden, protected from the harshness of life, would become such a very worldly and outspoken young matron.'

She laughed with him, glad that it hadn't deteriorated into a slanging match as it so often did. 'Let us just say that I had a lot of growing up to do in a very short time.'

He had positioned himself at the window and she heard him groan.

'Oh, God! Your Aunt Rachel is about to descend upon us.'

Susan hurried across to the window. 'So she is!' For a moment she considered going out to greet her aunt then instead waited for her to be announced.

Rachel MacFarlane was not given to making unexpected visits, preferring to await an invitation. She came in hurriedly, refused to part with her cloak, planted a kiss on Susan's cheek and offered her own to Edward who obliged with a brush of his lips. Waving away the offer of a comfortable chair she chose instead one with a hard back, declaring she would have difficulty getting out of the other.

'How are you, Aunt Rachel?'

'Well enough or I wouldn't be here. But never mind that. How bad is it? And don't treat me as if I were senile. Kindly remember that I am a daughter of the mill and what happens to it is of concern to me.' Her eyes bored into Susan.

'Our losses are substantial, Aunt Rachel, I won't hide that from you,' Susan said quietly. 'All we can do is hope that somehow we'll battle through.' She bit her lip. 'It's going to be a struggle.'

'If you have the determination – '

'Needs more than that,' Edward put in bluntly as he drained his glass.

'Drink dulls the intellect, Edward,' Aunt Rachel said severely. 'I hope this is not you drowning your sorrows.'

'Not at all,' he said stiffly, 'a small stimulant increases one's thought processes.'

'Does it indeed! We're always learning.'

Having dealt with Edward she turned her sharp gaze back to her niece.

'Susan, I want to help – '

'No, Aunt Rachel – '

'Kindly do not interrupt your elders.'

Susan murmured an apology.

'What I have will one day be shared between you and Matthew. However as your need is now – '

'No! You are not drawing on your money, I won't have it,' Susan said stubbornly.

'False pride will get you nowhere, my dear, and now be good enough to allow me an uninterrupted hearing.' She placed her feet in their tightly laced boots a little apart and looked down pointedly. Remembering then that her aunt liked a footstool, Susan hurried to bring one over.

'Thank you, that's much more restful. And now to what I

was saying. You, Susan, are not the only female member of this family to have a head for business.' She almost smirked. 'Against all well-intentioned advice and it is never in short supply, I invested my money in various enterprises. All were not successful I must admit but others paid a handsome dividend. An occasional flutter may not be considered ladylike but who was to know,' she twinkled, 'and from it I derived a great deal of enjoyment.'

Edward guffawed and Susan couldn't keep herself from giggling.

'Those misspent years mean that I am in a position to help you, Susan, but don't go imagining that I'm noble enough to risk becoming penniless in my old age because I am not. I'm too fond of my creature comforts.'

'May I say something?' Susan said meekly.

'You may.'

'Some capital would be a godsend but if I accept it, it has to be on my terms.'

'Go on.'

'This is to be a business transaction, the equivalent of a loan from the bank – '

'That's a bad joke,' Edward muttered.

'The Lomond Bank as it was and will be again,' Susan said, annoyed at the interruption. 'It means, Aunt Rachel, that the money is a loan and to be repaid with interest at the earliest possible date.'

'From one business woman to another I accept your terms,' she said smartly. There was a smug look on her face as she turned to Edward. 'Have no fears, Edward, just so long as there is a MacFarlane at its head, male or female, the papermill will survive.'

'I'm more than grateful,' Susan said as Aunt Rachel named a sum, 'but we should get by with less.'

'Very possibly but confidence will be quickly restored in the mill and out of it when you are seen to be paying your accounts at the normal time,' she said shrewdly.

'How very true, Aunt Rachel.' She hugged her aunt. 'You and I should have been partners.'

'Nothing would have suited me better, my dear, but I'm a bit long in the tooth for that now.'

At that moment the maid arrived to announce the arrival of Matthew and Winnie. There were kisses and hugs and a show of pleased surprise at seeing Aunt Rachel.

'Isn't this a dreadful business!' Winnie exclaimed, looking from one to the other as she loosened the buttons of her costume jacket.

'We're still reeling from shock,' Edward commented as he moved a chair forward for Winnie. 'How bad is it with you two?'

'Never have much in the bank, Edward,' Winnie answered for both of them. 'Most of what we have goes on stock.'

'Lucky you.'

'What about Moorend?' Susan enquired.

'Papa's a bit white about the gills, Susan, but that's delayed shock thinking what might have been.' Winnie smiled. 'Thankfully all the alterations and new furniture have been paid but as to how much they have lost I wouldn't know.'

Matthew took up the story there. 'Winnie's father is very close about what he has lost but neither he nor Mother seem too shattered. Why we really came over was to find out about the mill.'

Aunt Rachel moved her feet and managed to knock over the footstool and while this was being restored to its upright position, she spoke for Susan.

'Matthew, your sister has been telling me that the mill has lost heavily,' she said briskly, 'and a very worrying time it is for Susan and Edward too.'

Matthew nodded. 'That I can well believe and just because I opted out of the mill doesn't mean I don't care what happens. On the contrary I would be devastated to see the mill in real difficulties.' He smiled across to his wife. 'We discussed this before leaving home and we can raise some capital.'

Susan shook her head.

'Yes, Susan,' Winnie said gently, 'we do want to help.'

Susan swallowed hard but couldn't hold back the tears. 'Everyone is so kind,' she sobbed. 'Thank you from the bottom of my heart but it won't be necessary. Aunt Rachel has – '

'There! There!' Aunt Rachel said soothingly as if to a child. 'It's a woman's privilege to shed tears,' she said fiercely then swivelled to face Edward. 'Give your wife a handkerchief, there's a good boy, that apology she has in her hand is quite useless.'

Edward obeyed instantly, handing over a clean folded hand-kerchief and while doing so exchanged a look of resignation with Matthew. Shaking it open, Susan dabbed at her eyes then blew her nose and looked up shamefacedly.

'Sorry, everybody, I can stand the odd hard knock but too much kindness is my undoing,' she sniffed.

'Matthew and Winnie,' Aunt Rachel smiled to them, 'that was a very generous offer but I am in a better position to help. Anyway,' she added in her usual forthright manner, 'you farming folk are for ever pleading poverty, if not you're moaning about the weather, always something.'

The laughter that followed eased the strain for Susan and had Winnie wiping her eyes.

'When I found you here, Aunt Rachel, I rather thought you would be giving Susan a bit of help just as you did – '

'That is quite enough, Matthew.' She glared at him fiercely. 'That was strictly between us.'

Susan had suspected that their aunt had been financially supportive when Matthew was contemplating the purchase of Holmlea. Like her brother she hadn't wanted her nephew to be dependent on Euan Clapperton.

Refreshments were offered and declined. Aunt Rachel declared that she wanted home before darkness fell and shortly after her departure Matthew and Winnie decided it was time they went too.

'The old dear's bark is worse than her bite,' Edward laughed. 'My relatives would have offered sympathy but not much more whilst the old lady comes up with the hard cash.'

'She's a dear. Matthew and I have always adored her.'

'And she dotes on the pair of you.'

'Edward, shouldn't you be going over to Croft House?'

'Why?'

'Surely the fate of the distillery means something to you.'

'Under different circumstances it would.' He shrugged. 'Let Thomas and the old man get on with it.'

'I was just going to say that I would have gone with you but if you've made up your mind – '

'I have.'

'Then if you'll excuse me I'll retire. It's been a long day and I'm worn out.' But it hadn't finished yet.

'Unless I'm very much mistaken that is brother Thomas's voice I hear.'

They were both startled to their feet as Thomas barged in unannounced leaving the maid open-mouthed. He looked on the point of collapse. Like his brother he was normally fastidious about his appearance but his coat had been flung on and his necktie was askew. Though the night was chilly, sweat sat in beads on his forehead. And on his chalk-white face the freckles stood out like a disease. He stood in the middle of the room and babbled.

'We're ruined, everything's gone. Oh, God! Edward, can't you understand, we've lost everything. We haven't a hope in hell – begging your pardon, Susan – ' The words were pouring out and there was a froth of spittle at the corners of his mouth.

Edward looked at him with distaste. 'Get a grip on yourself, Thomas.'

'Susan.' His reddened eyes sought hers. 'S-sorry – ' His hand went out and she caught it in hers then began leading him gently to a chair.

'Edward, get Thomas something to drink,' she ordered, then to her brother-in-law, 'Don't try to speak for a few moments.'

Edward handed his brother a drink but Thomas's hand was shaking so much that he was in danger of spilling it and Susan guided the glass to his mouth. After a while he gave a shudder and a little colour reached his face. He tried to smile as he began to apologise.

'It's understandable, Thomas, we are all in shock.' Then added, 'Have you eaten at all today?'

'Eaten?' He seemed to be pondering the meaning of the word.

'Are you hungry is what Susan is asking.'

'No, I'm not,' Susan snapped. 'I asked if he had eaten which is quite different.'

Thomas looked from one to the other. 'I haven't but I couldn't anyway. Susan, what about the mill?'

'It's too early to say,' she said carefully, 'but I believe with a bit of luck we'll come through.'

'Luck,' he said bitterly, 'we'd need a miracle to get out of our mess.'

'Maybe things aren't as bad as you imagine.'

'Oh, they are I assure you, Susan, as bad as they can be. Tell me, what happens when one can't pay the workers?'

'They walk out,' Edward volunteered calmly.

'Surely you can raise – '

'Nothing, Susan, we can raise nothing,' he said hopelessly. 'Everybody is clamouring for what is due them, there's no goodwill left.' He cradled his chin with his elbow on his knee. 'We could have been all right; well, not all right but in a position to carry on. It was that hiccup with the new machinery and we refused to pay any part of it until the fault was corrected.'

'Which is precisely what we, ourselves, would have done,' Susan said.

'Is it working satisfactorily now?' Edward wanted to know.

'It has been for months but Father felt they should be penalised and withheld payment longer than I, personally, thought to be reasonable.' He shrugged. 'That has always been Father's way.'

'Hence the mess you are in now!'

'You are hardly in a position to speak,' Thomas said heatedly. 'If I recall correctly you favoured that policy yourself.'

'That is perfectly true, Thomas,' Susan said calmly. 'Edward tried to introduce it in the mill but I put a stop to it.'

Thomas smiled and looked at his sister-in-law with unconcealed admiration. 'You take after your father. I was a great admirer of his, you know.'

She was surprised. 'Thank you, Thomas.'

He turned to his brother. 'Life plays queer tricks. Don't think for a moment that I haven't known all these years that you resented the position I hold in the distillery. Well, thanks to Susan, you're sitting pretty while I and my family face ruin,' he said bitterly.

'How is your father, Thomas?' Susan hastened in with.

'Difficult to say,' he said broodingly. 'Look, I'm sorry for the ass I made of myself but I was feeling almost suicidal.' He looked at Edward. 'We don't all react in the same way.'

'Thomas, I am ringing for the maid. I insist you have some food inside you. On second thoughts I'll see Mrs Carson myself. Excuse me.'

It was a chance for her to get out of the room and leave the brothers together. For all his brother's boorishness Edward would want to be of assistance. She left Mrs Carson preparing sandwiches from the cold roast and the maid waiting to bring them.

'That's taken care of,' Susan said as she closed the door quietly behind her.

Thomas smiled as she sat down. 'Father has a bit behind him, Susan, but he is keeping quiet about it.'

Susan nodded. 'Sensible in the circumstances I would have thought. No use calling on reserves until it becomes absolutely necessary.'

Edward laughed. 'Take it from me, Father won't risk his all. He'll keep what he has to see himself and Mother in reasonable comfort for the remainder of their days.'

'Forgive me asking, Thomas, but does Elizabeth have money of her own?'

'A little but it's earmarked to pay for the alterations. The extra wing we had built is only just completed. In fact we were in the middle of arranging to have all the family over to see it.'

'You are having it hard. How is Elizabeth bearing up?'

'She is as worried as I am, Susan, but she tries to hide it from me. Elizabeth is quite marvellous really.'

The maid arrived with a tray and Susan served Thomas then poured a cup of tea for Edward and herself. As well as sympathy for Thomas and Elizabeth, Susan felt a helpless pity for all those small depositors whose dreams had been shattered like the fragments of a valued article lying in pieces at their feet.

'Thank you, that was very nice,' Thomas said after eating one small sandwich.

'Thomas, try to eat, please.'

'No, really, that was just fine.' He finished off the tea then stood up. 'I must get back to Elizabeth.'

'What is the next step?' Edward asked, getting up from his chair.

'You tell me! What does a bankrupt usually do, apart from committing suicide?' he said with an attempt at humour.

'Sell off.'

'And that, believe me, is a real possibility.' He kissed Susan and surprisingly Edward shook his hand. 'Susan, you look exhausted.'

'We all are, Thomas.'

Edward put his arm on his brother's shoulder. 'Anything I can do that doesn't require cash and you'll find me more than willing.'

'I'll take you up on that. If you can manage it, call at the distillery tomorrow and see for yourself just how bad things are.'

'I'll do that.'

In the weeks that followed the commercial life of the west of Scotland and beyond came to a virtual standstill. Warehouses and factories put up their 'For Sale' signs. And those firms struggling along were laying off workers. Trade dwindled, the small shops were feeling the pinch as customers' spending power dropped alarmingly. No one escaped, forced sales became the order of the day. It was a buyer's paradise. Those selling had to accept a fraction of the

305

real value of their premises. For many no buyer could be found.

The Aranvale Papermill struggled on. Wages had fallen to just above an unacceptable level but no worker was paid off. At Aran Heights, Miss Wilson enthusiastically carried out Susan's wishes. Food bills were almost halved and unheard-of economies were now taking place in the kitchen. Surprisingly, Edward made no complaints; indeed he declared that some of the meat dishes, favourites with the servants, were tastier than the more expensive cuts of beef. Polly was kept busy altering gowns and even cutting up one to make a dress for Victoria. New clothes were not even considered.

'Well, Edward, did you see your father and Thomas?'

'Yes. Everything's in the hands of the solicitor.'

'You mean,' she said aghast, 'the distillery is to be sold?'

'Yes,' he said heavily and she saw by his face that he, too, was shocked.

'It's so sad, it's a tragedy. One just can't imagine the Brodie name disappearing from the distillery. I could weep.'

'After that exhibition of Thomas's – '

'Unkind, Edward, very unkind.'

'Wait for it! I was going to say that he's remarkably calm considering the possibility that no buyer may come along.'

'Nonsense, its name alone will bring the buyers.'

But it didn't. The Brodie name was not enough and fears were growing as day after day went by without a genuine enquiry.

Susan's fair head was bent over papers and she frowned as the door opened and her concentration was broken. There was no need to look up. Edward was the only one who entered without first knocking.

'Busy?'

'As you can see.'

'Thought you'd want to hear the news. Thomas informs me that there is a prospective buyer for the distillery – maybe that is over-optimistic but a firm enquiry has been made.'

Her blue eyes widened with genuine relief. 'I'm so glad, but I knew it was just a question of time. One enquiry usually leads to others.'

'Father said something of the sort.'

'I feel sorry for your father but it is Thomas who has my real sympathy. He stands to lose most whatever happens.'

'And he's a born worrier.'

Edward perched himself on the corner of the desk and turned the top paper to read it. 'What is all this?'

'I'm authorising the wages clerk to restore the workers' pay to what it was.'

'We're not out of the wood yet. A bit premature I would have thought. Weren't you going to repay your aunt first?'

'All other economies will continue, Edward, but I want wages restored. The workers have been very supportive all this time but I don't want their hardship to continue.'

'Well, you're the boss,' he said, getting up from the desk. 'I'll go and get my head down too.'

The change in Thomas was unbelievable. He was almost jubilant when he called at Aran Heights.

'Who is it? Who is interested in the distillery?' Edward asked.

'Can't tell you that,' Thomas said, accepting a whisky. 'The information we have is that an English firm of solicitors is making enquiries on behalf of a client.'

'Someone looking for a bargain,' Edward muttered.

'More than likely but beggars can't be choosers,' Thomas said, pushing back his unfinished drink. 'Need to keep a clear head anyway.'

Susan nodded her approval and as if in silent protest Edward drained his glass.

'The arrangements are tentative,' Thomas continued, 'but I expect to be showing the prospective buyer round the distillery on Tuesday and then Father suggested we invite him to Croft House if it looks promising.' He smiled. 'You'll be kept in the picture.'

*   *   *

True to his word Thomas arrived at Aran Heights with the latest news, choosing a time when both Susan and Edward were to be at home.

'Thomas, you look a lot better.' Susan smiled as they moved into the sitting-room.

'Hope, however slim, has that effect and I've discovered the identity of the interested party.'

'Who is it?' Edward asked.

'Percy Carruthers.'

'The cotton king? Edward said disbelievingly. 'What would that lot want with a distillery?'

'It's the son-in-law who is interested; apparently he comes from these parts.' Thomas looked at his brother. 'I'd appreciate it if you could be there.'

'Of course you must go, Edward.'

'You, too, Susan. Father made special mention of that and Mother would be glad of your assistance.'

'Won't she have Elizabeth to help her?'

'Didn't Edward tell you?'

'Sorry, my humble apologies, I forgot,' Edward muttered.

'Elizabeth went over her ankle rather badly, Susan, and she's having to keep the weight off it for a few days.'

'I'm sorry to hear that. You could both do without that at this time. Poor Elizabeth.'

'You'll come?'

'Yes, of course I'll come, Thomas.'

CHAPTER NINETEEN

Croft House, home of the Brodies, was a large mansion on the fringe of Airdrie with a view of Airdriehill, the town's highest point and from which Arran, fifty miles away in the Firth of Clyde, could be seen on clear days. The house was surrounded by trees and set in spacious well-kept gardens, but for all its grandeur it lacked the commanding position enjoyed by Aran Heights.

Over the years Lilian Brodie had paid out a small fortune on clothes yet never even approached the look she was striving for. So it was with her home. Whatever took her fancy she purchased without thought as to how it would appear with the existing furniture and furnishings. An example was the Brodies' drawing-room. Large and well proportioned, it had a magnificent frescoed ceiling, priceless Persian carpets and a handsome Italian fireplace. Yet for all that it looked cluttered and untidy and there was the constant danger of falling over small spindly legged tables or embroidered footstools.

Susan and her mother-in-law were alone and sipping tea in the drawing-room.

'I don't see much of your mama these days.'

'I don't see a great deal of her myself.'

'That new husband is getting all the attention,' she said plaintively, 'and her friends have to take a back seat. I must say I'm surprised, Susan, Hamish was such a fine man.' She paused. 'Speaking for myself I could never replace John and I'm sure you must feel the same way about Edward.'

Could she replace Edward? Would she want to? No, she thought, Edward and I are often at each other's throat, we've hurt one another unbearably, yet I'd be lost without him. It was a comforting thought and she smiled.

'Yes, Mama Brodie, of course I do, feel the same way I mean.'

Just then the door opened and John Brodie came in followed by Edward.

'Good of you to come, my dear,' the elderly man said, kissing Susan on the cheek.

The weather was cold for late autumn but a fire took the chill off the room. Susan had given a lot of thought as to what she should wear and finally had decided on a costume in a lightweight material, thinking if the room got uncomfortably hot she could discard the jacket. The slightly full skirt was in royal blue and with it she wore a cream silk blouse with pleats down the front and leg-of-mutton sleeves ending in a tight-fitting cuff. Her hair was still her crowning glory but now it had darkened slightly and she wore it plaited and coiled in the fashion of the day.

For all his determination to appear at ease Susan thought that her father-in-law looked defeated, the broad shoulders drooped and his eyes were tired.

'Terrible times we live in, Susan, and this is a sad day for the Brodies,' he said heavily.

'I'm sorrier than I can say,' Susan said gently. 'I just can't believe that the Brodie Distillery is to be no more.'

'Only the name, Susan,' Edward corrected her, 'and that is only if anything comes of this.' His tone suggested his hopes were not high.

'Negotiations wouldn't have gone this far unless someone was really interested. Do try to be optimistic, Edward.'

'Like John I'll hate to see the Brodie name go,' Mrs Brodie said, 'but Thomas seems quite resigned to seeing the distillery in other hands.'

'Mother, has he an alternative?' Edward asked. 'After all, he is the one most affected.'

'Of course it is hard on Thomas,' his father said, fixing him with a baleful stare, 'and if I sense criticism you are rather too quick to allocate blame. My God!' he exploded. 'The bank, who would have believed it? The whole affair needs a thorough investigation and those responsible for this disaster put up against the wall and shot. Criminal incompetence, that's what it is.'

His wife looked shocked. 'John, what a dreadful thing to say!'

'Father is absolutely right, Mother. Personally I could cheerfully see someone swing for it.'

To change the subject Mrs Brodie turned to Susan and pointed to the cabinet. 'That is the most recent photograph, Elizabeth sent it over. Aren't the girls sweet and the baby is a little darling.'

'I must have a proper look.' Susan crossed to the cabinet and was remarking about the middle girl's resemblance to Elizabeth when Thomas arrived with his guest. Before turning round Susan carefully replaced the framed picture. Then she froze.

For a moment she gazed wildly round the room as though looking for an escape. She had to be dreaming, this was a nightmare, it couldn't be happening. She felt numb with shock and swallowed convulsively. Gooseflesh ran up her arms and she gave a shiver. The years had only enhanced his dark good looks and given him poise and assurance.

The voices carried – Thomas was doing the introductions, introducing Mr David Cameron first to his parents then to Edward. Thomas looked over to where she was. They were coming over and she felt a fluttering in her chest like a trapped bird.

'Mr Cameron, I would like you to meet my sister-in-law, Mrs Edward Brodie.'

In the moment their eyes met, his slightly amused, Susan knew instinctively that David Cameron was leaving it to her. What should she do? Claim to have met – suggest a vague remembrance of someone of that name having been employed as an accountant by her father? No, she couldn't bring herself to do that. In any case he had the advantage; just this possibility must have occurred to him.

She managed a thin polite smile as to a stranger and he bowed stiffly. Both his manners and his clothes were impeccable, the old David had gone. This one was smoothed and tailored by success.

She was only dimly aware of Thomas speaking: '. . . owns and manages the papermill, we are all very proud of her.'

Susan smiled to her brother-in-law, inclined her head to David Cameron and watched them move away. That was the moment tea arrived. Quietly and efficiently the maids poured the Indian blend to requirements, handed round plates of small cakes and biscuits then at a nod from the mistress of the house withdrew. During this time the conversation had been mainly of the vagaries of the weather.

'I believe you know this part of Scotland, Mr Cameron,' his hostess said.

'Yes, Mrs Brodie, I do.' A smile played round his mouth. 'This house was once well known to my mother.'

'Really!' Lilian Brodie's eyes widened. 'How very interesting. I don't recall the name but one meets so many people socially then sadly one loses touch.'

'My mother did not meet you socially, Mrs Brodie,' David Cameron said quietly. 'She was a maid in your service.'

'Oh!'

There was an awkward pause while Lilian Brodie recovered but she quickly rose to the occasion. 'Perhaps if you told me the name,' she said uncertainly.

'Cameron, Eliza Cameron.'

'Eliza – yes, I think – ' Her eyes were puzzled. 'Your mother's service at Croft House would be before her marriage.'

'My mother was unmarried.' Turning abruptly to face John Brodie he said, 'The name should mean something to you, sir.'

Susan caught her breath. What was David Cameron saying? What was he implying? A picture of the young David danced before her eyes. She remembered almost running to meet him from Aunt Rachel's and as they'd walked together he had pointed out the tiny speck of a cottage that had been home to him and his mother. And the rest – she was afraid of what she would hear – afraid of what she was just beginning to think. Her father-in-law's voice brought her back to the present.

'Hardly, young man, the servants were and are my wife's concern,' he said dismissively.

Dark smouldering eyes levelled on the older man and remained there. There was a stillness in the room as though everyone were waiting. Edward sat beside the window, Thomas a little apart and nearer to where David Cameron sat. Susan had deliberately chosen a chair some distance from the others. Mrs Lilian Brodie looked in bewilderment from the stranger to her husband.

'My mother should have been very much your concern, sir,' David Cameron said slowly and deliberately.

The elderly man had been sitting in an armchair but now he stood up and his hands were clenched fists.

'How dare you insinuate anything improper in my house,' he said in a peculiar breathy quiver.

Without haste David got up to face him.

'For a few paltry coins, sir,' he laid emphasis on the sir, 'you bought my mother's silence.' He paused but his eyes never wavered. 'You got her pregnant then all you cared about was getting rid of her as quickly as possible.'

In that room the silence was absolute. Susan could feel the hammering of her own heart. Beyond the curtains the rain lashed the windows but no one noticed. Those present watched the colour drain slowly from John Brodie's face. With an enormous effort he fought for control but Susan thought she detected a silent plea as he allowed his eyes to settle briefly on his wife. If she was aware of it she gave no sign. Her face was as white as his.

Locked in battle there was a strong similarity in the way each held himself. Both were powerfully built with the same jawline and each was engaged in weighing the other up.

It was in a blinding flash that it came to Susan. Dear God! Of course, that fugitive sense of recognition that had always just eluded her during those hours in the library with David. He had reminded her of someone but it had been too fleeting and it had drifted away. Now she knew that someone was her father-in-law.

Another thought struck her and its impact had her almost

313

crying out. No wonder Paul resembled the Brodies. He – was – a – Brodie. Paul was John Brodie's illegitimate grandson. Too much was happening, there was a buzzing in her ears and her mouth felt parched.

'This is absurd, young man,' John Brodie spluttered. 'Servant girls are all alike, get into trouble with one of their own kind and try to blame – ' He stopped at the look on David Cameron's face. There was hatred and contempt.

'You'd better be careful what you say,' David said threateningly, his eyes glittering with a dangerous light. 'For the sake of your health I'd advise you to sit down for you are going to hear the rest.'

Almost choking with rage and was it fear, John Brodie did sit down and once he had David returned to his own chair.

'My mother was incapable of lying, Mr Brodie.' He paused and leaned forward. 'Look at me! Go on, look at me closely. I look more like you than your two legitimate sons.' He laughed mirthlessly. 'The law of genetics is not to be ignored.'

No one could deny it, Susan thought, seen together the likeness was striking.

The face that had been the colour of porridge took on a purplish tinge.

'What do you want?' he rasped.

David threw him a glance of utter contempt, ignored the question and continued.

'My mother kept her vow of silence and took her secret with her to the grave. All she ever told me in answer to my questions was that my father was a gentleman. I find that amusing I must say but perhaps I do you an injustice, sir. Many in your place would have put a servant girl out in the street with nothing. You, in fact, handed over a few gold coins and a little extra to educate – excuse me, ladies – the bastard she was about to bring into the world.' He paused for breath and Susan could see that this was costing him too. He swallowed before he continued. 'My mother guarded that money and worked her fingers to the bone to add to it. Her only concern was that I should be well educated.' His voice cracked. 'No one could have had a better mother.'

No one spoke. No one took their eyes away and after a moment he was composed enough to carry on. 'My grandparents wanted nothing to do with a daughter who had disgraced their name. Fortunately an aunt was more charitable and she was the only one in whom my mother ever confided. After my mother died my aunt saw no reason why she should remain silent and it was she who told me the identity of my father.'

With a strangled sob Lilian Brodie got up and without looking at anyone went out, closing the door behind her. Susan made as if to follow but Edward shook his head warningly and she sat down again.

'Do you see what you've done, you've upset my wife.'

'Yes, but her suffering will be considerably less than that which my mother had to bear,' David said harshly.

'How much are you trying to get out of me?'

David laughed. 'Out of you? Do you imagine I would touch a penny of yours even if I were starving?'

'You don't really have an interest in the distillery, do you?' Thomas said bleakly.

'But I do, a very real interest I assure you. It is always prudent to have an additional financial concern.' He smiled but without malice. 'As you know to your cost there is no such thing as certainty in business.'

'No offer of yours will be considered,' John Brodie shouted. 'We have others – '

David shook his head. 'According to my sources and they are reliable, you have had no offers and in the present climate none seems likely.'

'That's quite true,' Thomas said quietly. 'False pride may suit you, Father, but it won't keep my wife and family.'

Edward was the most relaxed, almost as though he were enjoying the scene.

'Thomas is right, Father.'

'How long before – ' Thomas began anxiously.

'My solicitor will be in touch.' He got up and spoke directly to John Brodie. 'I am no more anxious than you that our

315

relationship is known and should it go further than this room it won't be through me.'

John Brodie opened his mouth to speak, changed his mind and just nodded.

Before leaving the room with Thomas, David's eyes rested on Susan for a long moment then he was gone.

Shocked by all the disclosures yet amidst it all feeling a rush of compassion for her father-in-law, Susan went over to put a comforting arm around his shoulders. He acknowledged it by patting her hand.

'Skeletons in the cupboard, Susan.' He sighed. 'And I'm too old, the fight's gone out of me.'

'Why fight a losing battle, Father? You haven't denied his claim, couldn't really, not with the resemblance.'

'Damn it, he could have faced me without dramatising it in front of my family.'

'And forego his moment of glory! In his position I would have done the same thing.'

'I'm quite sure you would, Edward,' he said cuttingly.

'Yes, Edward, you would be as ruthless as your half brother.'

'He's certainly a success story.'

'You two had better get on your way and I'll go and make my peace with Lilian, try to anyway.'

They saw him square his shoulders before going through to his wife.

Edward was flushed and his eyes bright as they left Croft House. The rain had stopped but there were puddles everywhere and a darkened sky suggested more rain wasn't far away.

'Quite an afternoon wasn't it?'

Susan's head was throbbing and all she wanted was to get home and be on her own. 'Yes,' she said wearily, 'quite an afternoon.'

'It's incredible! Who would have believed it? Mind you, Susan, it could be well worth while cultivating a friendship with my new-found half brother. Just think of the connections. He must be rolling in money.'

She didn't answer but he didn't seem to notice as he went on. 'After all he can't hold us responsible for Father's small peccadillos.'

'Edward, even if Mr Cameron were to take over the distillery, and I'm not all that sure he will but just supposing he did, the likelihood is that he would put in a manager and return to his own interests.' That was wishful thinking. She wanted David Cameron as far away as possible lest one day he met his own son.

CHAPTER TWENTY

With Caroline gone from his life, Edward turned again to Susan and though at first the shared nights gave her little pleasure, gradually she forgot his other women and warmed to a satisfying relationship.

Edward was asleep beside her, his breathing regular and she was able to think about those hours at Croft House. All her fears were for her son. Was there any threat to Paul? But how could there be? With her brain now working clearly she could see she had been worrying needlessly.

David would never know that his son was at Aran Heights. How could he? It was her secret, hers alone. David was out for revenge on the Brodies. What was he planning? Remembering how fiercely protective he had been towards his mother she should have felt more sympathy but curiously enough her heart had gone out to that broken old man.

David Cameron's arrival on the scene had affected them all. In David Cameron John Brodie had met his match. Edward was impressed, perhaps even envious. Rags to riches. Poor Thomas's only hope of selling the distillery. And what of herself? Sleep was beginning to overtake her but before it did her last waking thought was of David's wife. What was she like? Was she beautiful or had the attraction for David been the immense fortune that would one day be hers?

In a hotel in Hillhead, the aristocratic west end of Glasgow, David Cameron was also having a disturbed night. With his hands clasped behind his head he gazed into the grey dark and wished for the morning. For so long he had lived for this moment when he could humiliate John Brodie and had marvelled at his incredible luck in reading about the Granton

319

Distillery and the Brodies' financial difficulties. Later when the business came on the market he determined to get it whatever the cost.

Percy Carruthers had a great respect and liking for his son-in-law and with no son of his own he was involving David more and more in the running of his empire. There was little chance of the cotton industry falling into bad times but even so there was no harm in acquiring other interests. On that they both agreed.

When David spoke about the distillery in Scotland, Percy Carruthers had been surprised but then again the lad belonged to those parts so perhaps it was natural. In any case he raised no objections.

Now with everything working out as he had planned David could could only feel regret and sadness. Why hadn't he just kept in the background and used the Carruthers' name to acquire the distillery? That should have been enough but it was too late for regrets. Then his mood changed and his brow darkened. This was the revenge he had promised himself for his mother and he determined not to weaken. In his hand was the perfect tool. On him rested the future of the distillery. He could watch the proud Brodie empire topple, the ruined buildings all that would remain of a once prosperous concern or he, the bastard son of the owner, could take it over. How would John Brodie feel then? How would he feel about Eliza Cameron's son being the new owner?

If only he didn't keep on seeing Susan's face. It worried him that he couldn't stop thinking about her yet he'd accepted the possibility of seeing her on some occasion. Once she had been his youthful torment but gradually her memory had faded as a new and exciting life had claimed him. Seeing her again had surprised an ache in him. There was something about her, a proud dignity that set her apart and the passing years had only made her more beautiful.

His aunt was dead, her family scattered and away from Aranvale. But of course he would never set foot in the village that had once been home. And he would never go near the papermill, there was no reason why he should. He smiled. Somehow he didn't think anyone would connect him with the raw country lad he had once been. The distillery was far enough away and if he should decide to take up accommodation for part of the year then he'd buy a house in Airdrie or nearby.

The bed was too narrow and he moved restlessly, wishing he could reach for Gwen. Having her near, her warm body pressed to his, he wouldn't be thinking of Susan Brodie. A thought struck him and he smiled. Married to his half brother, Susan and he were related. There he was thinking of Susan again and it must stop. Gwen was the best wife a man could have and she was the one person in the world he would never hurt.

When Edward came down for breakfast, Susan was already seated at the table. Apart from a reference to the brightness of the morning they ate in silence until the maid went out.

'Did you get any sleep?' He smiled.

She laughed. 'It didn't keep you off yours. I was long in getting over.'

'What were you thinking about?'

'Thomas mostly,' she lied. 'I wonder how he'll come out of this.'

'Will Cameron offer him a position?'

'What do you think?'

Edward shrugged, examined the bacon on his fork then popped it in his mouth. 'He'll need someone who knows the business. A come-down for Thomas taking orders but as he said beggars cannot be choosers.'

Before the end of the week Thomas was at Aran Heights and looking happier than he had done for weeks.

'How is Elizabeth?' Susan asked as they joined Edward in the sitting-room.

'The ankle's improving and she can take the weight on it for short spells.'

'Oh, that's good but she'll have to go carefully.'

'You're looking cheerful, good news is it?' Edward asked

as he went to the drinks cabinet and began pouring whisky into two glasses. Susan shook her head to his unspoken question.

'Yes, Edward, the deal's gone through and though he must have known he could drop us further he didn't.'

'Not a complete rogue then our half brother?' Edward grinned as he handed Thomas a glass.

'He is an astute business man, that's evident by the conditions he's had drawn up.'

'What conditions?'

'Nothing that in his position I wouldn't have insisted on myself.'

'What are Mr Cameron's plans?' Susan found herself asking.

'He's bringing his wife and if she likes the area he'll consider buying a house and spending part of the year here.'

Susan felt a sinking sensation. No matter how often she told herself there was nothing to fear she couldn't rid herself of a feeling of impending danger. 'What about your own position, Thomas?'

'I'm to carry on with the day-to-day running and financially I'm to be better off than I dared hope.'

'What about Father? How is the old man?'

'Ignoring the whole situation, maybe feels it is the only way. And – wait for it – for the first time in his life he's allowing Mother to make the decisions and she thinks they should get away for a long holiday.'

'Best thing they could do,' Susan said approvingly.

CHAPTER TWENTY-ONE

For those companies fortunate enough to survive the collapse of the bank there was a gradual upturn in fortunes. Hard lessons had been learnt and those lessons would not be easily forgotten. Foremost among the survivors was the Aranvale Papermill. The undercurrents of discontent had largely disappeared and Susan was now respected by management and workers alike. She was the 'boss lady' but it was said with affection, for hadn't she fought to keep the mill going and shared in their hardship.

Now that she was sensible about delegating work, Susan was spending more time at Aran Heights and she had just come downstairs to find a letter from her cousin Hannah. Picking it up she took it through to the small sitting-room where a log fire gave out a welcome heat. She was anxious to know what Hannah had written, apprehensive too. Hannah and Samuel had been married for almost fifteen years but to their great disappointment the union had not been blessed with children. And now, wonder of wonders, Hannah was pregnant but amidst the joy there was worry. Hannah wasn't strong, she was in her mid thirties and early on there had been two miscarriages.

Susan slit open the letter, scanned it quickly then gave a sigh of relief. Hannah was well though tired, the doctor was pleased and Samuel, a worrier at the best of times, was much more relaxed. Susan went back to read the letter properly. Happiness leapt out of each page and Susan felt a lump in her throat. Please, God, she prayed, make everything go well.

Putting down the letter she began thinking of her own life. For eighteen years of it she had been married to Edward yet in spite of all its ups and downs there had been happiness between the dark times. And the family was growing up; well, not James. James would always be a child but sometimes looking at him Susan thought he was probably the most contented. It took so little to please him and his affection for them, in particular Paul, was touching. She supposed Nanny was right. James didn't have enough intelligence to worry, his own little world was secure and that was all that concerned him. Pretty vivacious Victoria was very different to the spoilt, pampered child she had been. True, there were still occasional tantrums when she would toss her red-gold curls in rage but these outbursts were quickly over and she was always sorry afterwards.

When her thoughts turned to Paul, Susan's eyes softened and her heart turned over with pride. At seventeen Paul was a tall, handsome boy and according to his tutor a very able student. Just recently Susan had seen a surprising change in Edward. It was as if he were anxious to get on a better footing with Paul. Only the other evening at dinner he had gone as far as seek his opinion and had been disconcerted by Paul's polite but cold response. Keen to help matters along Susan decided to discuss Paul's future education with Edward.

'Edward, are you to be at home tonight?' she asked as the clock chimed eight and he'd made no move.

'It would appear so. Why?'

'I'd like your opinion on Blackhall College.'

Lowering his newspaper he leaned back, looked at her and when he answered his tone was thoughtful. 'One of the Lansdown boys was there and did well.'

'That's encouraging. I've been impressed with what I've read but I wanted to be sure that it is educationally sound.'

He shrugged. 'As far as I know they teach the usual academic subjects but the main aim is to prepare the students for future responsibility.' He paused. 'Would do Paul good and give him more confidence to deal with people.'

'Y-yes. Of course he may hate the idea.'

'Or again he may be glad to get away from Aran Heights for a bit and have a chance to mix with others.'

324

Glad to get away, she didn't like the sound of that. 'Perhaps.'

'Leave it to the lad himself,' Edward said dismissively. 'And now to a change of subject. When are you going to buy yourself some new gowns? You've been to the Urquharts' twice recently in the same one. Surely the penny-pinching days are over?'

'Yes, of course they are and I do apologise if I've appeared careless about my appearance.'

He frowned. 'I didn't say that.'

'But you are absolutely right and it is high time I renewed my wardrobe and Victoria could do with some really nice dresses. She's only fifteen but she's getting so many invitations.'

'Break a few hearts that one,' Edward said fondly.

'But she'll do it gently.' Susan laughed. 'Deep down she's quite tender-hearted our Victoria.'

'Another snippet of news for you.'

'Oh!'

'David Cameron has bought the Beeches.'

Susan's heart plummeted. With the passage of time she had been lulled into a false security, convincing herself that David's wife would be unwilling to leave her friends to settle among strangers even for part of the year.

'It's not too far from the distillery or Croft House for that matter.'

'The house has been empty for months and needs a lot done to it but apparently an army of workmen are about to descend on it.' He paused. 'It would be a nice gesture on our part, Susan, if we were to invite the Camerons to Aran Heights. Make it a dinner party with the Maxwells and the Urquharts.'

She was playing for time. 'Edward, wait until they are settled in for a while before asking them.'

'That's just an excuse not to invite them. You don't like him, do you?'

'If you want the truth I think he's ruthless and he's made an old man of your father.'

325

'That's going a bit far,' Edward said reasonably. 'Cameron has only been making short trips up north and the two have never clapped eyes on each other since that day at Croft House.' He paused to throw a log on the fire. 'In his heart I bet the old boy is proud of his illegitimate son and if there's a ruthless streak in David Cameron where do you think he gets it from?'

'Your father, yes, I suppose you're right.' Edward and David had the same ruthlessness, Susan thought. She was beginning to see similarities in the half brothers. Thomas was the odd one out.

'We don't invite them?'

'Not yet. I'd much prefer if we waited.'

'Paul, when you've finished your lessons come along to the sitting-room. I have something I want to discuss with you.'

'Do I get a clue?'

'No, you don't.'

Susan was amused to see Paul take Edward's chair and stretch out his long legs in much the same way Edward did.

'It's about your education, Paul. This is just a suggestion and if you are not keen then you can continue with your tutor for another year or two.'

'What is the alternative?'

'There is a college in York, Blackhall College. I've made enquiries and your father and I thought two years there might be good for you. I'll let you have the literature to look at – ' She broke off. 'Paul, we want what is best for you but if you'd rather stay here – '

'No, Mother,' Paul put in swiftly and firmly. 'Two years at this Blackhall College would suit me very well.'

Susan felt unreasonably hurt. 'Aren't you happy? Is that why you want away from Aran Heights?'

'No, Mother,' he said gently, 'it isn't that at all. I love Aran Heights but I want to – I need to – broaden my life. Surely that's not wrong?'

She shook her head. 'Not in the least wrong and I'm just

being selfish. College would be good for you but I'll miss you so much and as for James – '

'You'll all have to spend a bit more time with him,' Paul said with a new outspokenness. 'Viccy knows what I've been doing with him and she can take over.'

Susan felt a rush of guilt whenever James was mentioned. It wasn't that she neglected him, she told herself, not a day went by without her seeing him either in the nursery or the garden but her visits seldom exceeded fifteen minutes. The truth was she hadn't the patience and was only too happy to hand over to others. It wouldn't do though, she must make a bigger effort.

'Then that's settled,' she said in a tone she would have used in the mill and was unaware of it until Paul laughed.

'Yes, m'am.'

'Oh, dear, I really must leave my office manner behind.'

Victoria was picking at her food and eventually pushed her plate aside.

'Why does Paul have to go to that hateful college? I don't want him to go.'

'That's because you'll have no one to fight with,' Paul grinned, his own appetite in no way affected.

'We haven't had a fight for ages.' She turned to Susan. 'Why are you making him go?' she snapped.

'Calm down, Victoria,' Edward said sternly, 'and don't use that tone of voice to your mother. Paul had no pressure put on him.'

'Well, it isn't fair and what about James?'

'James will miss Paul for a week or two then he'll begin to forget,' Susan said gently. 'Children like James have very short memories.'

'I don't want him to forget me.'

'He won't,' Edward said surprisingly. 'And for heaven's sake let's keep things in perspective. Paul will be home for Christmas and no doubt he'll find a spare minute to write home.'

'Will you, Paul? Will you write to me?'

'If you promise to reply.'

'Of course,' she said, her cheerfulness returning as well as her appetite. She brought the plate back. 'Might as well eat this.'

Blackhall College took in its new students in September and Susan was busy ticking off the items on the list, a very long list. Quite amazing, she thought, how much a student at Blackhall College required.

Like her father before her the family accepted that Susan did not wish to be disturbed when she was in the library and she was surprised to get a visit from Paul.

'Am I disturbing you?'

'Not at all.'

Before sitting down he looked appreciatively at the shelves of books and at the large desk.

'This is rather nice. I don't blame you disappearing up here.'

'I've loved it since I was quite small and kept it much as your grandfather had it.' She smiled over to him. 'One day it will be yours, Paul, but now I can see you have something to say.'

'Yes, Mother.' She could see that it was taking an effort for him to begin and suddenly she felt uneasy. 'I couldn't bring myself to ask this before but now that I am going off to college – ' He bit his lower lip. 'There's something, isn't there? I mean there has to be a reason for the way Father treated me.'

'Paul, your father has gone out of his way to be pleasant to you and you haven't responded.'

'Maybe he's just waited too long, Mother.' He was pale and sitting forward in his chair. 'I used to hear the maids discussing me.'

'What do you mean?' she said sharply.

'They could hardly fail to notice the difference. I mean he made a big fuss of Viccy, even James came in for some attention but I was ignored.'

'What did – they say?'

'Between giggles – that someone other than Father must have – must have fathered me.' She could hear the tears in his voice and he gave an angry brush to his eyes. 'At the time I was too young to understand but I remembered.' His dark eyes were anguished. 'There has to be a reason, Mother, I'm seventeen and I have a right to know.'

Susan's fingers began nervously pleating the material of her skirt. What she had always dreaded was happening and she was totally unprepared.

A wave of fury towards Edward swept over her. Damn you, Edward Brodie, damn you! she swore silently. If only you'd shown some compassion and not ignored the child this wouldn't be happening. But it was happening and Paul was waiting, his eyes on her face.

Unconsciously squaring her shoulders, Susan looked into that young, vulnerable face for a few moments in silence then she let out a small sigh.

'I had prayed this would never be necessary, Paul, but in this world sooner or later one must pay for one's mistakes. Other than to say I was very young and innocent I'm not going to make excuses for myself.'

Paul seemed to be holding his breath waiting for her to go on.

'Your – '

'My real father,' he said gently.

'Yes, your natural father and I were totally unsuited and perhaps that was where most of the attraction lay. Anyway we began to meet secretly, not often – '

'But you must have been in love?' It was dragged out almost pleadingly and she knew what he wanted to hear.

'Yes, Paul, we were in love but it was an immature love, mine was anyway. Much as I imagined myself in love I couldn't give up all that was dear to me – my family and Aran Heights – and make no mistake about it I would have had to give them up.'

He got up and began moving about the room restlessly.

'It was the time my father fell ill and he knew himself that it was serious, that he might not have long to live. You see,

329

Paul, it was his dearest wish to see John Brodie's son and his daughter married.'

'You could have objected, told him,' he choked.

'I did object at the beginning but you can't know how difficult it was for a girl to go against her parents' wishes.' She gazed ahead, thinking back to that time and for the moment forgetting Paul.

'Don't stop there, Mother, go on,' he said irritably.

'Try to be patient and try to understand. I adored my father, more than anything else I wanted to please him. I thought he might get better if I agreed to marry Edward and it did make him very happy. Then he couldn't get us married quickly enough. He wanted all his affairs in order before he died and my mother was barely given enough time to make the arrangements.'

'What about –'

'He must have seen the engagement and forthcoming marriage announcement in the newspaper because shortly after that he left Aranvale.'

'You never saw him again?'

'Never,' she lied. She gave a small shiver. 'What I didn't know, Paul, was that I was already carrying you before I married Edward.'

He looked stunned. The colour had left his face. Before he had been pale but now his face was chalk white and she felt sick inside herself.

'Not something I'm proud of, Paul, but I would never have married Edward if I had known.'

'What would you have done?'

'Confessed and taken the consequences.'

He tried to smile. 'In a way I feel better and there's a lot I can understand, about Father's attitude to me I mean.'

'Paul, remember this. Your father was a fine and an honourable man and he never knew about you.'

'A bit of a shock for – for my adopted father and no wonder he couldn't stand the sight of me.'

Susan gave a small hysterical laugh. 'Oh, yes, it was a dreadful shock for Edward.'

'Decent of him allowing me to take his name and of course that way he spared you – ' He broke off, appalled at what he was going to say.

She finished it for him. 'The disgrace. Yes, Edward spared me that,' she said flatly.

Paul got to his feet awkwardly.

Susan felt drained. 'I'm sorry, Paul, sorrier than I can say that you've had to learn all this.' She swallowed the lump in her throat, determined not to break down but it was costing her. 'You must be very disappointed in your mother.'

'No, really, honestly I'm not. All the pressures, I mean it couldn't have been easy for you.'

Susan gave a sad smile and nodded but they both knew that something precious had gone. Before he reached the door she stopped him. 'Paul, about Victoria – '

He looked surprised. 'Viccy won't hear it from me – no one will.'

'Thank you, Paul.'

Paul closed the door behind him and leaned against it. His mother! How could she? How could she have given herself like some cheap – he stopped, appalled at his thoughts yet powerless to shut them out. For miserable moments he felt something very close to disgust. It would pass, she was his mother and he still loved her, adored her, but just now his feelings couldn't be denied.

Yet deep down hadn't he suspected something of the sort but hoped desperately that there would be some other explanation? The secret was between the three of them but did that make it any easier to bear? He knew what he was and would carry the stain for the rest of his life. A maid looked at him standing there and, moving away, he went quickly outside. He needed the fresh air. He needed to get away from Aran Heights. College! How he welcomed it.

Long after her son had gone Susan remained where she was. She knew something of what he was feeling. Suspecting the truth yet hoping, always hoping for a different explanation. Sitting there she saw herself through

331

Paul's eyes. She looked the same. Like a painting, she thought, one that had an imperfection pointed out and no matter how one tried to forget it the eyes were drawn there.

CHAPTER TWENTY-TWO

I n those last weeks before leaving for college, Paul had been very conscientious about visiting relations and friends and Susan found herself wondering if it were deliberate, a way of spending less time at Aran Heights, then dismissed the thought as unworthy. Of course Paul would want to spend more time with his friends, it was only natural.

When Edward suggested that Paul's tutor should accompany him to Blackhall College and see him settled in, Paul readily agreed. Mr Erskine, with three weeks to spare before taking up his next appointment, was only too happy to oblige.

The night before his departure Susan organised a dinner party. Those present were Edward's parents, John and Lilian Brodie, Susan's mother and her stepfather, Euan Clapperton and Matthew and Winnie.

September was only a week in but already the evenings were shortening. Susan had the heavy plum-coloured curtains closed in the dining-room and the candle-light gleamed on the silver dishes and crystal glasses. There was game soup, white fish, saddle of lamb with garden vegetables and, to follow, apple pie, a favourite of Paul's.

After the meal Mrs Carson had been summoned and complimented on the splendid meal. In her great white apron and with her round face wreathed in smiles she had accepted her due.

'T'was for Master Paul,' she said, her small beady eyes seeking him out. 'For what he'll be gettin' to eat in one o' them establishments I wouldnae like tae think.'

Paul grinned. 'Don't worry, Mrs Carson, if it's too dreadful I'll sneak out a letter and you can send me – '

"deed and I will,' she said, not letting him finish. 'And now I'll be getting on.'

'She's a gem, Susan,' her mother said once the door closed.

'Yes, she is.' Susan laughed. 'And quite a character too.'

With a chilly wind blowing no one lingered in the courtyard and once the carriages were down the driveway the family went indoors. Victoria skipped away to see Polly about an alteration to a gown and Susan, Edward and Paul went along to the drawing-room. Here too the curtains were drawn and a fire burned brightly.

After some small talk Edward turned to Paul and said heartily, 'Bit of a change for you, lad, but I'm sure you'll soon settle down and begin to enjoy the life.'

'Yes, sir, I'm sure I shall.'

Edward frowned. 'Paul, just because you're going off to college there is no need for this formality. To be honest I don't much care to be addressed as "sir", at least not in my own home.'

Paul gave a slight smile that was not lost on Susan. 'Since you are not my father what do you suggest I call you?'

Edward's eyes bulged then he turned abruptly to Susan. 'You told him!' he said incredulously.

'I asked Mother,' Paul hastened in with. 'I've known for a long time that there was something about me – all Mother did was confirm my suspicions.'

Susan looked from one to the other. Paul was pale but at ease and she saw with a grim satisfaction that Edward looked absolutely shattered.

Her lips curled and she said with an icy calm, 'If you find this upsetting, Edward, you have no one to blame but yourself.'

'I don't blame you, sir. I mean accepting someone else's son can't have been easy and I should be grateful to you for giving me your name. No,' he shook his head, 'that wasn't what I wanted to say at all. I am grateful.'

Edward cleared his throat but his voice was oddly hoarse. 'Yes, Paul, I did treat you badly and I'm sorry about it now, but it wasn't for the reason you imagine. What I wanted was to hurt your mother as she hurt me and the way to do that was through you.'

'You can believe that,' Susan said bitterly.

Edward ignored her. 'Paul, if only you knew how often I've looked at you and wished you were my son instead of that – that idiot we have upstairs.'

'How dare you call James an idiot,' Susan shouted, her blue eyes glittering with anger. 'He's slow, he's backward but he's not – '

'Susan,' Edward said patiently, 'you can call James slow, mentally retarded, it all comes to the same thing, he'll always be a child.' He paused. 'Maybe you've learned to accept it but I haven't. God forgive me, he's my own son but I'm ashamed of him.'

'You're both ashamed of him, that's the trouble,' Paul said quietly. 'You can hardly bear to look at him that's why you spend so little time with James. Well, he has feelings too, you know, and thoughts too; no one knows what goes through his head. He's someone to me. I love him and that's why he's happiest with me.'

'Very noble, Paul, and I'm sure you genuinely believe it. But you can't know and I hope you never do know what it means to have a son like James. To be told that you have a son, all your hopes and dreams centred on that new life then to be told that he'll remain a child all his life.'

'I do understand, I understand only too well. If James had been born normal then he would be the heir, the rightful heir.'

'No! No! No!' It was torn out of Susan. 'The mill was your grandfather's and now it is mine. Mine to hand on to you. James's birth wouldn't have altered that.'

'You're wrong, Mother. I'm afraid you're wrong. Illegitimate sons have no claims, I do know that.' He walked out of the room.

A minute or two later Edward went out too. Susan didn't know that he had gone to Paul's room.

*   *   *

335

The bookshelves had a number of spaces.

'You're taking some reading matter with you?'

'Yes.'

'Paul?' Edward extended a hand. 'We can be friends, can't we?'

'I hope so.' The handshake was firm.

Uninvited Edward sat down. 'As a favour would you drop this 'sir' nonsense?'

'That shouldn't be difficult, I've had seventeen years of calling you Papa or Father.' He smiled. 'It would be difficult to change now.'

'Thank you – son.' He got up. 'You'll have some last-minute packing to do so I'll leave you to get on with it. See you at breakfast. Goodnight, Paul.'

'Good night, Father.' Paul watched the door closing. Tomorrow he would be gone and it was for the best. They all needed a breathing space.

Susan was busy checking the household accounts while Victoria stood at the window looking out. Quickly tiring of that she began to move restlessly about the room.

'Victoria, can't you settle to do something?' Susan said in much the same tone of voice her own mother had used when she had been that age.

'There's nothing to do and I miss Paul.'

'You could reply to his letter.'

'I've done that but I won't see him until Christmas and that's ages and ages.'

Susan sighed. After three attempts at the same column of figures she gave up and put down the book. The child did look miserable and remembering the dark storms of her own girlhood she looked at her daughter with an exasperated sympathy.

'Darling, haven't I just bought you two lovely new gowns, that should make you feel on top of the world.'

'When am I going to wear them?'

'You've never been short of invitations.'

'I'm going to be now,' she said sulkily.

'And why should that be?'

'Oh, Mama, you don't know anything,' she burst out. 'They all wanted Paul because he's better looking than the other boys but they couldn't invite him without me.'

'What nonsense. You're very pretty and well you know it.'

'And that's why – oh, never mind, you'd never understand.'

Susan smiled to herself. She knew well enough that the less attractive daughters of their friends envied Victoria her beauty and it was possible they were none too keen to invite competition. Then she laughed out loud. How ridiculous! Fifteen-year-olds and jealousy already rearing its ugly head.

'What are you laughing at?'

'You! Paul has never been keen on parties but you made such a fuss that he only went to please you.'

'I know.' She made a circle on the carpet with her toe, examined the mark left until the pile recovered. 'Mama, do you know what I really wish?'

'What do you wish, Victoria?' her mother said kindly.

'That Paul wasn't my brother then one day we could get married.'

'Now that is just silly.'

'It's not silly, I love him.'

'We all love Paul.'

'Not that way,' she said scornfully. 'I love him, you know – different.'

'Then all I can say is you've changed. As a young child you were positively horrid to Paul.'

'Only because Nanny and everybody liked him better than me. Not Papa though,' she said thoughtfully. 'Why was that, Mama?'

'Lots of fathers don't fuss over their sons.'

Victoria had her mother's full attention now and wanted to make the most of it even though she looked a bit wary when she said, 'Mama, you won't be angry if I ask you something, will you?'

'I don't know until I hear it.'

Her eyes dropped to the floor and her voice was little more than a whisper. 'Why is it Papa and you sometimes use different bedrooms? Rachel said her parents always use the same one and Mina said hers do too except when they have a quarrel.'

Susan was appalled. 'Victoria, I sincerely hope you do not discuss your parents. That is a private matter.'

'Well, I had to say something so I told a lie. I said you did – all the time. But why don't you?'

Losing her temper would be a mistake, this had to be handled delicately. It was obvious what they had been discussing. Rachel was older and possibly her mother had decided the time had come for that kind of talk. Informing Victoria of what lay ahead was something she had hoped to put off for a year or two.

'I am a business woman with very different interests from Rachel's mother or Mina's.' What on earth was she going to say?

'I know you need to be on your own to think out the day's problems,' Victoria said importantly.

Susan clutched at it. 'That is exactly it, my dear,' she said, relieved to have the matter settled so easily.

'You don't want any more children after James, that's another thing, isn't it?'

'Victoria, I do not like this conversation.'

'Then you're not like Rachel's mama, she says mothers have a duty to tell their daughters about babies and everything in case they get themselves into trouble.'

'I'm aware of my duties and we'll discuss these matters when I consider the time right.'

'I know most of it anyway,' Victoria said as she went out the door.

CHAPTER TWENTY-THREE

The gilt-edged invitation was on the mantelpiece; putting it there was a habit Susan had picked up from her mother. She knew Edward would be pleased, he always was when an invitation came from Robina and George Walker. Very comfortably off, the Walkers entertained lavishly and although Susan enjoyed their company she often felt sorry for George. Love of money, not of George, had been the attraction for Robina, almost a head taller than her slightly built husband. They looked an ill-matched couple and neither seemed to have much to say to the other.

That Robina was attracted to Edward, Susan was in no doubt, but whether those feelings were reciprocated she didn't know. Edward liked women and Robina was undoubtedly a fine-looking woman though there was a hardness about her mouth that made her look calculating. Somehow she didn't see Edward seducing his best friend's wife though on the occasions he did tease Robina the invitation in her eyes was plain enough.

One of the new gowns was laid out on the bed and after a leisurely soak in the perfumed bathwater Susan dressed with care. The perfect cut allowed the gown to mould to her figure rather than cling and the vivid blue was startling against her fair hair and creamy skin. The choker of real pearls, a gift from Edward's mother, added the final touch.

Edward's face lit up with pleasure when he saw her. She knew that she was looking her best but she still liked to hear Edward's opinion.

'Yes, I do like that, it's perfect on you. Now aren't you glad I persuaded you to get something new?'

'Yes, of course I am,' she said, half turning to get a view of the back. 'Let me look at you. Yes, very smart.' She flicked a tiny speck from his shoulder.

There were more than a dozen people in the Walkers' drawing-room when Susan and Edward arrived. Susan had only taken a few steps into the room when her fingers dug into Edward's arm and hearing her startled gasp he looked at her quickly.

'What's the matter?'

'You might have told me,' she hissed.

'Told you what?' Then enlightenment dawned. 'Oh, the Camerons! I didn't know they were to be here but what of it? To hear you one would think you had a personal grudge against him.'

'I'm totally indifferent to Mr Cameron,' she said frostily.

'Doesn't look like it the way you carry on. For heaven's sake, Susan, David Cameron had a perfect right to do what he did and it looks as though they are to be in our social circle so you had better try to be a bit friendlier.'

'Darlings, lovely to see you,' Robina enthused as she kissed Susan then, raising her face, waited for Edward's kiss on her cheek. Her vivaciousness wrapped them in a closeness Susan found slightly ridiculous. After the greetings Robina studied Susan's gown. 'This is new? But of course it is and quite, quite charming.' Her eyes swivelled. 'Your wife has excellent taste, Edward. And now come along and let me introduce the newcomers, Mr and Mrs Cameron.'

'Robina, Susan and I have already met Mr Cameron.'

Robina clapped a hand to her mouth like a child caught out in a moment of naughtiness. 'How silly of me, George did mention something about Mr Cameron and the distillery but any talk of business bores me, goes right over my head. We're not all like you, Susan,' she said waspishly.

Edward's fingers touched the bare shoulder.

'You could introduce us to Mrs Cameron. Neither of us has had that pleasure.'

'Then come along. She's a sweet little thing,' she said

dismissively, then when Edward was passing a remark to a couple who had just come in, Robina whispered to Susan, 'She's nothing but isn't he gorgeous?'

The Camerons were at the far side of the room but as if on cue David Cameron turned. Their eyes met and Susan found herself unable to look away.

'He is, isn't he?' Robina nudged her.

'S-sorry – '

'Having that effect on you too, my dear, I can see.' Then playfully, 'Don't be greedy, Susan, you have a handsome man of your own.'

'Robina, you make the most outrageous remarks.'

'Oh, I'm quick, Susan, that's my trouble. I can interpret a look,' she said meaningly.

Susan drew in her breath sharply but was saved an answer by Edward's reappearance. Robina took Edward's arm and tucked it in hers then marched him across the room with Susan a step behind. Everything about this evening was beginning to irritate Susan. Normally Robina's over-possessiveness didn't trouble her but just now she needed Edward. The prospect of being in David's company had her feeling curiously defenceless.

Gushingly Robina made the introductions and would have lingered had not George joined them. The talk became general until Robina said pointedly, 'George, have you seen to everything?'

'I very much doubt it, my dear, but we'll both go and check. They moved away and Edward immediately engaged David in conversation. The two women looked at each other and smiled. Gwen Cameron was small and fragile with large brown eyes and the sweetest of smiles.

'Do you think you'll like living here, Mrs Cameron? It must be a big change for you.'

'It is but I think I'll settle all right. David spent his early years in this area. Not that he's told me much about it but you know what men are.'

Edward and David broke off their conversation. 'We're not likely to be eating for some time so I suggest we find

341

ourselves a place to sit.' Edward's eyes went to four chairs and with David's help he placed them so that they could converse easily.

Once seated Gwen spoke in her soft voice. 'Do you have a family, Mrs Brodie?'

'Yes, we have three. Two boys and a girl.'

'Our eldest, Paul, is seventeen and in his first term at Blackhall College,' Edward said with all the pride of a father.

'We have two lovely daughters and a son to complete the family was our dearest wish but it wasn't to be,' Gwen said wistfully.

'These things can't be made to order.'

'No, Mr Brodie and more's the pity.'

'How old are your daughters?' Edward asked.

'Sylvia is fifteen and Amy is nine and as different as chalk and cheese. 'Aren't they, David?'

'Our Amy is a fighter, she'll hold her own with the best of them,' he said with the lopsided smile Susan remembered. 'Should have been a boy my father-in-law says.'

Gwen Cameron took over. 'Sylvia is inclined to be reserved and she's going to miss her close friend. We're hoping she'll find a companion of her age, someone to bring her out of her shell.'

'Look no further,' Edward said, deliberately avoiding Susan's eyes. 'Victoria has just turned fifteen and full of life, too full at times.'

Gwen's face lit up. 'How nice if the girls could meet.'

'That should be quite easy to arrange,' Edward said with a smile to Gwen.

Mrs Cameron looked at Susan.

Susan was beginning to feel panicky, everything was getting out of hand but she strove to hide her disquiet. 'Of course your daughter must come to Aran Heights and meet Victoria.' Then felt forced to add, 'Indeed you must all visit us one day.'

'That would be an honour,' David Cameron said gravely and she flushed. Did she imagine it or were those dark eyes mocking her?

'I'm afraid it's going to be a long time before we have our house-warming party, there's such a lot to do. But we very much hope that you and your family will come.'

'We'd be delighted,' Edward said warmly, 'and *I* speak for us all.'

'How much of the year are you to be spending in Scotland, Mr Cameron?'

'Quite a lot I expect, Mrs Brodie. There's much to be done and expansion is very much on the cards. However, once everything is running smoothly and I have someone trained to take control then we'll see.' As if it had just occurred to him David turned to Edward. 'If you are worrying about your brother's position then don't. I need someone with his experience.'

'But not the one you had in mind to – '

'Take over?' He shook his head. 'With due respect your brother is not decisive enough.'

'Don't you mean ruthless?' Susan shot at him.

'Perhaps I do, Mrs Brodie, but there are degrees of ruthlessness and to succeed in business a measure of it is essential. In your position you should appreciate that.'

'You may have gathered from that, Mrs Cameron, that my wife is a very competent business woman.'

'I had heard.' She turned to Susan. 'You can't know how I envy you. To succeed in a man's world is a great achievement.'

'Once one cuts through the prejudice, Mrs Cameron, it isn't so difficult and I was fortunate. My brother's interest is in farming and my father had me trained to take over from him.' David's eyes were on her; she could feel them but her attention stayed with his wife.

'David has engaged a tutor for Sylvia and I can tell you that raised a few eyebrows back home.'

'Did you object?'

'Not at all, I backed him all the way. Sylvia has a good brain and with no son to take over it seemed a sensible idea. There's no pressure on Sylvia but at least she'll be properly educated.' She grimaced. 'All I'm capable of is

343

sewing a fine seam and giving a moderate performance on the piano.'

'My wife underestimates herself. She is as shrewd as they come.' David laughed. 'Enough about us, you mentioned another son. How old is he?'

Susan had been expecting the question and her face shadowed. 'James is the youngest and I'm afraid he – he's backward,' she said, getting the words out with difficulty.

Gwen Cameron became flustered and looked helplessly to her husband.

'A great tragedy but these things happen,' David said, quietly sympathetic. 'At least you have the means to care for your child.'

'Unless one has first-hand experience one cannot begin to understand the anguish,' Edward said drily.

They were silent, an uncomfortable silence and it was a relief to all when their hostess came in to announce that they should go through to the dining-room.

For the remainder of the evening Edward and Susan were claimed by their friends.

Back at Aran Heights Susan and Edward went through to the sitting-room to discuss the evening.

'Enjoyed it I must say, though Robina is a bitch the way she humiliates poor George and embarrasses everyone else.'

'She annoys me,' Susan said, 'I often wonder how George puts up with it.'

'He won't for much longer.'

'Why? Is there something I don't know?'

'I got it in confidence a few months ago but no harm in telling you now. George has been seeing a young widow, seems pretty taken with her and this one isn't after his money. She has more than enough of her own.'

Susan's eyes widened. 'You mean George and Robina are parting?'

'Seems likely.'

'I know Robina has only herself to blame but I can't help feeling sorry for her. Do you think she suspects?'

Edward guffawed. 'Robina! She would never dream that George would look elsewhere.'

'When the blow falls she'll need a shoulder to cry on.'

'Don't look at me, I'm keeping my distance.'

'I'm very glad to hear it.'

Susan was beginning to feel guilty at the way she was neglecting her mother and with work well forward at the mill she decided to take the day off and visit Moorend. She wore a burgundy corduroy costume and a small matching hat and looked both attractive and warm. The day was cold and bright and pleasant for walking. Arriving at Moorend she was welcomed in by Mrs Dunbar.

The cluttered homely look had gone from Moorend to be replaced by quiet elegance. Even its owner had a new look. Long gone were the comfortably shabby suits and now Euan Clapperton wore fine tweed for the house, rough tweed out of doors. He was a gentleman farmer and should look the part as his new wife pointed out.

Susan kissed them both and dutifully remarked on the pleasing appearance of the drawing-room which had recently been in the hands of the decorator. It was the same room where she and Winnie had so often sat and chatted with the tabby cat stretched out before the warmth. There was no sign of a cat now. With no gift for small talk Euan Clapperton made little contribution to the conversation. Fortunately that morning a letter from Paul had arrived at the farmhouse and the talk centred round it. After a little over an hour and promising a longer visit next time Susan took the short cut across the fields. Matthew saw her and broke off what he was doing to greet his sister.

'Don't mind the back door do you? We're very informal here.'

'I don't.' she laughed. 'But I bet you don't bring Mother in this way.'

'Oh, no, it is the red carpet for her ladyship.'

She stood on the stone floor watching him use the scraper for his muddy footwear and change into other boots.

'Winnie has you well trained.'

'Henpecked.' They went through the door and into the kitchen where at the sink a girl in a coarse apron was cleaning vegetables. Along the passage Matthew opened the door of a square-shaped room dominated by a desk and a pile of papers clipped together.

'Winnie does the accounts here. Like you with the library this is her den and out of bounds to the rest of us.' They went out and into the sitting-room.

'Where's Winnie?'

'In the village. Aunt Tina is poorly and Winnie is suggesting she closes up the cottage and come to us at least for a while but she wants to hang on to her independence.'

'Matthew, they're all getting old; sad, isn't it? For a long time they seem to remain the same then suddenly you notice them ageing. Mother's slowing down.'

'Can't say I've noticed,' he said carelessly. 'Sit down and give me the news. How is Paul?'

'Enjoying life or says he is anyway. He'll be home for Christmas.'

'Young Peter thinks his big cousin Paul is marvellous. He's made up his mind he's going to college too. Could be he's like you; he certainly isn't interested in the farm.'

'But Duncan is so you've nothing to worry about.'

'Incidentally you didn't tell me the new owner of the distillery is that accountant chap who gave you the occasional lesson at Aran Heights.'

'Didn't think it would interest you.'

'I like to know what is going on. Have you met him?'

'Briefly and in company. I'm not sure if he recognised me or not. Anyway I didn't say anything about him having worked for Father.'

'Prefers to forget it?'

'Perhaps, perhaps not; anyway it isn't important.'

'Funny though, you have to admit. I mean why a distillery in this area when their main concern is in England?'

'Saw a bargain and snapped it up.'

'More to it than that I think. Here's Winnie,' he said as she tapped at the window. The back door opened, they heard her voice then she was with them.

'Susan, how lovely! Has your big brother offered you a refreshment?'

'Sorry, the thought never occurred to me.' He got up. 'No rest for the wicked. I'll leave you to your gossip.'

'Notice, Susan, how men talk and women gossip?'

'True though.' Matthew grinned.

'On your way out tell Edith or Annie to bring in tea.'

'How is your Aunt Tina?' Susan said when her brother had departed.

'Quite chirpy but at her age it isn't easy to throw off a chill. I pop in most days and oh, isn't it lovely news about Hannah! Your mother came over to tell us.'

'A little daughter, very tiny but gaining weight.' She paused. 'I'm very honoured and proud that the baby is to be called after me.'

'Congratulations! No surprise though, I mean you two were always like sisters.' She turned her head. 'Thank you, Annie and no, don't pour I'll give it a little longer.'

During the drinking of the tea the talk was of babies and family matters then Winnie put down her cup. 'Susan, that Mr Cameron at the distillery, is he your one-time heart-throb?'

'He was the accountant who came to Aran Heights,' Susan said stiffly.

'I know, Matthew mentioned it.' She looked at Susan in surprise. 'Sorry! Sorry! If I said anything out of place it was only intended as a joke.'

'No, you didn't. It's just a little embarrassing remembering the silly things I said to you at that time.'

'Well, you needn't be. Heavens! When I think of the times I've told you things I wouldn't want anyone else to hear. Have no fear, this is between us and no one else.'

'I almost fainted when I saw him.'

'You hadn't a clue?'

'No, the name was never mentioned – just a client and his solicitor.'

'Where did you meet him?'

'Croft House. Thomas introduced us and to be honest I knew that he was leaving it to me and I, coward that I am, decided to meet him as a stranger.'

'Maybe that suited him too?'

'I've a feeling it did.'

CHAPTER TWENTY-FOUR

Having missed one week which would have been noticed by the minister, Susan and Edward braved the storm to attend the kirk. The sermon was long and uninspiring and the worshippers were glad to leave the poorly heated place of worship. Rachel's parents were there and Victoria went off to spend the day with them and their two daughters. After waving them off Susan and Edward hurried to their own carriage. In spite of the warmth of her cloak Susan shivered in the November damp and her fingers, locked together inside the fur muff, tingled painfully.

November was a dreary month heralding the cold, dark wintry days. The promise of snow was in the air and once it came the Shotts hills would be cloaked in white but just now they looked drained of colour, brooding and depressing.

The scalding hot Scotch broth awaiting them helped to take the chill away and after changing into more comfortable clothes they sat at either side of the huge log fire.

'We must discuss this dinner party, Susan. Have you thought about whom to invite with the Camerons?'

'Really, Edward,' Susan bristled, 'after the way Mr Cameron treated your father, and your mother too for that matter, I'm surprised that you should wish to entertain them.'

'And I'm surprised at your attitude, it's totally incomprehensible to me.'

'Then it shouldn't be.'

'Like it or not, Susan, David Cameron is my half brother and I for one intend – '

'To keep in with him because he is Percy Carruther's son-in-law. Had he been a penniless nobody it would have been a different story.'

349

'Granted, but then he isn't a penniless nobody and he happens to be the new owner of the distillery.'

Susan pursed her lips but said nothing.

'David and his wife are to be invited to Aran Heights, I insist on it, so there's an end to it.'

Still she said nothing.

'Before that you had better ask Mrs Cameron and the girls for afternoon tea or are you against that too?'

'Not at all,' she said frigidly, 'but I think it should have been left. At some stage the girls would have met in other company and decided for themselves if they wished to become friends.'

There was a dangerous edge to Edward's voice. 'I wish to God I hadn't mentioned the girls meeting and if that is the way you feel forget about it.'

'And be thought of as inhospitable? Certainly not. No, Edward, I'll go through with it though an afternoon away from the mill is an inconvenience.' With a kind of horror Susan listened to her own voice and felt a deep shame. Getting away from the mill at one time would have posed problems but not now. No wonder Edward was shocked and angry; she was behaving abominably. And it was all David Cameron's fault. Why did he have to come back to Aranvale? Hadn't he caused enough upset in her life? And then there was her secret fear, Paul's strong resemblance to David, what if it was remarked upon? Some days she felt that she would make herself ill with worry.

Edward knew that she liked entertaining and he must be wondering about her reluctance to have anything to do with Mr and Mrs Cameron. David's treatment of her in-laws was a good excuse and true to a certain extent but it wouldn't do much longer. She would have to watch her step and try to behave normally.

Feeling wretched, Susan was on the point of apologising but he had his face screened by the book he was reading and the moment passed.

*   *   *

350

Mrs Cameron and her two daughters were coming for afternoon tea. During the morning there had been intermittent squally showers and Susan saw to it that the maids kept up the fires. By afternoon the drawing-room was well heated and welcoming. Victoria was standing at the window and saw the carriage enter the wide gates.

'That's the carriage, Mama.'

'Then come away from the window.'

Some minutes passed before the maid announced the visitors.

Small though she was, Gwen Cameron held herself well. 'This is very kind of you, Mrs Brodie, and we have been looking forward to coming to Aran Heights.'

Susan smiled. She liked David's wife and wished the circumstances had been different. Introductions over they sat down, the three girls together on the Chesterfield sofa while she and Mrs Cameron occupied a wing chair on either side of the blazing fire.

'This is lovely and warm,' Mrs Cameron said, holding her hands out to the heat.

'The house takes a lot of heating, we are so exposed here.'

'Our other house is much warmer isn't it, Mama?'

'Yes, Amy, dear, but the Beeches lay empty and as your papa said, it takes a long time to get completely rid of cold and damp.' She turned away and spoke to Susan. 'Actually we are quite comfortable and I don't complain because David did suggest us waiting until the workmen finished but I prefer the discomfort and being with my husband.'

While Mrs Cameron chatted on about the alterations being made to the house Susan found herself studying David Cameron's daughters. The younger child, Amy, was by far the prettier. She had her father's blue-black curly hair and dark heavily lashed eyes. One day she was going to be a beauty, Susan thought.

The elder girl was very different and just escaped being plain. She was fair like her mother but without her gentleness. Sylvia's was an arresting face with hidden depths in the

351

NORA KAY

grey-blue eyes. Her long fair hair was brushed back, showing her high forehead and she wore her hair secured at the back with a ribboned bow. What was so startling in such a young girl and what made Susan feel vaguely uncomfortable was the quiet dignified reserve. That same quiet reserve she remembered in the young David and for no reason at all Susan felt a disquiet and a curious foreboding of trouble ahead.

A disapproving look from her mother stopped Amy swinging her legs and with a deep sigh the child responded by fiddling with the sash of her dress. Catching Susan's eye, Victoria tried to turn a giggle into a cough and noticing it, Amy gave her an impish grin.

Susan laughed and bent across to touch Amy. 'Victoria is amused, Amy dear, because that's what she used to do when she got tired sitting still.'

'Oh, she isn't – ' her mother began anxiously but Susan stopped her.

'I can still remember how difficult it was for me to keep still when I was that age. It's just a pity this isn't the summer and we could be in the garden but never mind, once tea is over Victoria will find something to amuse you.'

'We could play hide and seek,' Amy said hopefully.

'No!' Mrs Cameron said firmly and shook her head to Susan as if to say please don't encourage her. It was obvious that she found her younger daughter a handful.

A welcome distraction came with the arrival of the tea things. Amy's eyes widened in anticipation. The doily-covered plates were filled with dainty three-cornered sandwiches, tiny buttered scones, macaroons, iced sponges and an assortment of biscuits.

If Mrs Cameron ate sparingly the girls made up for her. Victoria had a good appetite and a sweet tooth and seeing her tucking in was the signal for Sylvia and Amy to do likewise. The sheer joy of eating did more than anything to chase away reserve, Susan thought as she watched their expressions. By the time the plates had shed most of their load the three of them were at ease and anxious to be on their own.

352

'Victoria, take Sylvia and Amy through to the small sitting-room. It should be quite cosy and you'll get freedom to do as you wish.'

'Amy can be difficult,' Mrs Cameron continued after the girls had gone. 'She's a dear but gets too much of her own way. My father spoils her terribly and David gives them both a great deal more freedom than I think is good for them.' She smiled. 'David had quite a hard life and was used, even at an early age, to making his own decisions. That is something I have had to get used to, Mrs Brodie. David's upbringing was so different from mine and he is adamant that the girls will not be over-protected.'

'Victoria has quietened down but she was very rebellious and we had a difficult time with her.'

'She is very like you.'

'So everyone says. Your father must miss you all?'

'He does.' A frown puckered her forehead. 'My mother died some years ago and I'm an only child but, oh dear, I'm talking too much about myself.'

'You're not, I'm interested. But do excuse me while I ring for the maid to take away the tray.'

'Not much left to take away.' Mrs Cameron laughed.

'Mrs Carson will be delighted, she likes to know that her baking has been appreciated. Tell me, Mrs Cameron, as an only child were you lonely?'

'Not really but I used to feel guilty not being a boy.'

'Hardly your fault.'

'No, but you know the silly thoughts you have as a child.' She fingered the ring on her finger. 'David and my father get on famously and incidentally he is very impressed with the way you are managing the mill. I think he is putting you forward as an example to Sylvia.'

'I think if your daughter puts her mind to it she would succeed at most things. She strikes me as being very competent for one so young.'

'Thank you.' The warmth of the room had brought a faint flush to Gwen Cameron's cheeks. 'Why my husband decided to take over a distillery of all things I'll never know.'

353

'Didn't he tell you?'

Gwen shook her head. 'He had discussed it with my father and a decision was made to offer for it. Only after the offer was accepted did I learn of it.'

'I would have been furious. Weren't you annoyed?'

Gwen looked taken aback at the suggestion. 'Not annoyed, surprised yes, but when David explained to me that he had spent his early years in this district and liked the thought of having an interest here I quite understood. At one time he had relatives here but they are all dead or moved away.'

Susan smiled. 'So you didn't try to talk him out of it even though it was uprooting you all?'

'I wouldn't have dreamt of it but I think my father might have been less keen had he known that David intended to spend part of the year in Scotland. Like me he thought that my husband intended putting in a qualified person and returning periodically to see that everything was running smoothly.'

'Instead of which he decided to buy a house?'

'Yes, he now thinks that the distillery needs constant supervision for a year or so.'

'And he'll be anxious to learn the trade for himself,' Susan said drily.

Gwen Cameron looked unhappy. 'Forgive me, Mrs Brodie, but I can't rid myself of the idea that you don't much care for my husband.'

Rather than meet those searching eyes Susan got up to straighten a crystal vase that was only slightly out of position. 'Distresses the eye, don't you think? I'm getting to be as bad as my mother, she can't bear to see anything out of place.' She sat down, feeling more able to meet those questioning eyes.

'I'm sorry if I have given you that impression. I hardly know your husband,' she lied, 'but I imagine he is a very astute business man.'

'Oh, he's that all right but I expect Edward is too.'

'A frustrated one. My elder brother died in an accident and Matthew, my twin, wanted to be a farmer. That only left me, Mrs Cameron. I was desperately keen to learn the business and my father had me trained to take over. Edward has a lot of pride and for a long time he found it intolerable to have his wife at the helm.'

'It couldn't have been easy for you?'

'It wasn't.'

'Does your brother-in-law resent taking orders from my husband?'

'Far from it. Thomas is only too grateful to have a position in the distillery.'

The clock chimed and Mrs Cameron glanced at the mantel-piece. 'How time flies when one is enjoying oneself. Thank you very much for a very enjoyable afternoon but now we really must go.'

'I'll ring for the maid to tell the girls.' Susan smiled and held out her hand. 'I've enjoyed meeting you.' And it was true. Mrs Gwen Cameron was a genuinely nice person and an intelligent one too.

CHAPTER TWENTY-FIVE

T he invitations went out to the Carmichaels, the Lawsons and the Baxters, all of whom had business interests in the area. Their acceptances came within the week as did one from David and Gwen Cameron. All were anxious to meet the daughter of Percy Carruthers and curious about the local lad who had made good.

The dinner was arranged for Thursday evening and on Monday Mrs Carson produced a menu. They went over it together but it was a mere formality and both knew it. Susan invariably agreed with Mrs Carson's suggestions. In the early days Susan's energies had been taken up with the mill and though she spent less time there now she saw no point in changing something that had worked so well in the past.

Miss Wilson continued to see to the smooth running of the house and Mrs Carson had a free hand in the kitchen. Proud of the confidence placed in her, Mrs Carson could be relied upon to produce a meal that would be hugely enjoyed on the night.

Seldom had Susan been in such a state of nervous excitement and Edward shook his head, puzzled by the change in her but wisely refrained from remarking on it, knowing that it would probably only make her worse. Women were unpredictable creatures.

What was David thinking as he prepared for this evening? Susan couldn't help wondering. Would he remember those other times when it had been the servants' entrance for him and then the back stairs to the library? Her lips curled into a smile as she stepped out of the perfumed bathwater and wrapped herself in the warm fluffy towel. Patting herself dry she stretched over for her robe and sat before the mirror studying her face and wondering how long her looks would last. Soon she would be forty. The thought both alarmed and saddened her. How would age affect her? Would her skin tauten or like her mother would her fate be the little pads of slack flesh? As if to reassure herself she touched the skin under her chin and felt its firmness.

Blue for so long had been her favourite colour but now she thought it suited her less well. It was too cold. Tonight she would wear the rose pink.

In the hall she met Edward on his way upstairs.

'Edward?'

Knowing it was his opinion she wanted he stopped and she twirled for his benefit. Desire quickened as he looked at her. She was still very beautiful and his eyes rested on the fragile material swathed over her firm breasts then to the gently nipped-in waist and the lovely full skirt.

'You'll do.' The words were nothing but his expression told her all she needed to know.

'Thank you.'

The Carmichaels could be depended upon to arrive first and when Edward and Susan heard the sound of the first carriage in the courtyard Edward grinned. 'Want to bet that's John and Lydia?'

'At least they never hold up the meal.' Susan laughed as they went along to the drawing-room to be ready to receive their guests.

'Surely we're not first!' Lydia said as she always did. She was a sallow-faced woman with a high nervous voice.

'Someone has to be, Lydia.' Edward smiled as he kissed her and shook John's hand. John Carmichael was a small dapper man who liked to flirt with the ladies but in a way that gave no offence. With charming old-world courtesy he raised Susan's hand to his lips.

'How very beautiful you look, my dear,' he murmured then, turning to Edward: 'Your wife has the kind of beauty that survives the years. I hope you appreciate her, old boy.'

'My wife's appearance has always been a source of pleasure to me,' Edward said smoothly.

'How lucky you are, Susan, to have a husband who still pays you compliments,' Lydia said plaintively. 'I can't recall the last time John paid me one.'

'Then he should be thoroughly ashamed of himself,' Edward said as he put an arm round her narrow shoulders which barely held up the flimsy straps of her burgundy gown.

They chatted together until Mark and Eleanor Lawson arrived, closely followed by George and Beatrice Baxter. George's booming voice and hearty laughter could be heard before he reached the drawing-room and Lydia gave a pained look.

'Fond though I am of George it must be dreadful to live with that voice. Poor Beatrice, she has my sympathy.'

'Sh-sh,' Susan said warningly, as both couples were about to enter. For the next few minutes there were shrieks of delight as friend greeted friend.

Susan was aware of Mark Lawson moving away from the others and waiting for her to do the same. But she didn't, she didn't want to give him any encouragement. Fond though she was of Mark it was no more than that, whereas he had made no secret of the fact that his feelings went deeper. His own marriage to Eleanor was dead. All they shared was a house and the children and occasionally a social occasion such as the invitation to Aran Heights. More than once Mark had said that he found it utterly inconceivable that Edward could look at another woman when he had a wife like Susan. At first his advances had amused her, he was never objectionable and she had been flattered at his persistence. Only once in a fit of depression when things had been particularly bad with Edward had she been tempted and how glad she was that she hadn't succumbed.

Mr and Mrs Cameron were barely inside the door when Edward was over to greet them. With a murmured 'excuse me' Susan followed.

'Welcome to Aran Heights, David,' Edward said heartily.

Then he kissed Gwen on the cheek and shook hands with her husband.

'Thank you, I'm delighted to be here. You know, Edward, as a young lad I always admired Aran Heights, there was something about it that made it stand out from the others.'

'As far as my wife is concerned you've said the right thing. Mind you, I have a great affection for the old house myself but Susan loves it.' While he spoke he took Gwen by the arm and was leading her over to where the others had broken off their conversation to meet the newcomer.

It left Susan alone with David and as she brought her gaze up to meet his she was mesmerised by those dark eyes observing her with a cool concentration. She felt angry that he should be so much at ease when her own heart was thumping painfully. Then she saw a nerve twitch and there was something in his voice – embarrassment – apology – she couldn't tell.

He spoke very softly. 'I'm well aware that my presence in your house doesn't give you pleasure but don't worry, Mrs Brodie.' He smiled into her face. 'You chose to meet me as a stranger and I find that suits me too.'

'You had the advantage. I was taken aback,' she said shortly, then with an effort managed to adopt her hostess manner and with a charming smile touched his sleeve. 'Do come and let Edward introduce you to the others and I must see to my duties.'

In the dining-room the guests sat in high-backed chairs at the long table covered in stiff, pure white damask. The silver dishes glittered in the light from the tall candles and it caught too the facets of the crystal glasses. Edward sat with Mrs Cameron on his right. No one could be more charming than Edward when he made the effort, Susan thought, and he was making the effort for Gwen. That it was appreciated was evident when her smile widened and her lips twitched at some amusing remark.

George Baxter enjoyed good food and when he got it it received the attention it deserved. He put in a word here and there but largely left the conversation to others.

Knowing how snobbish Beatrice Baxter could be Susan was highly amused at the number of times she drew David into the conversation. That she was impressed with his quiet courtesy and good looks was not lost on her husband who looked over to Susan and raised an eyebrow. She smiled back then answered a remark of John Carmichael's who then called on Beatrice for her opinion. Lydia, feeling neglected, decided to get in on the conversation.

'Excuse me, Mrs Cameron, but how is your son getting on with his tutor?'

Gwen smiled. 'We haven't a son, Mrs Carmichael, David engaged Mr Beveridge to teach our elder daughter.'

'A tutor for a girl!' Lydia almost gasped.

'Why not, Lydia?' Susan laughed. 'Have you forgotten that I shared a tutor with Matthew?'

'No, I hadn't,' she said, flushing because she had then excused herself by saying, 'but then you're the exception.'

'Your father must have been very forward thinking, Susan.'

Susan shook her head and leaned back as the maid removed her plate.

'I'm not so sure about forward thinking, Beatrice. Two for the price of one made economic sense.'

Lydia wouldn't leave it alone though her husband shot her a warning glance.

'Advanced education may have some advantage if a girl is unattractive and unlikely to marry, though even then – '

Susan saw Gwen Cameron's flush of annoyance. David looked amused.

'Lydia, both Sylvia and Amy are nice-looking girls, indeed Amy is going to be a real beauty.'

Gwen gave Susan a quick smile and David looked both pleased and surprised.

'In that case it is beyond me. I know we are perfectly satisfied with our governess,' Lydia said huffily, then turned to Beatrice for support. 'You are too, aren't you, Beatrice?'

Beatrice leaned forward with a soft rounded thrust of bare shoulders.

'Perfectly satisfied but then Mary is very talented musically.' She dismissed Lydia and rested her eyes on David. 'Forgive me for not quite agreeing but don't you think that giving young ladies a broader education can only result in them losing some of their femininity?'

'For heaven's sake, Beatrice,' Mark said almost angrily, 'how can you say that? No one could call Susan anything but charmingly feminine.'

'Why, Mark! Thank you, that was sweet of you but Beatrice may have a point. Edward thinks I've developed a hard streak.'

'What a lot of nonsense you all talk,' George boomed. 'Surely it all depends on the girl and if she has brains.'

'See what you've started, Lydia,' John said with an edge to his voice. 'That's all right between us, we know each other so well but Mr and Mrs Cameron don't.'

'No need to apologise,' David said quietly. 'Another viewpoint is always refreshing.'

'Good! Then perhaps, Mr Cameron, you wouldn't mind answering this,' Eleanor said coyly, twisting the rope of pearls at her throat. 'Would you have bothered the same about your daughter's education if you'd had a son?'

'I sincerely hope that the answer to that is yes. You see, Mrs Lawson, in my opinion there will come a time when everyone, irrespective of sex, whether rich or poor, will be educated according to ability.'

'Then I sincerely hope it isn't in my lifetime,' Lydia sniffed. 'I detest those feminist demonstrations.'

'You may well be right, Mr Cameron,' George said as he wiped his mouth with his napkin. 'Perhaps we should all cultivate our intellects, male and female. The country needs brains and God knows there aren't too many of our politicians over-gifted in that department.'

'Now! Now! George, that's dangerous talk.' Edward laughed.

'Susan, is Victoria to have a tutor?'

'Unlikely, Beatrice, but if she wished then of course.'

'You go along with that, Edward?'

'I most certainly do not. I would have forbidden it.'

'What nonsense, Edward. You've never been able to deny Victoria anything.'

Edward threw up his hands. 'I give in, and now for any favour let us talk about something else.'

CHAPTER TWENTY-SIX

Stifling a yawn, Victoria helped herself to bacon and scrambled egg and carried the plate to the table.

'Off porridge are you?' her father asked.

'I haven't taken it for ages, it's fattening.'

'It is not fattening, dear, and at your age you need a good breakfast.'

'By the look of what she's got there I wouldn't say she was doing too badly.' Edward grinned.

'This is from your brother, Victoria,' Susan said, waving a page of the letter.

'What is he saying?'

'He wants to bring a friend with him when he comes home for Christmas. Edwin somebody – ' She went back to the previous page. 'Edwin Martin. The boy's parents are in India and according to Paul he's going to find it a bit dull spending all his holiday with his grandparents.'

'And I know what that means,' Victoria said, pulling a long face. 'They'll go off on their own and leave me.'

'Then ask one of your own friends to spend a few days when this Edwin is here.'

'That's what to do, Victoria,' Edward said approvingly. 'Then if the young men are agreeable you can always make up a foursome.'

'Ask Mina, we're due her hospitality anyway.'

'Absolutely not, Mama, she's been sweet on Paul for ages and I can just see her making eyes at him, it would be sickening.'

'You'll have to resign yourself to Paul getting married one day, Victoria, and he could do a lot worse than choose Mina.' Her father grinned. Nothing delighted him more than teasing Victoria.

'I don't want her for a sister-in-law and she won't be if I can help it.' She frowned then brightened. 'I know, I'll ask Sylvia.'

'Why on earth do you want to ask Sylvia Cameron?'

'Why shouldn't she?' Edward bristled.

Now why had she said that? Susan could have kicked herself. She might have been able to dissuade Victoria if she'd handled it carefully but now Victoria had Edward on her side.

'I didn't mean it that way. I imagine the Cameron family will be going to Rochdale to spend Christmas there.'

'They're not. Sylvia's grandfather is coming up for Christmas and possibly staying for New Year too.'

'Then you go right ahead and invite Sylvia,' Edward said and was rewarded with a smile.

Susan bit her lip. No matter how hard she tried to keep distance between herself and the Camerons she wasn't succeeding. Victoria, looking smug, finished her breakfast then went out.

'I cannot understand you, Susan. Sylvia is a very suitable companion for Victoria, she's quiet and sensible. Her only fault seems to be that she is a Cameron.'

'Just leave it, Edward.'

'It must have been my imagination but I thought there was a thawing in your attitude to David.'

'He and his wife were guests in this house and I hope I know how to behave,' she said haughtily.

'Oh, you do, my dear, no one could be more dignified and charming. And may I add, though small and fragile, Mrs Cameron is astute; after all she is Percy Carruther's daughter and he doesn't miss a trick.'

'Astute about what? What do you mean?'

'She adores David and she must wonder what it is about him that you dislike.'

'You know, you don't have to wonder,' Susan said harshly. 'I don't suppose you've noticed but your father and mother have never got over that dreadful scene. That said, I have no objections to Sylvia coming here.' Susan got up, flicked a crumb off her skirt and left the breakfast-room.

* * *

The December weather worsened then came a reprieve. The cold east wind dropped and a pale sun glinted through the clouds. Aran Heights had undergone its Christmas cleaning and everything was bright and sparkling. Susan avoided what she called the over-Christmassy look but she had the gardeners bring in armfuls of holly. In one corner of the hall a huge vase was filled with the deep red berries and with the log fire burning cheerfully it was a welcoming sight. The tree she and Victoria had decorated was in the drawing-room and pieces of holly were spread over the picture frames.

Late in the afternoon of the sixteenth the carriage drew up at the front of the house. There were voices and instructions given as the carriage moved away and Paul and his friend entered. Waiting in the hall to greet them were Susan, Edward and Victoria.

With a start of surprise Susan saw that Paul had grown in the time he'd been away and his great height made him look older. She was the first to step forward to greet her son. Paul, looking happy and relaxed, kissed her on the cheek then gave her a hug. 'Wonderful to see you, Mother.'

'Welcome home, Paul,' she said softly.

He crossed to Edward. 'Hello, Father.' They shook hands.

'God, you're stretching, you're as tall as I am.'

Victoria had been standing aside but as Paul turned to her she threw her arms round his neck and kissed him. A bit embarrassed, Paul extricated himself and brought his friend forward.

Edwin Martin was of average height with thick brown hair, a pleasantly rugged face and a ready smile. After bowing politely to Susan he exchanged a firm handshake with Edward then looked at his friend's sister with open admiration. Paul and Edward exchanged looks and both grinned. In her dark skirt and high-necked white lacy blouse, Victoria looked sweet and fresh. She murmured a conventional greeting but her colour had risen and her eyes were shining.

'Where is James?'

'In the nursery,' Susan said. 'I thought you would see him later.'

'No, I want to see him now and introduce him to Edwin.'

'I'll bring him down,' Victoria said with uncharacteristic eagerness.

'Mrs Brodie, I'm very grateful to you for having me.'

'Edwin, we're delighted to meet a friend of Paul's. Your parents are in India I believe?'

'Yes. They're doing a four-year stint. My grandfather has a jute mill in Dundee and my father is looking after the family interests in India.' He smiled across to Paul. 'I'm an only son and this college lark is supposed to prepare me to take on some responsibility.'

'And is it succeeding?' Edward laughed. 'Or are your parents and Paul's pouring money down the drain?'

'Oh, no, sir, truly the money isn't wasted. I mean we really do have to keep our nose to the grindstone.'

'Edwin's right, Father. If we manage to retain a third of what we are taught we'll be doing well.'

'Your son has natural ability, Mr Brodie, I'm just a plodder.'

A disturbance on the stairs made them all look up. Victoria was dragging a reluctant James who grunted angrily. Paul crossed over to take charge.

'What a way to treat your big brother,' he said with mock severity. 'James, it's me! It's Paul.'

'Paul,' James said uncertainly then raised his arms and Paul bent down to clasp the short awkward body.

'I missed everybody, James, but you most of all and I've brought someone to meet you.'

Edwin joined them at the foot of the stairs and without being the least bit embarrassed held out his hand to James who slowly put out his left hand and Edwin shook it gently. 'Hello, James, I'm pleased to meet you. I've heard a lot about you from Paul.'

James looked bewildered but happy as he looked from one face to the other. Edward had walked away; the sight of his son always distressed him.

Paul took his hand. 'Come on, James, we'll take you upstairs. Mother, Edwin is getting the room next to mine, is that right?'

'Yes, I think you'll be quite comfortable, Edwin, but if you want anything be sure to ask.'

'Thanks very much.'

Gwen Cameron was puzzled. 'I thought you would have welcomed a few days at Aran Heights.'

'Mrs Brodie doesn't want me, she's only asking me to please Victoria.'

'What nonsense, Sylvia, Mrs Brodie is charming.'

'She is to you.' She saw her mother frown. 'There's no use looking like that; it isn't imagination, I just know.'

'Well it would upset me very much if I had to write and decline the invitation on your behalf.'

'Oh, I'll go,' Sylvia said resignedly, 'just don't expect me to enjoy it that's all.'

'Of course you'll enjoy the company. Victoria's brother Paul is home for Christmas and Mrs Brodie mentions a friend – ' She broke off as other matters claimed her attention.

Paul had expected a friend of his sister's to be fun-loving and pretty and was disappointed to find that Sylvia Cameron was neither. Not that she was actually plain, he told himself, but rather that her appearance was unremarkable, someone who would go unnoticed in a crowd. Also that cool manner of hers was a bit off-putting. He could see the time ahead being pretty heavy going with Edwin going soppy on Victoria.

Sylvia wasn't too happy either. Far from needing her company Victoria seemed to want to spend all her time with Edwin. It threw Paul and her together and she wasn't sure that she particularly liked him. She distrusted his good looks and resented his slightly condescending manner. Just because he had been away at college he seemed to think himself superior. Still, she was a guest in the house and the warning from her mother still rang in her ears so she made the effort to be friendly.

Becoming aware that she had made very little contribution to the conversation and with Victoria busy pouring out tea and being mother, Sylvia turned to Edwin and began questioning him about college. Some of the questions surprised and baffled him and he appealed to Paul.

'You take over, pal, I'm getting out of my depth.'

Victoria laughed. 'Sorry, you two, I should have warned you. Sylvia has dispensed with a governess and has a tutor all to herself. She's going to be like my mother and run the business.'

'Are you, Sylvia?' Paul asked.

'I'm hoping to and my grandfather has promised me a position in the cotton mill.'

'Not the distillery?'

'Oh, no,' she said dismissively. 'Once my father is satisfied with the running of that he'll get someone to take over and we'll all return to Rochdale.'

'Presumably you'll get married one day.'

'It's a possibility, Edwin, but what of it?'

'Maybe your husband wouldn't approve of his wife spending her days in the mill.'

'His loss then. I wouldn't marry him.'

'Could work all right,' Paul said thoughtfully. 'It hasn't damaged my mother and father's relationship.'

'Yes, it has, Paul. Papa's never liked Mama going into the mill,' Victoria said with a toss of her head. 'I'm not going to be like Mama.'

'Couldn't be, you haven't the brains.'

'Beast.'

'I'd quite like to see round the papermill if that wouldn't be asking too much.'

'Mother would be delighted. If Father is available he'll show us round or get someone else.'

'May I come?' Sylvia asked.

'Of course. We'll all go.'

'What a bore.'

'You can stay at home, Viccy.'

'On my own? Certainly not.'

Sylvia turned to Edwin. 'If you'd be interested in seeing over the distillery I could arrange it with my father.'

'Great! I'd like that, thanks.'

Paul felt strangely hurt that Sylvia hadn't included him – yet why should she? The distillery, until recently, had belonged to the Brodies and he'd been inside it many times.

'Does the invitation include me?'

She looked surprised. 'But of course, Paul. I'm sorry, I just imagined you'd been in it often enough.'

'I have but I'd like to see the changes your father has made.'

She looked at him sharply and he realised his mistake.

'My Uncle Thomas has nothing but admiration for the way Mr Cameron handles the workers, Sylvia. They like and respect him and I'm afraid that couldn't be said for my grandfather.'

'Your grandfather was never a humble worker, my father was and because of that he can understand their worries.'

'He's got the distillery back on its feet and that's what is important.'

She was certainly impressing him. Most girls would have tried to hide their father's humble beginnings but she seemed to take a pride in mentioning it.

He really isn't so bad, Sylvia thought, in fact he was really rather nice.

The next day the four of them went out. Victoria and Edwin went on ahead leaving Sylvia and Paul to follow.

'You don't get this kind of weather in Rochdale?' he shouted against the wind.

'It gets its share of blustery weather but there is a wildness about here that's exhilarating and I like it.'

Sylvia was laughing, her cheeks flushed as a frisky wind whipped her skirt round her legs.

'I'm glad Victoria invited you, Sylvia, and not one of her other friends,' Paul said, wondering how he could ever have thought her plain.

'Why?' she asked in her direct manner.

'You're much more interesting.'

'And not at all pretty. Don't deny it, Paul, it's what you thought when you met me. It was written all over your face.'

Paul had the grace to blush. 'That was your fault.'

'How could it be my fault?'

'That abrupt manner would scare anyone off.'

'Yes, I know.' She sighed. 'I have an unfortunate way of talking as my mother keeps telling me.'

'No, you don't. It's only a bit off-putting at first. I think you're delightful and it's marvellous to be able to carry on an intelligent conversation with a girl. Poor old Edwin won't get that with Viccy.'

'That won't worry Edwin. Victoria is lovely, Paul, and more important, she is nice with it.'

'Certainly seem to be smitten with each other, don't you think?'

'I do and if there is such a thing as love at first sight I'd say it's happened to them.'

'Maybe I'm beginning to believe in it too,' he said softly, so softly that he didn't know if she had heard.

With Victoria and Edwin out of sight Paul decided to risk it. Sylvia had taken off her gloves and he caught her hand in his. A tingling sensation shot up his arm and made him draw in his breath. Bewildered by it he said shakily, 'Sylvia, may I write to you when I go back to college?'

'Yes.'

'But will you reply to my letters?'

'Of course I'll reply; what a stupid thing to ask.'

The young people were entertaining themselves and were no trouble. Finding herself unexpectedly busy at the mill Susan saw little of them apart from meal times and not always then. Edward was being helpful and made himself available to show Edwin the various departments in the papermill. Peter, Matthew's younger son, should have been with them, Susan thought fondly. Young though he was, he seemed fascinated by the machinery and each time he was there demanded full explanations to his questions.

*   *   *

Hearing of his daughter's request concerning the distillery, David Cameron sent the carriage for the young people. The girls, if they insisted on coming, were to remain in the office while the boys did a tour of the distillery.

In the carriage they were laughing and talking about the visit ahead.

'Your Uncle Thomas is very proud of the distillery, Paul.'

'He is and when you get him started talking about it there is no stopping him.'

'I like hearing about it.'

'I take it you know then that only the finest natural ingredients are used in the making of Granton whisky,' Paul said, sounding intentionally pompous.

Sylvia laughed. 'Making it one of the best?'

'Not one of the best. The best. Incidentally have you been round it?'

'Of course she hasn't,' his sister said scornfully.

'No, I haven't. My mother would have fainted at the suggestion and even my father couldn't be persuaded but he did tell me about it.'

'Come on, Sylvia, tell all,' Edwin said, 'and let me appear a little knowledgeable.'

'Ask Paul, he's been through a number of times.'

'Him! I'd rather hear it from you.'

'All right, I'll do my best. The smell, the rich aroma of fermentation is what hits you first.'

'Go on.'

'I'm thinking, Edwin. You'll be taken to see the raw whisky before it is transferred into oak casks for maturation.' She paused and Edwin nodded. 'Apparently that is the point when the distiller uses his skill to make the crucial judgment that determines the quality of the whisky,' She nudged Paul. 'You now.'

'Ah, yes, well, the oak casks are left in a darkened warehouse for at least ten years.'

Victoria yawned. 'When do we get there?'

'In a few minutes,' her brother answered.

The long street they entered was dreary and dirty and the

warehouses had windows thick with dust and most had the added protection of iron bars across them. After another turn they were through the gates and into a cobbled court-yard. From the carriage windows they could see workers bent under their heavy sacks of grain and there was the constant rumble of empty casks being rolled along the cobbles. Further away could be heard the steady tapping of a cooper's hammer on the iron hoops of a cask. These the coachman, when he got down from his perch, informed them were the sights and sounds of whisky. Remembering his instructions, he led them through a labyrinth of corridors to the offices. Victoria giggled and wrinkled her nose. Before Edwin arrived on the scene nothing would have dragged her into this smelly place but now she thought of it as an adventure.

David Cameron sat in a swivel chair behind an enormous desk where once John Brodie had ruled with a harshness that he considered the only language the workers could understand. David had contemplated clearing away all that had belonged to its owner then he changed his mind, getting a curious pleasure from keeping it as it was. The desk and chair, together with the rest of the furniture, were very much to his taste as were the watercolours of old Glasgow, a reminder of a time when the Brodies were merchants and made their fortune in the tobacco trade.

Walking to the window David saw the carriage turn into the gates and a little later Mr Davies, the coachman, announced that his daughter and her friends had arrived.

Sylvia came in ahead of the others and David noticed that she looked flushed. She kissed him before making the introductions.

'Papa, this is Victoria.'

Just for a second the clock was turned back and he was with the young Susan MacFarlane. The girl was very pretty, he thought, but now that he studied her he noted the difference. She didn't have that gorgeous silver fairness, hers was a reddish fairness and the seriousness, the quick intelligent look, were missing.

'Delighted to meet you, Victoria, and may I say how charming you look.'

Victoria, smiling demurely, acknowledged the greetings and a tall, dark boy came forward.

'This is Paul, Papa,' Sylvia said, suddenly shy and David felt a quickening of interest. Gone was the brusque manner which her mother deplored, to be replaced with a softness that touched her face and was in her voice. David felt strangely moved at the thought of his daughter and Susan's son being attracted to one another.

'This is very good of you, Mr Cameron and much appreciated,' Paul said. They shook hands, each weighing up the other.

David liked what he saw. He liked this tall young man with his ready smile and the signs of strength in the firm chin. Sylvia was very precious to him but he would have no hesitation in trusting this boy with her happiness.

Paul, too, was favourably impressed. Mr Cameron was nothing like he expected and straightaway he liked Sylvia's father. Why his mother extended such a lukewarm welcome to the Cameron family was beyond him – beyond his father too. Edward got on well with them.

Edwin left Victoria's side to be introduced. 'Edwin is a college friend of mine, Mr Cameron.' For a while the conversation was about college then Thomas Brodie arrived.

'Hello, Uncle Thomas, are you going to do the honours?'

'Your uncle knows a lot more about the whisky trade than I do, Paul. For me every day is a school.'

Thomas smiled. He looks happy, Paul thought, there was certainly no bad feeling or even awkwardness between the son of the former owner and Mr Cameron and surely that spoke volumes.

'What about the young ladies?' Thomas hadn't expected to see his niece and David's daughter.

'They are going to stay in the office with me.' Then David began to laugh. 'If this is going to be a regular occurrence, Thomas, we'll have to do something about light refreshments.

As it is they are all too young to partake of the "water of life".'
    'What is the water of life, Mr Cameron?'
    'Whisky, Victoria.' David smiled.

Sylvia was no longer at Aran Heights. Her grandfather had arrived and she had returned home. She thanked her hostess rather stiffly for an enjoyable few days and left one young man feeling lost.
    'Edwin, will you have to go to India one day?'
    'I expect so.'
    'Is it terribly hot?'
    'Almost unbearable according to my mother but no one works during the hottest part of the day.'
    'Does your mother enjoy the life?'
    'Not much, Mrs Brodie, but she's in the minority, most of them do.'
    'What is it she doesn't like?' Edward asked as he buttered his toast.
    'She can't be bothered with the endless socialising and hates the emptiness of the life.'
    'Then why does she go?'
    'Considers it is her duty to accompany my father.' He grinned. 'He says it is to keep an eye on him.'
    Edward laughed heartily and Susan smiled.

They were in bed.
    'What do you think of Edwin, Edward?'
    'Nice lad.'
    'Victoria hangs on to his every word, have you noticed?'
    'Does that bother you?'
    'No, but I hope she realises that once Edwin is back in college that could be the end of it.'
    'Somehow I don't think so. It may well develop.'
    'Paul did very well entertaining Sylvia.'
    'I don't think he found it a hardship,' Edward said drily.
    'I'm afraid I've had to neglect them.'
    'Probably glad to be left to themselves,' Edward muttered from under the bedclothes.

'You could be right. Incidentally where did they go on Wednesday afternoon? I forgot to ask.'

'Sylvia suggested her father show Edwin over the distillery but in the event they all went.'

Her heart stopped then raced. 'They – all – went?' Susan said stupidly.

'That's what I said. David sent the carriage and he looked after the girls while Thomas showed Edwin accompanied by Paul the magic of whisky-making. And now, please, do you think I could get some sleep?' Turning away, he dragged the bedclothes with him but Susan was too shocked to complain. A kind of fury born of despair seized her. The unthinkable had happened. Paul and David had met. Father and son had come face to face. She tried to visualise it and failed.

Did kinship show itself in some way? Was there an invisible bond, something that would draw them together? But of course not. They were strangers meeting for the first time and if someone remarked on a resemblance there was nothing to fear. Paul was a Brodie, he took after his grandfather. Her head ached, she longed for sleep and in the morning her face was pale and there were shadows beneath her eyes showing how little she had slept.

Christmas Day. Mrs Carson had excelled herself. It was the traditional Christmas dinner but cooked to perfection. Edwin looked blissfully content as they rose from the table to sit in the drawing-room. Paul and Edwin both flopped into chairs.

'Mrs Brodie, I've been a proper glutton and I do apologise but you have a cook in a million.'

'Yes, Mrs Carson is a treasure.' Susan smiled.

'The cook my grandparents have is an old dear but she's past it. A burnt offering is nothing new but the old folk eat so little they hardly notice.'

'I'm quite sure it isn't as bad as that, Edwin, but I do think it helps with our cook that I don't interfere. Mrs Carson has a free hand.'

*   *   *

377

Paul and Edwin had gone. The house was quiet and there was the flat feeling of the end of a holiday. The postman had been and the maid arrived with letters on a silver tray just as they were finishing breakfast. Edward took them, glanced at the envelopes and handed two to Susan. He was well aware that Victoria was craning her neck to see the other envelopes.

'One for you, Viccy,' he said, examining the envelope and infuriating his daughter. 'Sloppy writing.'

'Papa, it's mine, please give me my letter.'

'Edward, give it to her and don't tease.'

'There you are.'

'Thank you.'

'Aren't you going to open it?'

She blushed. 'No, I'll wait I think.' Swallowing the rest of her breakfast she pushed back her chair and with an 'excuse me' hurried from the room.

CHAPTER TWENTY-SEVEN

Winter had held the countryside in its grip until well into March but now the cherry trees with their delicate pinks overhung the large trumpeted daffodils and there were the first glimpses of early red tulips.

'I wish it were Easter,' Victoria said wistfully as she followed her mother down the steps to the terrace.

'Well, you won't have long to wait.'

'It'll be nice when Paul and Edwin come. You do like Edwin, don't you?'

'I seem to have answered that before but yes, I think Edwin is a pleasant, well-mannered boy.'

'I wish he was to stay all the holidays.'

'His grandparents would be offended if he didn't spend some time with them.'

Victoria gave a little skip and took her mother's arm. 'Edwin is the nicest boy I know and it's even better that he's a friend of Paul's.'

Poor dear, Susan thought with a pang, she just can't hide her feelings. 'Victoria, it doesn't do to show your feelings. Let the boy do the running and he'll respect you all the more for it.'

'All right, I'll try and Mama,' the tone had become wheedling, 'may I have a new gown? One with a low neckline, not too low of course.'

'It won't be, you're far too young.'

'I'm not and you're just old-fashioned. This isn't the Victorian age now you know.'

Susan hid a smile. 'I'm well aware that this is 1903 but that doesn't mean we have to let Victorian standards go.'

Her daughter smiled knowingly. 'I know why the Queen liked going to Balmoral.'

'Oh!'

'She wanted to be with her ghillie, John Brown.'

'That is gossip. Rachel, I suppose?'

'Her mother says it is common knowledge.'

'It is only gossip and it is unkind. The Queen may have been lonely and liked to talk to her ghillie and some people had to make the most of it.'

'Sylvia had a letter from Paul.'

Another moment of unease for Susan. 'Just politeness, Victoria, and hoping that Sylvia enjoyed her few days at Aran Heights.'

Victoria looked at her mother thoughtfully. Mama didn't like Sylvia very much so she needn't say that Paul and Sylvia were corresponding regularly.

The longed-for Easter holidays. Paul and Edwin arrived. All that morning Victoria had been up to high doh but she had calmed down and Susan couldn't have faulted the way Victoria smiled and greeted Edwin. She was learning.

That same evening Paul announced calmly that he was going to the Beeches to see Sylvia and all Susan could do was watch him going.

'Mama, we're going to Moorend and we'll see Uncle Matthew and Aunt Winnie at the same time.'

'That's fine, dear. Give them my love.' She turned to her son. 'You'll be going too, Paul?'

'Not today, Mother.'

'What are your plans?' she asked after the other two had gone.

'I'll be seeing Sylvia.'

Susan moistened her lips and strove to keep her voice steady.

'Paul, dear, aren't you perhaps overdoing it? I mean Sylvia may be reading too much into your friendship and her parents may not be happy about you calling so often.'

380

'On the contrary, Mother,' he said coldly, 'Mr and Mrs Cameron have been extremely kind and I couldn't have had a warmer welcome. And what's more,' he added, 'Sylvia would come here if you invited her but you haven't.'

'Paul, you are very young – '

'The same age as Edwin and that relationship doesn't seem to bother you.'

'You're all far too young to know your own mind.'

Paul's face relaxed. 'Mother, I'm not contemplating marriage.'

'I'm very glad to hear it,' Susan said almost dizzy with relief but it was short-lived.

'That doesn't mean we won't at some time. I love Sylvia and I know I won't change.'

Something sour and choking filled her throat. 'You can't be,' she said harshly, 'it's out of the question. Sylvia is not right for you.'

'Let me be the judge of that, please,' he said, looking at her with the eyes of a stranger.

'Judge of what?' Edward asked as he came in.

Paul turned to him with relief. 'Mother strongly objects to my friendship with Sylvia.'

'Don't let that bother you. Sylvia's a fine girl but your mother, for some reason of her own, has no time for the Camerons.'

Susan saw the sardonic smile on Edward's face and if something had been to hand she would have hurled it at him.

Paul left the room without another word.

'If you're trying to drive a wedge between you and your son then you're going the right way about it. And another thing, Susan, if it comes to a choice between you and Sylvia I think we both know whom he'll choose.'

She shot him a look of pure dislike and walked out, almost banging the door behind her. As always when she was deeply troubled Susan climbed the stairs to the library. Sitting behind the desk she knew black despair. She was losing her son, losing his love and his cold politeness was breaking her heart. If there was a God in heaven why did he allow the Camerons

381

to come here and cause so much misery? She felt wounded and mortally hurt as she saw Paul turning more and more to Edward. To think that at one time she had prayed for such a closeness and now that it was happening she was jealous and miserable.

Next morning she went in to the mill earlier than usual. Work, plenty of it was what she needed to occupy her mind, and always before it had been successful but not this time. The problem was too big. It frightened her. What should she do? If she waited perhaps the attraction would die a natural death. They were at a romantic age. But if it didn't? She couldn't put it off much longer. Something would have to be done.

'Is Mother out?'

'Yes, Paul,' Edward said, looking up briefly from the paper. 'You're looking very smart.'

'I'm getting the nine fifteen for Glasgow.'

'Going on your own?'

'No, Sylvia wants to see Glasgow.'

'Cleared it with Mr and Mrs Cameron?'

'Just Mr Cameron. He said it was all right, that he considered me responsible enough to take care of Sylvia.'

'And so do I.'

'Thanks.'

'How are you for cash?'

'Not bad.'

Edward went into his pocket. 'Here you are, it doesn't do to be short when you are taking a young lady out for the day.'

'Thank you very much, Father, that is very generous.'

'I can recommend Green's in Gordon Street. It's a respectable place and the food is good.'

'I – um – haven't mentioned this to Mother,' he said awkwardly.

'Don't. If anything is said I'll handle it.'

'I'd better get going.'

'Enjoy yourselves but remember to behave.'

Paul grinned, feeling a surge of real affection for the man who had once treated him so badly.

'I can promise you that.'

Before getting on the train at Aranvale Paul bought three-pennyworth of Fry's creams from the small confectioners. And when the train drew in at Airdrie station Sylvia was on the platform looking anxiously the length of the train. He waved and she half ran towards him, looking fresh and pretty in a lime green dress and bolero. Soon they were sitting close together, Sylvia nearest the window.

'For you,' he said, dropping the paper bag in her lap.

'Oh, Paul, thank you. Fry's creams, I love them.' They looked at each other and smiled. A smile that told it all, happiness spilled out. They were together, a whole lovely long day ahead of them.

'Papa says it always rains in Glasgow.'

'Today it wouldn't dare.' He smiled as doors slammed, the guard blew his whistle, the green flag was waved and they were off. Sylvia watched the passing scenery and he watched her.

In what seemed a remarkably short time the rhythm of the train altered and they were slowing down before coming into Queen Street station. When it lurched to a stop Paul lowered the window on its leather strap, opened the door and they got out.

They hurried along with the other travellers until they were outside the station. 'Anything special you want to do, Sylvia?'

'Papa knew Glasgow well as a boy so I can leave the sightseeing to him. What's that place where the steamers sail from? Papa told me but I forget.'

'Broomielaw?'

'That's it,' she said, delighted.

'We can get a tram and go there after luncheon.' He touched the coins in his pocket. 'My father suggested I take you to Green's in Gordon Street.'

'Good, that's settled. Paul, let's just walk; anywhere, it doesn't matter.'

Arm-in-arm they walked along Sauchiehall Street busy with

shoppers. The windows were well stocked and pleasing to the eye. It would have been difficult to drag Victoria away but Sylvia barely gave them a glance.

They had a good lunch at Green's then they took the tram to Broomielaw. For a while the mist persisted then it cleared and the sun came through. With their fingers interlocked Paul and Sylvia watched the steamers and the swans circling the moored boats as if staking their claim. Others stood and watched and mothers grabbed at their children as if fearful of losing them.

'Paul, where did you go for family holidays?'

'It was difficult to get away for more than a few days with both my parents in the mill so we didn't go far. Gourock, Rothesay, Dunoon.'

'Lovely names.'

'Lovely places but I think I've outgrown them. I haven't been to London but I mean to put that right.'

'I've been several times. Papa worked there for some years so he was able to show us around.' She swung round to face Paul. 'Wouldn't it be wonderful to travel? Now when we're young, not wait as most people do until they are too old to enjoy it.'

'Which faraway places were you thinking of?'

'Oh, I meant Europe. Paris, Rome, Venice, Florence, so many places I've read about and would love to see and I'm lucky, Paul. My papa would never hold me back from something I really wanted to do.'

'What about your mother?'

'In the end she always gives in to my father.'

'Your mother is very gentle.'

'Not the right description. Beneath that gentleness there's quite a band of steel.' She dropped her voice and her eyes fixed on his face. 'I want to see your face when I say this.'

'Good gracious! You look serious.'

'This is serious. Paul, my father is illegitimate.'

'So?'

She laughed and did he hear relief? 'You mean you aren't shocked? Most people are. My father has risen above it or he pretends that he has. Deep down I know he does care, he cares terribly. Can you imagine what it must be like not to know who your father is? Whether he is alive or dead and worst of all what kind of person he could be to leave a young girl to bring up his child single-handed?'

Paul's face showed nothing of what he was feeling. Should he tell her, since she'd been so honest, that he shared the same fate as her father? Easier for him, he had a substitute father and a name to protect him. The urge to tell this remarkable girl was strong but he couldn't do it. The person to suffer would be his mother and he'd given his promise not to tell Victoria, not to tell anyone.

'A person is who he is and the accident of birth doesn't alter that.'

'I agree. You're like my father, Paul, maybe that's why I like you so much and my mother can't get over you being so dark. She says it is very unusual, almost unique, for both parents to be fair and produce such a dark child.'

'My grandfather, before he turned grey, was very dark and presumably that is where I get my dark good looks.'

'Conceited, aren't you?'

'No, I've nothing to be conceited about. Sylvia . . .'

'Yes?' she said as they began walking towards the tram stop.

'I've enjoyed everything about today.'

'And so have I. It's been wonderful.'

CHAPTER TWENTY-EIGHT

Another night of broken sleep for Susan. With her nerves raw at the thought of what lay ahead she determined to keep to the usual morning routine. Ramsay brought her back to Aran Heights at noon and after a pretence of eating luncheon she went up to her bedroom to change. On the bed lay the day dress she had decided to wear. Without Edward's persuasion Susan doubted whether she would have chosen it – amber wasn't a colour she favoured but she trusted Edward. He always knew what suited her.

By three o'clock Susan decided he wasn't coming but by quarter past he was being shown in by the maid.

'Good afternoon, Mrs Brodie.' He was very smart and businesslike in a dark suit.

'Thank you for coming.' She waved a hand for him to be seated and sat down herself.

'I'm here at your request, Mrs Brodie, or was it a command?'

She didn't rise to the bait. 'My reason for asking you to come alone concerns Paul and Sylvia. You must know, David,' she deliberately used his Christian name, 'that a serious relationship is out of the question.'

'May I ask why?'

'That should be obvious. Edward and you are related.'

'That isn't generally known and it only makes us half brothers and the young ones half cousins. Marriage between half cousins is not unusual.'

'I don't want it.'

His eyes glinted. 'Now we're getting the truth. You don't want a daughter of mine marrying into your family.'

'I won't deny that, but it isn't for the reason you think.'

'Ah, but I'm sure it is.' He leaned forward, his eyes fixed unwaveringly on her pale face and a harshness crept into his voice. 'You had better get this into your head, Mrs Brodie: my daughter's happiness means a great deal to me and if – and that is all I am saying – if Sylvia and Paul wish to marry some time in the future they have my blessing and my wife's too. We are both fond of Paul and he's assured of a welcome in our home.'

'David,' she spoke slowly and clearly, 'I can only tell you that marriage between Paul and Sylvia is impossible, it can never be.'

He got up abruptly. 'I've said all I intend saying on the subject. Now if you will excuse me – '

Susan half rose. 'No, David, don't go. Please sit down and hear me out then you'll understand.'

For a moment she thought he was going to refuse but he sat down, his face set in a hard line and watched Susan put a hand to her throat. Her eyes were on him, those beautiful eyes pain-filled as she fought for control.

'Susan, what's wrong? What is the matter?'

'Sylvia is a delightful and intelligent girl and you do me an injustice. In different circumstances . . .' Her voice trailed off and she closed her eyes. For so long she had kept her secret but now . . . 'David,' her voice was a whisper, 'Paul is your son.'

He stared at her. 'What in God's name are you saying?' he said hoarsely.

'I'd hoped even to the last moment that it wouldn't have to come out.'

What he was hearing couldn't be true! His hand was pressed over his mouth. He felt numb, stupefied, incapable of thought or speech. When he could speak his voice came out thick, muffled, as if he were drunk.

'Now you can understand my anguish, seeing those two – ' She broke off and gave a mirthless laugh. 'I married Edward not knowing that I was carrying your child. Can you imagine that, David? Can you imagine what I went through?'

She heard his swiftly indrawn breath. 'What did you tell Edward?'

'The truth or what I believed it to be then – that the father of my child was someone I knew for a brief time and would never see again. He wanted a name but I never gave him one.' Anger touched her voice. 'If only you hadn't come back. Revenge was what you wanted and you got it.'

'Perhaps.' He was pale and shaken but there was a light in his eyes she didn't like.

'You have no claim on Paul,' she said quickly. 'He believes Edward to be his father and that is the way it is going to remain.' It wasn't true, Paul knew that Edward wasn't his natural father, but she didn't care.

David's breathing was still heavy but his colour had returned. 'Susan, if only I had known, if only – '

'You'd gone from Aranvale and I was married to Edward.' She didn't know if he was listening.

'You can't even begin to understand how much I – we – wanted a son. My daughters mean the world to me but a son, I needed a son, Susan.' He stopped and said slowly, wonderingly, 'Paul – is – my son.' Susan saw the longing, the naked agony of suddenly being told of a son but a son denied him.

'We all have our cross to bear, David. Trying to discourage this relationship has cost me the love of my son,' she said brokenly. 'I've lost Paul and hurt him badly.'

David got to his feet and squared his shoulders. 'For what you have suffered, Susan, I am deeply, deeply sorry. Now it is up to me. Somehow I have to protect those two and keep them apart.'

'No matter what you do they are going to be miserable.' She got up to stand beside him and he gave a small smile.

'Mercifully the awful anguish felt by the young doesn't last for ever. I speak from experience. It took me a long time to get over you, Susan. No, that isn't quite true. I never really got over you, I thought I had but just seeing you again – Once you were a lovely girl but now you are a very beautiful woman.'

It was a dangerous moment and they both knew it.

389

'You made a good marriage, David,' Susan said unsteadily. 'I like Gwen.'

'We both chose well, Susan. Edward must love you very, very much to accept and bring up another man's child as his own.'

She nodded. They both smiled and the tension eased. Even so they were so engrossed with one another that they didn't hear the door opening until Edward spoke and they both turned.

Susan hadn't realised that it was so late and she was taken aback to see Edward.

'Well, hello there! What brings you to Aran Heights, David?'

'I invited him,' Susan put in swiftly before David could answer.

David gave her a quick look then spoke easily. 'We were discussing the young folk and I agree with your wife that the relationship should be discouraged.'

'Why?'

'We are half brothers.'

'Is that the reason Susan gave – ?'

'No! Stop it!' Susan drew herself up and held her head high. 'David, it's time for the truth and Edward has a right to hear it.' She turned to her husband. 'It isn't often I suggest you have a drink but I think you may need one.'

'Thank you but I'll manage without.'

'Very well.' She paused. 'You've always been desperate to know the identity of Paul's father so now I'm going to tell you.' Her lips were trembling but she kept a grip on herself. 'Edward, Paul is David's son,' she said clearly.

'Is this some kind of joke?' he demanded but he looked sick.

'No joke. You knew that David worked for my father but you didn't know he came to Aran Heights to teach me the business.'

'Why the secrecy?'

'The fault was mine. I was too shocked that day at Croft House to think clearly. I thought it better to pretend we hadn't met. Later I regretted it but by then it was too late.'

'Edward, you must believe me I knew nothing about it – I had no idea,' David said quietly, looking ill at ease. 'That is the truth. What happened was my fault and I was then and I still am deeply ashamed.'

'Spare me the details,' Edward said savagely.

'There are no details, Edward,' Susan said quietly. 'It was the only time and we were never together after that. By the time I knew that I was pregnant David had left the mill and Aranvale and I was married to you.'

Edward opened his mouth but no words came and abruptly he turned his back and busied himself with the decanter. His hand shook and some of the whisky spilled. He was remembering that unguarded moment when he had seen the longing in David's face and a dreadful fear took hold of him. What were Susan's feelings? Had he lost her? Was her seeming dislike of David Cameron just a cover for her real feelings?

With a murmured excuse David had moved towards the door but turned before reaching it.

'Susan, you mustn't worry. I'll do what has to be done.' Then he was gone.

Edward drained his glass and poured himself another. With it in his hand he walked to the window. After a few minutes he said tonelessly, 'David's coming back.'

He came in without an apology. 'I can't leave it like this.' He sounded agitated. 'Paul is my son and I must, I have to do something for him.' His eyes fixed on Edward. 'The only way I can do that is through you.'

'What do you mean?'

'One day I want my son to take over the distillery but it can only be through you. It's thanks to you that Paul has a name and I'm grateful. More than anyone I know what that means.'

'Where do I come in?'

'I gather from Thomas that you've always hankered after the distillery. Well I want you to take control of it.'

'Control of the distillery?' Edward said incredulously.

'Already we're making a fair profit with the potential for a lot more. Once my father-in-law is repaid in full for his outlay then the Granton Distillery becomes yours. No strings attached, Edward. I'll have the necessary papers prepared by my solicitor and ownership transferred to you with Paul inheriting one day.'

'David, how are you going to explain all this to Gwen?'

'Don't worry about Gwen, Susan. She'll be happy to go back to Rochdale to be near her father and she isn't one for questions.'

'You'll have to tell her something.'

'Yes, I'll have to tell her something but I don't yet know what that is. Be assured it will be what I consider gives least pain to all concerned.'

'And Sylvia?'

'Poor Sylvia. Poor Paul.' He sighed. 'Sylvia has always longed to travel so perhaps that is the answer for her.'

'Yes.'

'Once we are back in Rochdale all this will be forgotten.' He didn't believe it, not for a moment.

She didn't either. She loved Edward and knew she would be lost without him but David would always have a corner of her heart. Didn't one always remember one's first love?

There was a light tap on the door and the maid put her head round. 'A Mr Ritchie – '

Edward glanced at the clock and frowned. 'He's early but I'd better see him. Excuse me, I shouldn't be more than ten minutes.'

Left alone, David went over to Susan and very gently put his hands on her shoulders. 'Thank you for making such a fine job of our son. He is a young man to be proud of and don't worry, nothing will change his love for you.'

Feeling his nearness and knowing this could be the last time she saw him her eyes filled. She blinked them away but not before he had seen them. With a groan he gathered her in his arms and for a brief moment they were locked in an embrace. 'How I wish things had been different,' he whispered.

Gently she drew away from him. 'No, David, don't wish that. You have a good marriage, you love Gwen and I love Edward.'

'I'll never forget you but I like to think of our son in Aran Heights, the house that always held such a fascination for me.'

'One day it will belong to Paul.'

'He's gone then?'

'Yes, Edward, he's gone.' She tried to read his expression but failed. 'You must be very happy about the distillery?'

'I'm not sure I've taken it in.'

'Ironic though, isn't it?'

'What is?'

'You getting what you most want and through my bastard son.'

'Don't, Susan, please don't.' His eyes were bleak and he didn't look like someone who had just got his heart's desire. 'You're still in love with him, aren't you?'

'No, Edward.' She shook her head. 'Once I thought myself in love with David but that was a very long time ago. People change, we all do.'

'I couldn't bear it if you left me,' he said brokenly. 'I love you, Susan. Those others, Caroline included, meant nothing. It was always you but you never seemed to want me and God knows I don't deserve you after what I made Paul and you suffer.'

'Paul has completely forgiven you. He likes and respects you.' She paused. 'And as for me what I did to you was dreadful, unforgivable, yet you stood by me,' she said quietly. They had been standing well apart and without being aware of what she was doing she held out her hand. Slowly he came towards her and she gripped his hand. 'Edward, I need to tell you something.'

'No,' he said harshly, 'I don't want to hear it.'

'But you do. I love you, Edward, love you very much and I'm just sorry it's taken me so long to tell you.'

'You do mean it? Oh, God! You do, don't you?'

393

'You should know by this time that I only say what I mean.'

'Then tell me about David – the truth, please.'

'This is the truth. I shall remember David with warmth and affection and perhaps I'll remain a little in love with him but only in the way one remembers one's first love.'

He drew her close and she knew that he was satisfied. She could feel the thudding of his heart and a lovely warm feeling enveloped her. Life for them both had been fraught with difficulties but they had overcome them. Now she couldn't bear the thought of life without him. She hadn't known it at the time but her parents had been right. They had known that Edward was right for her.

'I've just had a thought, Susan. Paul will have to choose between the papermill and the distillery.'

'No, he won't. Paul is a Brodie and that changes everything. His place is in the distillery and maybe fate has taken a hand. Peter likes nothing better than wandering about the mill.'

'Matthew's son. That's fitting. So it will still be the Brodies and the MacFarlanes.'

Susan moved away from him to look into his face, her own worried. 'Tell me, Edward, am I doing the right thing or should Paul know that David is his father?'

'He should know,' Edward said firmly. 'Paul should know that the distillery becomes his in his own right and not through me.'

'And then he would understand about Sylvia?'

'Yes.'

With her head resting on her husband's shoulder Susan felt at peace, the burden of guilt gone. All the trauma, the fears and the heartbreak were in the past and buried forever. What lay ahead no one could say but together they would face it.